GILES, F.   Sundry
            times
AS 9/86   13.95

7/12   070.92⁴⁴

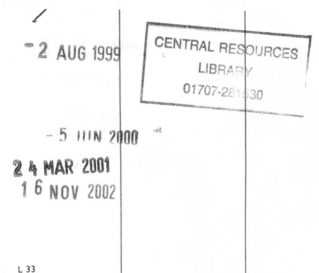

SUNDRY TIMES

By the same author

A PRINCE OF JOURNALISTS
The Life and Times of Henri de Blowitz
Faber & Faber, 1962

SUNDRY TIMES

Frank Giles

'I hope that I never ridicule what is wise or good.
Follies and nonsense, whims and inconsistencies
do divert me, I own, and I laugh at them
whenever I can'

Elizabeth Bennet in *Pride and Prejudice*
JANE AUSTEN

'. . . at sundry times and
in divers manners . . .'
ST PAUL'S EPISTLE TO THE HEBREWS

JOHN MURRAY

© Frank Giles 1986

First published 1986
by John Murray (Publishers) Ltd
50 Albemarle Street, London WIX 4BD

Typeset by Inforum Ltd, Portsmouth
Printed and bound in Great Britain
by Butler & Tanner Ltd, Frome

British Library CIP data
Sundry times.
1. Giles, Frank   2. Journalists——
Great Britain——Biography
I. Title
070'.92'4   PN5123.G5/
ISBN 0-7195-4289-8

For our children –
Sarah, Sebastian, Belinda

ACKNOWLEDGEMENTS

Among those who read part of the typescript of this book are Hugo Young and Brian MacArthur, formerly of *The Sunday Times*, and Peter Roberts, presently with the paper. They made valuable comments, for which I am grateful. J.W. Lambert, one-time literary editor of *The Sunday Times*, read the whole typescript and made detailed, numerous and thoughtful suggestions. I am deeply in debt to this old friend.

Hugh Trevor-Roper (Lord Dacre) took much trouble in commenting upon Chapter 9 (the Hitler Diaries), and kindly gave permission to quote from his letter to me. For various advice I am grateful to Lord Briggs (Provost of Worcester College, Oxford), Sir Edward Tomkins (formerly British Ambassador in Paris) and Mrs Field, who enlightened me as to the nature of Angels-on-Horseback (Chapter 6, p. 131). Lady Diana Cooper kindly allowed me access to her family album for photograph No. 9.

Michael Cranmer, Picture Editor of *The Sunday Times*, was extremely co-operative over some of the illustrations. Colin Wilson, Librarian at Times Newspapers, was equally helpful with archive material, especially my printed despatches from Paris and Rome to *The Times*.

The help and comments of these kind people, though highly valued, in no way diminish my responsibility for what I have written.

Contents

Illustrations

I am grateful to the following for making it possible
to print the following illustrations: Camera Press
Ltd: 7, 8, 10; Lady Diana Cooper: 9; *The Sunday
Times*: 13 (photo: Michael Ward), 16, 17 (photo:
Sally Soames), 18 (photo: Frank Hermann), 19
(photo: Sally Soames); Photos Raymond Darolle-
Sygma: 14

Improbable Appointment

One night in early October 1939, the authorities of the small British colony of Bermuda were in something of a flap. An unidentified ship of considerable size was approaching the island from the East. The Second World War had been declared a month earlier. Bermuda, a tiny outpost of about 150 islands, measuring in all no more than 19 square miles, 586 miles away from Cape Hatteras, the nearest point of land, is after St Helena and Tristan da Cunha probably the most isolated place in the English-speaking world. German warships on the prowl, such as, for example, the powerful cruiser *Graf Spee*, destined to meet her end at Montevideo two months later, could well choose Bermuda as a target for bombardment or even invasion. It had a Royal Naval dockyard and was the headquarters of the Royal Navy's America and West Indies squadron.

An easy target it would have been. Its defences, apart from the naval establishment, consisted of a detachment of a British infantry battalion, the local militia force, and various small supporting services, principal among which was a piece of coastal artillery, a single gun, suitable for firing at unfriendly ships. This unfortunately was not serviceable, and the main task that October night was to try to get it into working order by first light the next morning.

The effort proved unnecessary. The identity of the mysterious vessel was discovered. She was the RMS *Oropesa*, belonging to the Pacific Steam Navigation Company, thirteen days outward bound from Liverpool. Among her passengers was the newly arriving Governor of Bermuda, his widowed sister, his butler, his coachman, his groom, two housemaids, and his aide-de-camp, a youth of barely twenty who until a month previously had been an undergraduate at Oxford and about as ill-equipped to be an army officer and a Governor's ADC as it is possible to be.

Later in the morning the party landed, to the accompaniment of

ceremonial greetings, and the new Governor was driven to the Secretar-
iat buildings to be sworn in. This ritual was nearly made impossible by
the idiotic, though presumably well-meaning, action of the young
ADC, who decided, for reasons best known to himself, to send the
briefcase containing the Royal Warrant straight up to Government
House, a mile distant. By the time it had been retrieved and sworn
upon, tempers in the crowded Council Chamber were becoming frayed,
uniforms, in the sticky October climate, darkened with sweat.

Unbelievable though it seemed then, and indeed seems now, I was
that ADC, and the sequences of that day are stamped upon my memory
with all the incision and clarity of the engraver's art. It was my first
experience of public life. How on earth had I got there?

Born in 1919, I grew up a sickly child. My father, a regular Sapper
Officer who died when I was ten, was abroad most of the time mapping
out the post-war frontiers of Albania or being Military Attaché in
various Balkan capitals. My recollections of him are hazy, except that
he was a good linguist, played the piano quite well, was a fine shot and
cricketer and considered the then nascent League of Nations to be a Bad
Thing. For those days he must have been, I think, a slightly unusual
soldier, given to reading and even the arts in a way often associated with
Sappers who, according to military legend, tend to be mad, married or
Methodist.

The only one of these categories which fitted my father was marriage.
My mother was the younger daughter of Anglo-Welsh parents living in
Glamorganshire. That is, they were not really Welsh but their forebears
had chosen to live there – in the case of the Allens, my mother's family,
initially in Pembrokeshire – so that they, and their like, occupied much
the same social and territorial position as the so-called Anglo-Irish
ascendancy in Ireland.

I remember my maternal grandparents and their setting extremely
well. Grandfather could hardly be considered a squire, even though his
enlarged and beautified ex-farm house was called the Manor House; its
fields and gardens amounted to no more than 20 acres. He was not
particularly well off. He had no profession and never, I think, had had
one. Except for the days when he had to perform his duties as a
magistrate on the local bench, he spent his time in his study, smoking
and reading the newspaper. But the standard of living at the Manor
House, at least in terms of people to look after you, was lavish: four
servants indoors (cook, scullery maid, parlour maid, housemaid), two
outside (chauffeur/handyman, cowman/gardener), two cars, four

courses every night at dinner. A 'dressing gong' sounded half-an-hour beforehand, a second gong announced the meal itself. Life was as boring as it was predictable; yet the sheer predictability imparted, to a childish mind, a solid and on the whole satisfying feeling of form and substance.

It was not until later, when I began to read the novels of Anthony Trollope and still more of Ivy Compton-Burnett, that I realised I had been witness to what, with the exception of a few modern adaptations such as cars and the telephone (until 1929 the Manor House had no electric light), was in essence a Victorian household. (But, though the ambience of the place resembled that of a Compton-Burnett novel, the people in and of the house – owners, servants, children – failed by a very long distance indeed to think and act like the extraordinary creations of that author's imagination.) Though by no means the pious and strait-laced paterfamilias of Victorian tradition, my grandfather, in some of his autocratic ways, was the archetypal patriarch. What was less usual about him was the Regency vigour, not to say coarseness, of his language: he was continually inviting my gentle grandmother, a saint on earth if ever one existed, to "kiss my arse". "Oh Charlie," she would say reprovingly, but she had become so used to the expression that I believe she would have begun to suspect that something was wrong if it had not been regularly forthcoming.

Grandfather's eccentricity often took the form of making himself into an even greater monster than he was naturally. At the age of fourteen I had written him two letters, and he had replied: 'There is much too much kiss my bottom nonsense in both your letters. You should only write letters when you have anything to say. What do you mean by lots of love and kisses? [This must have been a provocation on my part.] Only a general servant would put that in a letter, and who cares whether the wireless is mended or whether you have been cleaning the garden. Do something useful that will help you in after life. If you behave yourself, you can come for two nights. You must bring your own petrol and if you want any books you must pay for them yourselves, and not take away our library ones. If you carry out my instructions, *perhaps* you may have some cider. Your grandma is very well, and very busy trying to catch cold, but so far she has failed.'

My father's early death left my mother extremely hard up, so that many of my earlier memories are coloured not by the comparative luxury of the Manor House, where we spent much of the time, but by the austerities of home. This meant, until I was fifteen, a large

Edwardian house at Fleet, near Aldershot, where the social setting was far removed from the Trollopian, 'county' style of life in Glamorganshire. My poor mother, in an effort to make ends meet, tried intermittently to take in paying guests, who would be apt to find my sister and myself, late at night, washing up the unusually large number of dinner plates and dishes and insisted good-naturedly on helping us. The paying guest experiment was not a success, but such an impression did it leave that I am able today to persuade myself, quite easily, that I spent nearly all my school holidays at the pantry sink.

School meant, initially, a small and slightly cranky establishment at Cockfosters, north of London, in those days a rural neighbourhood not yet suburbanised by the encroaching Tube. It was chosen because of my poor health, on the grounds that the stresses and exertions were likely to be less there than in a larger, conventional school. A bout of rheumatic fever had left behind a murmuring heart, over which Harley Street specialists gravely shook their heads. A good deal of the time before I was eight was spent, on doctor's orders, lying in bed. When I did get to The Grange, with its handful of pupils, I was such a poor physical specimen that specially nourishing food was ordered, including supplies of fresh cream, with which to build me up. Whether it did so or not I cannot recall, but remember vividly the embarrassment caused by the reactions among the other boys to this privileged regime. Why, they asked, eyeing with envy and malice the cream on my porridge, the delicious malt extract which made such an enjoyable aftermath to a meal, should they be confined to the road to Sparta while scrawny Giles was allowed to tread the path to Sybaris? (They did not of course express themselves in these terms, but their meaning was painfully clear.) Occasionally, there were spectacular fainting fits, followed by more head-shakings in Harley Street. From time to time, I would miss a whole term, spending the time instead in bed at home, waited on and fussed over by my devoted and anxious mother.

Attendance at this school conferred one great and lifelong boon. When I was about ten, one of the masters – there were only two, other than the headmaster, an austere but kindly Christian Scientist who must have regarded my starts and turns with suppressed disapproval – generously presented me with his own, rather worn set of records (78 rpm – there was nothing else) of the Mendelssohn violin concerto. The soloist was Fritz Kreisler. On my portable gramophone, I played these scratched and hissing discs over and over again. Each time seemed more wonderful than the last. The slow movement above all, with its plangent melody soaring above all earthly cares, seemed the equivalent of an invitation to pass through the gates of paradise. Naturally, I was unaware then that the Koran defines paradise as the sensual garden of delights promised to the faithful after death. But though far from being half in love with easeful death, I would not have been at all surprised or displeased by such a definition. *Musik ist heilige Kunst*,* sings the Composer in the Prologue to *Ariadne auf Naxos*. Though as ignorant at the age of ten of the existence of Richard Strauss and his works as I was of Islam's holy book, I was nonetheless conscious, in a very special way, that a landscape had been revealed which once seen could never be forgotten. It would always be there to be revisited with new vistas continually opening up. It was the beginning of an experience which has never ceased to develop, becoming broader in scope and more profound in significance as the years have come and gone.

Though generally bad about administering her own affairs, especially money (another lasting and unpleasant memory is of trying to turn away duns who came to the door demanding payment of long overdue bills), my mother fought like a tigress to ensure that my sister and myself were 'properly' educated. This meant battling with trustees, who were threatened with the dire words 'grammar schools', to release exiguous funds. These efforts succeeded to the point that when the time came to move on from prep school I finished up at Wellington College, the huge nineteenth-century baroque creation standing amidst the Berkshire pines and silver birches and heather. From here after four years, at the age of seventeen and a half, I won a major open scholarship in history at Oxford.

The choice of Wellington, a tough and disciplinarian establishment, given to sending its products to Sandhurst and Woolwich, seems very odd. It was hardly the place for delicate children, even though I was excused most games. An early medical report from the Wellington doctors spoke, in addition to other troubles, of rheumatism, flat feet and colour-blindness. For this reason Marlborough (too rugged) and Eton (too damp as well as too expensive) were ruled out. But Wellington, whence, in my first year, Giles Romilly ran away to found an anti-public-school movement which created a sensation, seemed a curious venue for someone like me, who was moreover not destined for the army. The real reason, it seems, was that my mother, after leaving Fleet, settled in a village near Wellington, whither she could easily

* Music is holy art

come to my rescue in the event of sudden illness.

I had shown no particular talents. What was certain was that I was already an enthusiast for classical music and was rather better read than most children of that age. My lifelong affair with Jane Austen was already launched and I was familiar with most of Dickens. A young tutor I had had at home during one of my periods of illness had mocked at the sentiments of Kipling's *If*, the text of which my mother had had framed and hung upon my bedroom wall. So naturally I mocked too.

Wellington in the thirties has been well described, among others by T.C. (Cuthbert) Worsley.* It was probably no worse than other schools of its kind and period, but it was pretty terrible: rampant with philistinism, homosexuality, sadistic masters and games worship. Fortunately, as in nature action usually begets reaction, so a rather self-consciously precious counter-movement of would-be aesthetes and intellectuals grew up to balance the tough army types. Having survived the first two or three years of personal mediocrity, it was towards this group or school of thought that as time went on I naturally gravitated.

Nearly every school, whatever its other defects, has or has had one great teacher and Wellington was no exception. Rollo St Clair Talboys – the very names bring an immediate touch of romance and improbability – fitted into no category of schoolmaster: a bachelor, he was not sarcastic or cynical or hearty (though, with a characteristic desire to tease, he pretended that if he had to spend a week in London with any section of the school, he would choose the Army Class "for then I should really see life"). As the historian of Wellington has written: 'humanistic in outlook [he] tended to stand apart from the community, faintly mocking [its] routine with quaint sardonic humour, becoming thereby irritating to [his] colleagues and idolized by the older boys who were permitted to share his amusement.'†

Once I began to be taught history by Talboys, a whole new world was revealed, in which a fair measure of fantasy was mingled with a strict attention to taste and style. His teaching of Tudor history, of the Reformation and counter-Reformation, above all his extolling of Thomas More, not only caused me to regard that statesman as the greatest of all Englishmen – an opinion I still hold today, despite modern tendencies to devalue More – but led me, at the age of sixteen or so, into wishing to join (or thinking I wished to join) the Roman

---

Flannelled Fools (Alan Ross, 1967)
†*A History of Wellington College* by David Newsome (John Murray, 1959)

Catholic Church. With much tact and kindness the Master, F.B. Malim, who was on record with the confession that he was 'an impenitent Victorian', talked me out of it.

When King George V was buried at Windsor in January 1936, a detachment of the Wellington Officers' Training Corps, of which I was an undistinguished member, was called upon to line some of the route. Despite my earlier anti-Kipling tendencies, I was vastly moved and impressed by the occasion and later committed my impressions to paper. Read today, these show clearly the effect of Talboys' reading lists: ersatz touches of Clarendon, Macaulay, Greville, combined with a sentimental and overwritten style of which Talboys would certainly not have approved. None the less they do give a contemporary impression of a royal funeral by a sixteen-year-old.

The Wellington Guard-of-Honour was lined up on the upper slopes of the Long Walk, just below the Castle. After a long wait, the strains of the Dead March in Saul were heard, heralding the arrival of the funeral procession. Shortly afterwards, the first lot of troops by the Cambridge Gate are called up to attention. The schoolchildren in the crowd slacken their unending chatter: there is only a dull murmur of voices now. The music is louder: thud! goes the gun. At last – No. 2 Company [i.e. Wellington] – Atten-Shun! Three minutes later we are resting on reversed arms. The funeral procession has started. The temptation to look up is terrific, as the feet trudge by. First the Life-Guards, their long cloaks billowing in the breeze. Tramp-tramp, thud booms the gun. Those feet are muddy and dusty. They have walked over four miles today. Then out of the corner of my eye, I can see the gorgeous heraldic uniforms of the Puirsuivants approaching. I notice the wrinkles in their black stockings. Now rank upon rank of Army, Navy, and Air Force Representatives are passing, still at the same steady tramp. Oh Joy! we are at the present, and at last I can see something. Here come the members of the Army Council, swords reversed, heads bowed. Now the Admirals of the Fleet, some of whom are talking and looking back. Thud – says the gun. The bagpipes are playing now – a highland lament. Sir John Kelly [the principal naval ADC] walking completely alone, is followed by more Life-Guards and then the silent bands of the Guards, their drums heavily crêped.

Now the noise from the bagpipes is deafening . . . the Heralds are passing now. There is one very old one with a beard, and another very tall starchy one walking by himself. Now the valets, a sombre contrast in their plain black coats: Mr Tubb, the Sergeant Footman, has a handkerchief peeking out from his breast-pocket. But now, it is upon us! First the colours, and then the naval ratings. But as soon as I fix my eyes upon these, my vision is obstructed by a gigantic mass of bearskinned humanity – a line of Grenadiers. Then as suddenly as the vision was obstructed, so it is cleared. There is nothing save a gun-carriage pulled by naval ratings, the silver mountings gleaming, and on it rests a plain coffin. It is draped with the Royal Standard and on it, on a purple cushion, is the emblem of monarchy, the State Crown. I cannot take my eyes off it. Underneath it lies George, a faithful servant of the British Empire, who never again will see the light of day. But then I realise, as never before, that kings may come or kings may go, but the British monarchy and all that it stands for, goes on for ever. And as if in correspondence to my thoughts, there comes a dejected figure in naval uniform: the eyes are drawn, the face is pale. That is my King! [Edward VIII]

The continuing influence of Talboys must have led to improvements upon this rather novelette-ish style, for I began to win prizes for essays, compositions, historical treatments. At the annual speech-day, these prizes were distributed by the President of the Governors, the aged Arthur, Duke of Connaught, Queen Victoria's third son. "Well done, my boy," he would say, handing over a pile of book prizes, to which the response was: "Thank you very much, sir." This enables me, or any other prize-winner of the time, to establish an unusual link of longevity. In Windsor Castle hangs the Winterhalter portrait of the First Duke of Wellington, in whose memory the college was founded, handing a christening present to his godson, the infant Prince Arthur, later Duke of Connaught. The Queen is holding her little son in her arms, while the old Duke, in full dress uniform, proffers a casket containing his present. Now, it is reasonable to suppose that the Duke said something, even if it was only baby language, to the child; and equally reasonable to suppose that the Prince is making a few glugging noises in return as he reaches out with a marked degree of interest and anticipation towards the present-bearing Duke. On these assumptions I can claim that someone who had had conversation with the victor of Waterloo spoke to me on several occasions, and that I replied, as he, in his time, had answered the old Duke.

In the spring of 1937, Talboys decided to put me in for an Oxford history scholarship. I was considered too young to have any serious chance, but a canter round the course seemed a good idea, and I could make a serious attempt a year later. The examination was held in Christ Church hall and I have no recollection of the papers. I posted one of them to Talboys at Wellington and got a typical reply: 'we find no questions in it that are possible to do really well, chiefly because of their tired phrasing. Such a pity, this lack of vitality in a General Paper set without any real grasp of a VIth form boy's range or mentality. It may be due to the weather.' The letter concluded with the advice to go 'into Codrington Quad at All Souls and look up . . . "Quam dilecta tabernacula tua, Domine virtutum"* you will exclaim with the psalmist.'

Back at Wellington, I got a letter a few days later from the Principal of Brasenose informing me I had been elected into an open history scholarship. It seems that Christ Church had also been ready to give me an Exhibition, and much anxious discussion now ensued as to what was the best thing to do: accept the scholarship, accept the Exhibition or try for a Christ Church scholarship the following year. My mother knew little about Oxford, but at least she knew Christ Church had a social cachet, whereas she had only vaguely, if ever, heard of Brasenose. "I am an officer's widow," Talboys, in his mocking way, described her as saying to him, though what that had to do with it is not clear. I really did not mind. It looked to be a remarkable feat to have won a whole scholarship and on balance seemed better to hold what I had rather than chance all in twelve months time and perhaps lose all. Talboys thought likewise, so Brasenose it was. I spent a final term at Wellington, resting on my intellectual laurels, and went up to Oxford in October 1937.†

Among the letters of congratulation on winning the scholarship was one from my great-aunt, my grandfather's sister, who lived in the same village as he in Glamorgan. She, too, was a Victorian, by age as well as by life-style. She always wore a hat, a great wide-brimmed, high-crowned affair, and carried smelling salts in a reticule. 'I know nothing about that Coll. [Brasenose],' she wrote, in her flowing, nineteenth-century script, but 'Uncle Tom [her late husband] always said they were very strong and could hit out well . . . my dear Boy, I hope you will have a very happy time there and think Oxford the happiest place in the world.'

---

* Psalm 84: How amiable are thy dwellings, O Lord of Hosts
† Thirty years later, I was proud to be made a Governor of Wellington, an appointment which Talboys, with characteristic hyperbole, always described as equivalent to the award of the Garter.

The old lady struck the nail on the head twice over. Brasenose did hit out well, in the sense that it was full of cricketers, oarsmen, rugby players, some of them owing their admission to their athletic prowess or promise. They tended intermittently to get drunk and make a great deal of noise in the quads. As a result something of the Wellington story repeated itself: I made friends and went around with a group of people who were not primarily, often not at all, games players, but who liked music, wine, good talk . . . We even formed ourselves into a loosely constructed club, called the Lotophagi (Lotus-eaters who, according to Tennyson, dwelt in 'a land in which it seemed always afternoon'). I don't believe the club ever met but it bound us together, or so we priggishly imagined, by indissoluble links of fastidious taste and appreciation.

The great difference with Wellington was that there was no real opposition. In an atmosphere of mutual tolerance, the hearties went their way, we went ours. The College was presided over by its Principal, W.T.S. Stallybrass (Sonners), a distinguished academic lawyer and a man with a genius for friendship, above all with the young. He taught me a much needed lesson that the world is not made up of diametrically opposed opposites, but on the contrary consists of many differing sizes and shapes and kinds of people, few of them being demonstrably superior (or inferior) to the others. Certainly his own dinner-parties, large and lavish, sometimes too lavish in the matter of wine and vintage port, leading to youthful excesses and distressing regurgitations, were striking examples of his catholicity. Like many Brasenose men, I became very fond of him, and he of me.

Sonners (stemming from his family's original name of Sonnenschein) was one of the great formative influences at Oxford between the wars. In appearance ungainly and rumpled, traces of fallen cigarette ash marking his waistcoat, his rooms in their clutter and disorder representing an extension to his own personality, he knew how to win and retain the respect and affection of the athlete and the aesthete, the exuberant and the grave. During the war, he willingly added hours to his already overcharged working day by composing long, handwritten letters to Brasenose men scattered by military exigencies all over the world. A lifelong bachelor, he delighted in the presence and friendship of women. When, early after the war, I became engaged, one of the first priorities was to take my fiancée to Oxford to meet Sonners. Predictably, he went out of his way to welcome and charm her. When in 1948 came the news that he was dead, killed in a fall from a train while the worse for drink, it seemed that a light of unrepeatable quality had been extinguished.

Others of the Brasenose dons were good for one's education, and not merely in tutorials. The generous Maurice Platnauer taught me to love the music of Delius and how to tell one fine claret from another. Alan Ker took me to concerts and widened my musical knowledge. I had at Wellington developed a good singing voice, a light, high baritone, and began to be in demand as a soloist at Oxford concerts and in the Brasenose chapel. I even went to entertain the amazed inmates of Oxford gaol with a recital of folk songs. Unfortunately, I could not, and still cannot, make anything but a very poor effort at sight-reading. When later I became a leading member of the university madrigal singers, I was strongly dependent upon my friend Harry Fisher,* who stood next to me and who, though possessing only modest vocal gifts, had unerring musical sense and ability.

In the midst of all this freedom and pleasure-making at Oxford, I worked hard at my history and became convinced (the dons did not demur) that only bad luck or some unforeseen cataclysm could prevent me from getting a first. This combination of work, fun and friendship gave reality to my great-aunt's second observation about Oxford being the happiest place in the world. So it was and so, in my memory, it has remained. I had panelled rooms giving, on one side, on to one of the most pleasant if not the most distinguished seventeenth-century quads in Oxford, and on the other to the Radcliffe Square, an urban landscape which has, in my view, a claim to be the third most beautiful public place in Europe after the Campidoglio in Rome and Place Stanislas in Nancy. My style of living was modest, nothing like the sound-of-broken-glass school of Oxford reminiscence or fiction. But it was all I wanted, or could have dreamt of. All I desired was that it should go on, preferably for ever.

But by the time the University reassembled after the summer vacation of 1939, the country was at war. By then I was in Bermuda, pining for Oxford. What had happened was that soon after the outbreak of war my guardian, Major-General Sir Denis Bernard, who had earlier in the summer been appointed the new Governor and Commander-in-Chief of Bermuda, got in touch with me to know whether I would be interested in accompanying him as his ADC. A serving officer, he had

* Later Sir Henry Fisher, former High Court judge and sometime President of Wolfson College, Oxford

already chosen a young man from the regiment of which he was Colonel. But the coming of war meant that this officer had to rejoin his battalion. Bernard, who had shown a fatherly interest since my own father's death nine years earlier, and who therefore knew of my health troubles, thought it probable that when the time came for me to be called up I would not be passed fit for active, front-line service; and so he made his proposal.

What was the right thing to do? I could probably have completed my third year at Oxford, got my degree and then joined or been conscripted into some form of national service. On the other hand, the Bermuda offer, although I knew nothing whatever about the job or the place, was an opening into the unknown which would almost certainly be more interesting than some eventual pencil-pushing job in the services at home. I cannot recall clearly the pros and cons process which must have gone on within my mind. What I did do was to secure a military medical examination. As expected, this showed that I was in a low medical category. So the choice had to be made: Oxford or Bermuda? The coin, so to speak, came down with Bermuda uppermost. This was the very beginning of the war and, in a way that would certainly not have been possible later, the General was able, through his War Office contacts, to get me a Second Lieutenant's commission on the General List, that varied assortment of people whom for one reason or another it is not practical or suitable to appoint to a regimental or corps commission. The badges are simply the royal arms, and the wearers of the uniform thus designated are often, and sometimes scornfully, referred to as belonging to 'Fortnum and Mason's' or 'Crosse and Blackwell's'.

A big rush was now on. My mother, 'the officer's widow,' threw herself whole-heartedly into a spending spree on my behalf. Visits to civil and military tailors and bootmakers soon made me the possessor of winter-weight uniforms, tropical uniforms, ceremonial white uniforms, summer mess jackets (white), winter mess jackets (scarlet), boots, spurs, white and khaki pith helmets, a scarlet plume to adorn the white one on special occasions, sword-slings, aiguillettes (gilded and tasselled ropes worn on the right breast to denote attendance on the Sovereign's representative), a morning coat, a tailcoat, a red arm-band bearing the letters 'ADC', tin trunks and uniform cases to carry all this clobber: I could have been equipping myself to be Viceroy of India, or at least the Colonel of the Bengal Lancers. In addition, I insisted on taking all my Oxford books, in order as far as possible to continue with my studies so that when the war ended (perhaps in a matter of months) I could return to Brasenose and pick up where I left off.

These preparations made, the Governor's party embarked on the *Oropesa* at Liverpool. The next thirteen days were spent steaming first in convoy and then, more dangerously, alone. The intervals afforded ample opportunity to get to know better my new employer. Aged fifty-seven, he was a deeply disgruntled man. Up until a few months ago, he had been commanding the 3rd Division, based on Salisbury Plain. Replaced in this post by a youngish Major-General called Bernard Montgomery, he was continuously irritated by the thought that this man, instead of himself, would be leading his troops in France. This was not a matter only of professional pride, though that certainly entered into it; after a lifetime of devoted service to the army, why should he be cheated of potential battlefield glory and sent instead to govern a tin-pot place in the middle of nowhere? But there was also the question of money. As the *Oropesa* chugged westwards, blacked out at night against the threat of German submarines, so HE (His Excellency), as I now called him, began to talk more and more bitterly. The thing that seemed to irk him most was that being Governor of Bermuda would cost him not only all his pay but some of his private income, whereas in France, leading his division, he would have been incurring very little expense. To make himself economically secure and to win as much kudos as possible were his not unreasonable ambitions. As Bermuda would provide for neither of them, the poor little island came in for a fair measure of abuse.

This makes Denis Bernard sound dislikeable. He was not. Within the limits imposed by being a conventional, rather old-fashioned soldier, wedded to his regiment, disapproving of young officers marrying, given to wearing very highly polished field boots, he was a man of integrity and high standards, who drove himself hard and expected the same of others. Patience was not his strong point. Irascibility could easily develop into a show of bad temper. But once this was over, he could display a certain bear-like charm, enlivened by some gruff and bluff humour. The blow that fate had dealt him was indeed a cruel one. To cap it all he had voluntarily saddled himself with a baby-faced ADC who was so ignorant about military affairs that he failed, and had to be rebuked for failing, to notice that in the course of the voyage HE changed the insignia of rank on the epaulettes of his uniform from those of a Major-General to those of a Lieutenant-General, the rank borne (in those days) by the Governors of Bermuda.

Mrs Brooke, the future chatelaine of Government House, I also knew quite well, for in recent years she, a widow, had kept house for her bachelor brother in his various commands. A little older than he, she made a slightly scatty impression, heightened by her habit of half-closing her eyes against the smoke which was drifting upwards from the Turkish cigarette perpetually depending from her lips. The Bernards came of Anglo-Irish aristocratic stock, and Mrs Brooke was obsessed by class distinctions and a great name-dropper. But at heart she was a good and kindly person who longed to be more cultivated than she really was. On practical matters, she was extremely, and rather charmingly, vague. On board ship, this showed itself in an absolute lack of any sense of locality, an inability to tell port from starboard. Consequently she was frequently to be found, cigarette at the droop, wandering up and down one of the long companion ways off which the staterooms opened, in an attempt to find her cabin or the Ladies, an effort usually unsuccessful because both were on the opposite side of the ship.

The last memory of the voyage, just before the unidentified *Oropesa* gave the authorities in Bermuda such a fright, was of a small but alarming mishap suffered by HE. He went out on deck about 9.30 p.m. to get a breath of air. Having stepped out of a brightly lighted saloon into the utter darkness of a blacked-out ship, he naturally could not see anything. Inclined to be impetuous, instead of waiting until his eyes had adjusted themselves he charged forward, straight into a sturdy iron pillar, one of a row supporting the upper deck. The point of impact was his nose and, given the brisk pace at which he was travelling, the effect must have been exceedingly painful. For a moment it seemed probable that the citizens of Bermuda, in their first sight of their new Governor, would find that his nose curiously occupied well over half his face. Restoratives applied by the ship's doctor, however, soon had the nose under control.

Meanwhile the *Oropesa* steamed on through the subtropical night, taking me further and further away from Oxford, my friends and everything which was dear and familiar. It was a funny, you could say preposterous, way of going to war: little or no connection here with Alfred de Vigny's *Servitude et Grandeur Militaires* (although he, too, never saw action). With the optimism and adaptability of youth, I was not especially depressed or even apprehensive. Above all, I was not astounded in the way I am today, surveying the past from the belvedere of the present, at the sudden and unpredictable change which had come over my life. Those uniforms and ludicrous accoutrements lying in the hold in their tin boxes, the tendency of the immensely stately butler to come to my cabin and ask whether there was anything I wished him to do for me (thus compelling me, in desperation, to hand over for polishing already brightly gleaming shoes), the immeasurable difference in degree which separated all this from everything I had known before – nothing seemed to bother or surprise me. The predominant thought, as the long voyage drew to a close, was that despite a very real risk we had not been torpedoed. That was quite enough to be going on with.

2

An Island Story

I gave the handle of the private telephone connecting Government House with the stables several sharp turns and when the person the other end, summoned by these persistent rings, answered, I spoke confidently into the mouthpiece. "Good morning, France. We'll want the victoria and pair for His Excellency at nine forty-five, Mrs Brooke wants Sutton and the surrey at eleven to go calling, and this afternoon there's the formal opening of the House of Assembly so we'll need the landau with you and Sutton on the box in your best uniforms."

France was the coachman (he had previously been driving the Lord Mayor of Liverpool's coach-and-four) who had come with us from England, Sutton a soldier-groom who had served the General in his former command. Why bring a coachman, of all things? For the good and simple reason that in 1939, and for many years after, Bermuda was a horse-drawn society. All cars and lorries, except for fire engines and ambulances, were forbidden. The less affluent citizens got around by bicycle, the better-off by one-horsed vehicles with a fringed cover on top, an American contraption known as a surrey. The really well-heeled ran to a carriage and pair. For those who possessed no horse but needed occasionally to drive behind one – in order to dine at Government House, for example – there were livery stables for hiring purposes. (For the younger or more impecunious guests, even dinner at Government House did not call for four legs: on a fine night, there was nothing amiss with a bicycle, even for the ladies, who gathered up their long skirts and hung them, like a pile of washing, over their arm.) I may have been brought up partly in the Victorian setting of my grandparents; but that was nothing compared with this sudden excursion into a yet more distant past, with its prevailing and Dickensian smell of horse-droppings, horse sweat and saddle soap.

Yet the colony's legislators who decreed these arrangements had acted wisely. Had fully fledged motor traffic been permitted (still not completely the case today) you would have got from one end of the island to the other in about forty minutes. As it was, it was the best part of a day's work to walk and trot from Hamilton, the capital, to St George's, the only other town, a distance of thirteen miles. And a very pleasant way it was of spending a day. No one who has not driven regularly behind a horse or horses can have any idea of the continuous felicity of the experience. There is ample time for observation, yet if the horses are trotting the pace can be exhilarating. Bowling along the white coral-based roads of Bermuda, their verges lined by hedgerows of flowering oleander and hibiscus, was a delight that never palled. If the occasion was formal and we were in the landau, a graceful four-seater with two men on the box, drawn by two, and even occasionally four grey horses, then a feeling of effortless superiority was unavoidable as we overtook lesser mortals on their bicycles or in their one-horse surreys and traps. As a result of this, I know from personal experience, in a way that few other people can possibly know, just what it was that enabled the insufferable Mrs Elton, in *Emma*, to boast about the glories of travel in her brother-in-law's barouche-landau.

Bermuda was, and still is, a Crown Colony with a Governor, an Executive Council, a Legislative Council and an elected, single-chamber Parliament or House of Assembly. Despite these trappings, everyone knew quite well where the real power lay: with the handful of white merchant and banker families who dominated the financial, economic and social scene. (The blacks, although making up the greater part of the population, counted in 1939 for almost nothing.) These families were heavily intermarried, so much so that it was the height of folly ever, in Bermudian company, to express a personal opinion about anyone on the island, for who was to know you were not talking to the brother-in-law of the person concerned? Close-knit though this privileged circle was, it was shot through with family feuds and antipathies, and the danger was great of inviting to Government House two sections of a family who had not spoken to one another for years. Such a danger was, as I wrote home facetiously after about two months in the place, part of the risk incurred by a soldier in a great modern war; it could not be avoided.

The other characteristic of these Bermudian families was their intimate and personal connection with retail commerce. I had been brought up to regard people 'in trade' as belonging to another, inferior social class, and as in England, at Oxford or elsewhere, I had never met any such people socially, I had never had occasion to question this particular piece of snobbery. In Bermuda, it was quite possible to have as a dinner companion the lady from whom you have bought a pair of shoes that very morning. The scions of these aristocratic families regularly served behind the counter of their family haberdasher's shop or liquor store or ironmonger's establishment. So much was this true that the best time for a Government House tennis party – one of HE's favourite forms of entertainment, despite his own mediocre performance on court – was Thursday afternoon, early closing day in Hamilton. Trott, Trimingham, Tucker, Smith . . . the holders of these names, some of them traceable back to the early history of the colony (it was settled in the first part of the seventeenth century) deferred to no one in their pride in the past and confidence in the future. Yet they displayed (apart from their attitude towards the blacks) little if any class-consciousness, the result, no doubt, of their having absorbed so much of the American ethic, imported by generations of tourists and holidaymakers from the United States.

According to the Oxford Dictionary, an aide-de-camp is 'an officer who assists a general in the field, by conveying his orders, procuring him intelligence etc.' This definition obviously did not fit my case. Although I did do a little basic military training – such as learning to salute – with the detachment of the British infantry battalion stationed in the colony, I was manifestly unequipped to assist a general, or anybody else, in the field. Besides, there was no field. HE, though he often put on his red-tabbed uniform and went off to inspect a camp or barracks or some other part of his tiny command, could not be said to resemble in the faintest degree the general of traditional warfare, surrounded by staff officers on curvetting horses and surveying from some grassy knoll the serried ranks of his division or corps drawn up below him.

My job therefore turned out to be rather more like that of a private and social secretary. I had to arrange the entertaining, select and invite the guests to lunch and tea and dinner, greet them when they arrived, line them up (in the case of a formal dinner) for presentation to HE and Mrs Brooke, who like royalty entered the room only after all the visitors were assembled. I had also to supervise the household. In addition to the stable staff, the butler, the cook, the maids, this included three British soldiers dressed up as footmen, of whom I was nominally the commanding officer. I checked the wine in the wine cellar, the tennis balls in the tennis hut, the progress of the sixteen convicts who came from the prison every day to work in the gardens.

There was nothing and nobody to guide me in all this. There had been no handover with the outgoing Governor and his staff. Quite early on, I came upon a vital piece of equipment: a card index of all the people who had in the past been entertained. One side of the card bore their name and address and when and for what they had last been to the house. The other, much more compromising side listed their strengths and weaknesses: good bridge-player, drinks too much, over-free with ladies etc. By far the most frequent annotation was the cryptic marking 'GPO'. What could this mean? General Purpose Offering? Good Person for all Occasions? I cannot now remember how I discovered the damning truth, but discover it I did. Those letters meant that such people were unsuitable for any specialised form of hospitality and should be bidden no more than once annually, to the summer Garden Party Only.

Life began to settle down into a sort of pattern. HE continued to mope and in private to despise the Bermudians for their lack of warlike spirit. Mrs Brooke, on the other hand, was the life and soul of the island. There was no woman's committee of which she was not president, not a bundles-for-Britain meeting which she did not chair. Driving along in the landau, HE sitting quietly by her side, she would bob and bow and wave and smile at the passers-by, who gazed back with scarcely disguised astonishment. Some Sundays we drove to the garrison church, I wearing my immensely expensive field boots and sword, and there, after the service was over, scenes reminiscent of an Anglo-Indian cantonment were enacted. The British regimental band played on the parade ground, the officers and their wives and daughters and sisters walked about and chatted on one side of the greensward, the NCOs and other ranks being kept at a safe distance on the other. Then it was back for lunch at Government House, a large, airy, ugly building erected in 1887, surmounted by three towers which gave it the appearance, from a distance, of a Victorian workhouse or possibly a subtropical mental asylum. Perched upon a hilltop outside Hamilton, its windows and terraces commanded sweeping views of the sea to which the coral formations gave a light but brilliant green effect inshore, while further out, beyond the reef, a deep and marvellous cobalt colour prevailed.

When not at the garrison church, we – the Government House party – would spend many Sundays visiting the outlying parishes of the island. The scene could have been taken straight from the pages of any Victorian novel about country life. We set out in the landau, France and

Sutton ramrod-like on the box, and reached the favoured church in good time for morning service. A receiving committee of local dignitaries, their panama or straw hats doffed in respect to the King's representative, was waiting to escort HE to the front pew. If it was a Communion service (not popular with the General), the whites of the congregation received the Sacrament first, and only when the last one had been ministered to would the blacks file up for their turn. Lunch with a local bigwig followed and in the later afternoon, as the shadows began to lengthen and a cool breeze got up off the sea, the grey horses would be harnessed again and off we would trot, along the dusty lanes and past the pretty, pink or white coral-built houses, through the outskirts of Hamilton, and up the steep hill – the horses sweating by now – which led to Government House. Hooves clattered on the wooden blocks beneath the portico, the footman emerged to open the doors of the landau and another day's duty was over.

One of the few fully racially integrated institutions was the prison service. Black and white wrongdoers served out their sentences together in apparent harmony. The General, intent, if he could not lead his troops into battle, on exploring every corner of his toy principality, carried out periodic inspections, poking about with his whangee cane into swill buckets and latrine drains, asking the convicts what they were inside for. One such question, put to a red-haired Scotsman of cheerful demeanour, evoked an answer that was at first incomprehensible, so strong was his Glaswegian accent. Asked to repeat it, he said, more clearly and with what seemed to me a certain swagger, "Carnal knowledge of a mare, Sir." The General's face, which had a permanent tendency towards the purple, became even more suffused. He appeared to be undergoing some sort of inner struggle, though whether he was trying to suppress laughter or repulsion, I never knew. Winning the battle for self-control, he passed on to the next man, a lugubrious black convicted for the more humdrum offence of petty larceny.

In most ways the most conformist of men, HE had an astonishing capacity to surprise. One night I returned to Government House late, after dining with a girl-friend in the town. The big house was in pandemonium, lights blazing, footmen running, telephones trilling. What had happened was that the General, too, had dined out with friends and had stayed on for a rubber of bridge. Moved either by some masochistic urge, or because he genuinely shrank from turning out the coachman and horses to convey him a short distance, he decided to follow the Bermudian example and bicycle. Though a fine horseman, his sense of balance on two wheels was uncertain. Returning from his bridge evening quite late, perhaps emboldened by a whisky or two over the final hands, it seems he careered, unbraking, down a steep dip in the Government House drive, lost control and shot over the handlebars to hit his head hard against a hefty palm-tree. By the time I turned up, he was lying on a sofa in the drawing-room, mildly concussed, his head swathed in bloodstained bandages, awaiting the arrival of the ambulance to take him to hospital. He had finally, though not at all in the way he would have wished or expected, acquired a war wound. He was too groggy to upbraid me for being absent in the hour of need, but the normally benign Mrs Brooke cast a reproachful glance. It must have been soon after this that the General wrote to my mother, complaining about my frivolous social life and promising to impose a more disciplined regime in future.

Nothing could alter the isolated geographical position of Bermuda: three centuries earlier, Andrew Marvell had composed the lines

> Where the remote Bermudas ride
> In ocean's bosom unespied

with the result that the word 'remote' has been more often quoted to characterise the island than any other. But that very quality gave to wartime Bermuda an unexpected importance. The only safe link between Europe and the USA – safe, that is, from the threat of German submarines to allied surface traffic – was by air: Lisbon to the Azores, the Azores to Bermuda, Bermuda to New York, or vice versa. The service was assured by the flying boats of Pan-American Airways (and later on by British Overseas Airways, as it then was). These planes, huge affairs by the standards of the time, would glide down upon the waters of the Little Sound for their refuelling stop. Off them would step any transatlantic traveller important or rich enough to secure a passage to London or New York. Two or three hours later, they would take off again for the next leg of their journey. That at least was the idea. Sometimes mechanical troubles, but more often, on the eastward flight, the weather at the Azores, would mean that the plane and its passengers had to remain at Bermuda awaiting better conditions.

All this introduced a new order of things. The British wartime dirty tricks department took full advantage of this opportunity to examine the mail the planes carried. As the war went on, indeed, Bermuda became a huge censorship centre for surface as well as airmail. Hundreds of censors from the United Kingdom, the more senior ones working at a high level of secrecy, moved into one of the big hotels to which the tourists no longer came. In another way I became personally involved. Because it was thought politic to show special courtesies to Very Important Persons travelling by the air route, I would, after examining an advance copy of the incoming plane's passenger manifest, don my uniform, bicycle down to the harbour, board the Governor's launch and chug over to the island where the flying boat base was housed. Then, on the arrival of the plane, I would single out my man (or woman), give him the Governor's compliments, take him to a special refreshment lounge, and remain with him until it was time for the plane to leave again.

By these means I met and talked to a great quantity of people from the real world. Sometimes, when they were delayed, we had them to stay at Government House whence they obligingly carried letters to loved ones in England. Among these was Robert Menzies, the Australian Prime Minister (very critical of Churchill's overbearing methods), Henry Morgenthau, the US Secretary of the Treasury, Sir Keith Murdoch, the Australian newspaper owner whose son Rupert was, forty years on, to become my employer at Times Newspapers, the Norwegian Prime Minister, Lord Halifax, Attlee, then Deputy Prime Minister (he left his shaving brush and shoes behind), Gil Winant, the beetle-browed American Ambassador in London . . . But before him there was an earlier US envoy from London: Joseph Kennedy, the father of the future President. Subsequent history has shown that he held anti-British, or at least defeatist, views. A note I kept at the time (November 1939) recorded that, though he seemed extremely affable, his general view of the situation was depressing. He thought the war would be 'abominably short', that there would soon be carnage both in France and in England, and not until that happened would the warring nations find a joint meeting ground and become united by a common demand for peace. With the gift of hindsight, we can see that these judgements were spectacularly wrong.

It was not only from the air that distinguished visitors were apt to drop in. In addition to my other duties, I was the Governor's cipher officer, spending long hours unbuttoning secret cables from London, most of them containing war news that was often stale. One day in July 1940, after the fall of France, I deciphered a cable from the Colonial Office that read as follows:

Arrangements have been made for the Duke of Windsor and party to

1 Bermuda 1940: the Duke of Windsor and the Governor, F.G., opposite, in the landau

2 Bermuda 1940: the Windsors' stay at Government House: Mrs Brooke, left, the Governor and F.G. in uniform, Captain Wood (the Duke's A.D.C.) and wife standing

3 Bermuda 1940: the Windsors at the Cathedral, the Governor behind

sail from Lisbon on August 1 by ship of American Export Line to be diverted to land him at Bermuda. Arrangements are being made here for HRH and party to proceed to Nassau by *Lady Somers* (which it is understood leaves Bermuda on August 13) or by warship. So far as known at present party will consist of Duke and Duchess, Major Philipps, Captain and Mrs Wood, maid and valet. Grateful if you could inform me what arrangements can be made for party between arrival at Bermuda (possibly about August 11) and departure.

This message had varying effects upon those in Government House. HE, in his bad-tempered way, declared that he for one would take to his bed if *that* woman came into the house. (In the event, he obviously had no choice but to reply to London that the royal party would be welcome.) Mrs Brooke, though outwardly loyal to her brother, was secretly excited by the prospect. So, in larger measure still, was I. Here was a welcome change from the parochial round. Though they had since their marriage been to England privately, this would be the first time that the Windsors would be officially received on British soil. Anticipating a good news story – had not the Bishop of Bermuda two years earlier stalked into a newspaper office in Hamilton and torn down pictures of the Windsor wedding? – American reporters and photographers began arriving in the colony.

On the *Excalibur*'s arrival, I went out by launch and greeted the Duke and Duchess. He looked very different to the lonely figure I had seen four years earlier, ambling dejectedly along behind his father's coffin at Windsor. The party included a Special Branch man, Detective Inspector Holder, who had been sent from London to Lisbon to join them. He electrified me, before we left *Excalibur*, by drawing me on one side and announcing, in a dramatic whisper, that the Duke and Duchess were in danger every moment of the day and night and should never be allowed out of his or my sight. At this time, of course, we in Bermuda knew nothing of the previous month's goings-on in Lisbon, when the Germans had made various clumsy or far-fetched attempts to dissuade or prevent the Duke from taking up his post as Governor of the Bahamas; they hoped, apparently, that they could make use of him to bring about, or preside over, a negotiated peace.

A full-scale greetings ceremony had been laid on for the visitors when they landed from the launch at the Yacht Club steps: guard of honour, band, colours . . . The Duke, not surprisingly, carried out his inspection and did all that was required of him in a manner made perfect by a

lifetime of training. But his brow darkened when he saw what he could
not avoid seeing: the failure of Mrs Brooke or any of the greeting wives
to curtsey to the Duchess. Later that evening, at dinner at Government
House, the clouds turned darker still when, the ladies having withdrawn, the talk turned to the war situation: "If I'd been King, there'd
have been no war," said the Duke emphatically. HE went scarlet with
rage and clearly had to exert a great effort of self-control to stop himself
from slamming out of the room. It is now known from public sources
that the Duke had made this sort of remark before; it did represent his
sincere opinion. But that made things no easier at the dinner table that
August night, only two months after the débâcle of Dunkirk. Only the
tactful interventions of a specially invited guest, Charles Lambe,* who
had been a royal naval equerry when the Duke was on the throne and
who was temporarily in Bermuda in command of a cruiser, partly
defused the electric atmosphere.

In the week that followed, while the Windsors waited for a ship to
take them on to the Bahamas, my special duty was to look after them,
accompany them on their public appearances and generally act as their
guide and factotum. As a result, I had ample opportunity for observing
them and every night made some copious notes about my impressions.
They included the curious fact, imparted by seeing the Duke take a
shower after a game of golf, that he had absolutely no hair on his body,
even in the places where one would most expect it to be. Whatever the
correctness or defects of my observations these do at least have the
advantage of being immediately recorded.† Red-hot, indeed, were my
sensations when, just after we had all arrived at Government House
from the landing ceremonies, the Duke appeared in my office where I
was busily catching up on the deciphering. He was still smarting from
the discourtesy (as he saw it) shown to his wife. "Who ordered this?" he
asked me, angrily. Nothing that had ever happened to me could be a
help in answering such a question from such a person. At the age of
twenty-one (it would have made little or no difference, I believe, had I
been forty-two or eighty-four), I was totally dumbfounded. Without
saying anything, I reached into a file of deciphered cables and handed
him the one we had received from London, giving instructions on
etiquette and modes of address. The Duke, it said, should be accorded a

* Later Admiral of the Fleet Sir Charles Lambe, Chief of Naval Staff 1959–60.
† I lent some of my notes to my friend Frances Donaldson for her biography of Edward
VIII (Weidenfeld & Nicolson, 1974).

half-curtsey, but not the Duchess, who should be addressed as 'Your Grace'. The Duke read the cable, uttered a wordless expression of disgust and turned on his heel.

Later, discussing the matter with Mrs Brooke, he asked her, almost pathetically, to assure him that we had not sent for such instructions and seemed relieved when assured they had come unsolicited. "It's all the Queen," he burst out. "My brother is perfectly all right, it's the Queen who is behind this." And he added, half in gloom and half in anger, "I don't know whether we will be able to stick it down at Nassau if this sort of thing is going to go on all the time." He said he had never, in all his life, heard of anything called a half-curtsey, and if the Duchess was not to be addressed as a Royal Highness, she should be called Duchess or the Duchess.

The person who appeared, externally at least, to be oblivious to all this was the Duchess herself. 'She is a very clever woman', run my notes, 'and like all clever women contrives to hide her real feelings behind what is, in her case, a highly polished exterior . . . She is not intrinsically beautiful or handsome, but she has a good complexion, regular features and a beautiful figure . . . She is of course beautifully dressed, and this does not mean just extravagantly dressed, but dressed with a canny sense of fitness, with a knowledge of how to avoid the bizarre but strike the original. The coiffure is superb . . . she has good legs and ankles and moves well . . . More than all the charm of her physical appearance, though, is her manner: she has, to an infinite degree, that really great gift of making you feel that you are the very person whom she has been waiting all her life to meet. With old and young and clever and stupid alike she exercises this charm and during the week she was here, during which she met a number of people, I never saw anyone who could resist the spell – they were all delighted and intrigued . . . She does not talk much, unless she sees you want to talk, and she is always quiet and dignified and composed . . . she is never anything but stately, and when she had to wave to the crowds on her arrival, and subsequently whenever we drove through the town, she did it with ease and charm and grace which suggested that she had been at it all her life.'

It was fascinating to watch this famous couple together and assess the impact of each personality upon the other. 'He is more in love with her than she with him,' I noted, though her feelings assumed 'a watchful, almost maternal devotion'. Each night, before the Government House party went to bed, she would ask me about the arrangements for the next day, in particular the time of the Duke's first engagement – "for I am the alarm clock in this family." As well as timekeeper, she was also watch-dog. One night after dinner, when she was involved in a bridge four in another room, he sat on in the drawing-room, talking ceaselessly to Mrs Brooke and myself, when he should have been preparing the speech he would have to make on arrival in Nassau. (He was describing, in graphic detail, his months as King at Buckingham Palace when, spurning a proper lunch, he would use the lunch hours to roam the corridors and explore the cellars. In the latter, he found a troglodyte race of little men, nominally in charge of the electricity supplies and drains, who lived there permanently in encampments formed of the piles of tinned food and other supplies they had purloined or been given by the cooks and store-keepers.) Presently the Duchess, dummy for that hand, appeared at the drawing-room door. Her expression was reproachful.

"Now, David, what about that work?"

"All right, darling, I'm just going up now."

The Duchess returned to the bridge table.

Of course, the Duke did not go up, and it was nearly midnight when he finally said goodnight. As he walked up the stairs, he looked across to the bridge table the other side of the hall and said, perhaps a little guiltily, "Now you see, darling, I'm going to attend to my speech." His wife made no reply but 'just looked at him . . . like a nanny whose charge had forgotten the precepts she had taught him, thereby grieving more than annoying her'. It was small wonder that, in the course of a shopping expedition one morning, the Duke, having bought a pair of bathing trunks, explained that he had "better have some of these. It's I who wear the shorts in this family, you know."

After a week, the Windsors sailed away, but before long another royal ménage arrived. This was ex-King Carol of Romania and his red-haired mistress, Magda Lupescu. The protocol authorities in London, ever-vigilant, had ruled that she could not be received at Government House, so the party was accommodated at an hotel. HE gave a stag party for the King, the King gave a stag party for HE, the officers of the garrison entertained the King at a guest night in the Mess; and all this time Mme Lupescu remained immured in her hotel room, in company with two poodles and two Pekes. The King, I wrote in my notebook, was a dull dog: 'to shake hands with him was like gripping hold of a piece of wet cod'. My ambition to meet Mme Lupescu was finally achieved when she and the King stood me a drink in their cabin on the ship that bore them away from Bermuda. Henna and mascara in large quantities had been called in aid of her appearance, but, I noted, 'she is very easy to talk to, and her gestures and movements are at least happy and vivacious, compared with Carol's courtly but lugubrious bearing.'

This was the period of the war when Winston Churchill persuaded a still neutral United States to make over to the Royal Navy fifty old destroyers, considered vital for the battle of the Atlantic, in return for the right to instal US bases in Bermuda and some of the West Indian islands to the south. By midsummer 1941 large numbers of American ships and sailors had begun to clog the anchorages and overrun the streets. They were followed by numerous American soldiers, still wearing the dimple-dented, wide-brimmed hat associated with First World War doughboys. Though the Bermudians did not at all like what was happening, everyone – British, Bermudians, Americans – were on their best behaviour; it was important not to provide any fuel to the isolationist critics of Franklin Roosevelt's policy of giving maximum aid, short of co-belligerence, to Britain. But despite these efforts, an air of unease prevailed. HE was a serving Lieutenant-General and Commander-in-Chief, yet he commanded far fewer men and resources than the American Rear-Admiral and Army Brigadier-General whom he outranked. Though sensing that something was amiss, I did not know at the time and still do not know today what brought things to a head. What is certain is that one day a top-secret cable arrived from London, with the instructions that HE was to decipher it himself.

It was, in effect, the sack. The Government had decided, in the changed circumstances, that the tradition of appointing a very senior army officer to govern the colony must be abandoned. The new Governor would be a civilian, Lord Knollys. Dolefully HE and Mrs Brooke prepared to depart, which they did in September. In his case, regrets and recriminations were outweighed by relief at relinquishing a job he had never wanted or liked. In a revealing letter from the ship taking him homewards, he wrote: 'I am very pleased indeed with the way you discharged your duties as ADC. If only I had been able to devote more of my time to the profession which I really do understand, I might have been able to teach you more about it, but at any rate you have got an inkling of it and realise how straight and honourable it is compared with ordinary "business" and how vastly more honest than the life of petty intrigue of which I have seen so much in the last two years.' He ended: 'I am very happy. It is nice to be in a completely English atmosphere.'

Knollys asked me to stay on and see him in, an invitation which was renewed repeatedly, until I finally left in November 1942. A very different regime now ruled at Government House. The son of a famous courtier, Knollys was only forty-two (he and his wife Margaret later became close personal friends), and had wide business experience, particularly in the USA. His ability to get on with Americans was probably one of the determining factors in the appointment. Good-looking and good-mannered, he lacked a dominant personality; if anyone did the domineering, it was his wife, who had a quick temper and did not mind what she said to anyone. They brought their young children, and the whole atmosphere of the house brightened notice-ably. I certainly appreciated this at the time, but looking back now I can see that the Knollyses, though far more of the world and flexible than their predecessors, lacked some of the colour and eccentricity of the latter. They were not such good 'copy' as Mrs Brooke, who had been told in youth, and apparently still believed, that when a train stopped in the middle of nowhere in the countryside, you should immediately dismount for fear of being run into by the train behind. They differed, too, from the General, with his almost childlike impulses, enthusiasms and aversions; the only oddity of 'Edgey' Knollys (the name was an elided form of those bestowed on him by his royal godfathers, King Edward VII and the Prince of Wales, later King George V) was to conclude almost every remark, however simple or portentous, with the phrase, equivalent to a nervous tick, "in that way".

Apart from this change in style, and the import of another, naval ADC to share my duties, the texture of life did not change much. Cables still had to be deciphered, airborne VIPs watered and fed. One of these created quite a stir. We had a cable from Washington telling us that Lord Louis Mountbatten, as he then was, who had been in the USA superintending the repair of his bomb-damaged ship HMS *Illustrious*, would be flying through on his way to London. He would be travelling under the assumed name of Mr Mountain (not a foolproof cover, one would have thought) and it was essential that nothing should impede his onward journey. The reason for all this secrecy and haste was that the War Cabinet in London had decided to create the new command of Combined Operations; Mountbatten was being summoned to lead it.

Even the priorities of war could not control the weather in the Azores, which was too bad to allow the plane to fly onwards from

Bermuda. There was nothing for it. Lord Louis would have to stay at Government House until such time as the plane could take off again. Here, there was an added complication. That night there was no possibility of giving any guest his dinner at Government House; the Governor was going off to some function, the servants had been given the night off, and Margaret Knollys and myself, together with a few friends, were going to have dinner in Hamilton's main restaurant. Despite the risk of blowing his cover, Mountbatten would have to come too.

The prospect caused him no dismay whatever. Elated by the thought of his new job, full of pride and battle honours for his wartime naval career up to then, he was clearly out to enjoy himself. We arrived at the restaurant, had some drinks in the bar and went to our table where very soon Mountbatten's voice, which had a particularly resonant, booming quality, could not fail to be heard by the other diners present. "You'll be getting *Indomitable* here next week on her shake-down cruise," he bellowed, "a fine ship, and a tremendous addition to our air-strike capacity." He was referring to a newly constructed and commissioned aircraft-carrier, which was 'working up' in the comparatively safe waters of the Western Atlantic, before joining the main fighting strength of the Royal Navy.

This piece of news was not news to me. I knew about it, as a result of my reading of secret telegrams and intelligence which passed through my hands on the way to HE. But I also knew that this was not something that should be talked about in public places. Only a couple of weeks earlier, the British Naval Commander-in-Chief in Bermuda had issued a circular warning everyone in his command against careless talk, and enjoining them to report any example of such talk that ever came to their notice, no matter who might be involved.

It was therefore with a sinking feeling that I saw a young naval officer whom I knew slightly, and who was dining with a companion in the restaurant, leave his table, come across to our table and ask me if he could have a word with me outside. We went into the bar and he explained that he had heard clearly – how could he not have done so? – the remarks made by a member of the Government House party. These were highly prejudicial to naval security and he must ask me the identity of the maker of the remarks (everyone in the restaurant was in civilian clothes). Mindful of the need to conceal Mountbatten's presence, I told my friend that it was not possible for me to give him the information he wanted, but that I could personally assure him that, however questionable the practice of shouting out the names and movements of warships in public, the stranger who had just done so was a person of the utmost importance whose identity must be protected. The young naval officer looked unhappy but accepted the situation and we both returned to our respective tables.

Mountbatten continued to talk in stentorian tones and *Indomitable* again came into his conversation. I suppose it was because she was an aircraft-carrier, the sister ship of his own *Illustrious*, that he was so excited. However that might be, the young naval officer again came to me and asked me to step outside with him. Again I tried to assure him that, whatever the appearances, this was not a case where his very proper sense of vigilance should be exercised. This time he refused to be assuaged, and said that he was going immediately to contact the civil and naval police. As with the Duke of Windsor and his demand to know who had issued instructions about his reception, so now I felt profoundly troubled and perplexed. What was worse: revealing the name of someone whose true identity we had been instructed to preserve at all costs or seeing Lord Louis Mountbatten arrested and marched off from a public restaurant? Faced with that stark alternative, perplexity soon ceased. I told my friend who the stranger was, emphasising that he was England-bound on a mission of the highest importance.

Rather to my regret, he collapsed into a fit of horror and remorse. Only a few minutes before, he had been full of the resolve and fearlessness – "I don't mind who it is, he is endangering the safety of His Majesty's ships" – which a good case engenders. Now all he wanted to do was to meet Mountbatten and explain his part in this protracted episode. I therefore went back into the restaurant, gave Mountbatten a hurried whispered account of what had been going on, and asked him if he would come out and speak to the officer. He did so, and although I was not present at their conversation, my friend told me afterwards what had happened. Mountbatten congratulated him upon his attention to duty even when off duty, said that he, the young man, had behaved entirely correctly, and, ordering drinks from the bar, washed away the whole affair in a flood of *bonhomie* and pink gin. Several decades later, in London, I reminded Mountbatten of this contretemps when I met him somewhere. He did not like the recollection at all and changed the subject quickly.

These tales of ex-Kings and other exalted persons might give the impression that they were all that mattered in wartime Bermuda. This was not so. The hand of war, though physically absent, inevitably made itself felt. It was painful to be in the sunshine and calm of the subtropics and listen to broadcasts about the blitz in London or Coventry. It was still more painful to get news of the death in action or capture of friends. Sometimes such tragedies occurred, as it were, on the doorstep.

Towards the end of 1941, the Free French submarine *Surcouf*, the largest submarine in the world, put into the dockyard in Bermuda. Something of a white elephant in naval terms, she had had a chequered career since escaping from Brest in the summer of 1940. In Devonport, where she fetched up, two British officers were killed by French gunfire in a fracas on board. After 1300 French sailors had died at Mers-el-Kebir in Algeria, victims of British shells, only 14 of *Surcouf*'s complement of 150 volunteered for Free France; the rest sabotaged much of the boat before being taken prisoner. Thereafter *Surcouf*, with a new crew and assigned to Atlantic patrols, was riven by Vichy-versus-Free French differences within the crew which took their toll on the actual operation of the boat. In Bermuda, the Knollyses were invited by the Captain to lunch on board and I accompanied them. Though a splendid show of French culinary hospitality was put on in the cramped wardroom, the general tension was almost tangible. It had already been the subject of adverse reports by the British liaison officer on board, Roger Burney RNVR, with whom I had been at Wellington.

Roger, only twenty-two and a former conscientious objector, was a deeply troubled and lonely young man. Caught in the withering crossfire of divided French loyalties, he had no one to trust or confide in, except the two British naval ratings providing him with a communications link on board. While the boat was at Bermuda, we did our best at Government House to cheer him up, entertaining him, having him to stay. A few weeks later he wrote to me from a Canadian port. 'I have been experiencing a reign of terror ever since I left you,' he wrote, 'and not a soul to talk to, nothing to do but mope in my loneliness and read and read my beloved Italian history . . . I'm afraid you did me no good at all because I feel this loneliness far more keenly now. I begin to pine for the autumnal corruptness of New York or else for the academic solidarity of beloved Cambridge . . . I could write of the many amusing and horrifying incidents that have already occurred since I left [Bermuda].'

Two months later *Surcouf* was lost with all hands, Roger included, while en route to Tahiti via the Panama Canal. What really happened is one of the war's unsolved mysteries. She may have collided with a US army transport vessel, she may even (though this is pure speculation) have been sunk by joint British and American naval action after a mutiny on board had threatened to deliver or had actually delivered the boat into Vichy hands. What is certain is that poor, lonely, perplexed Roger was missing, presumed, and then confirmed, dead. From what he had told me of the conditions on board while under way, it was not surprising that he had premonitions of mortality. Though he perished, his name is perpetuated in one of the most splendid memorials imaginable. Benjamin Britten dedicated his War Requiem to him among others, 'in loving memory'.

Roger had ended his letter with the words 'for heaven's sake don't commit the folly of angling for your return to the Motherland.' This is just what I was doing. Without indulging in false heroics, I was beginning to think, as the war dragged on, that there must be something useful I could do at home. Never to have heard a bomb drop or an anti-aircraft battery explode into life, never to have eaten a dried egg omelette or stood fire-watch during a raid, was going, later on, to create unbridgeable gaps in experience between me and my friends. Without knowing what it was I would be doing when I got there, I began to prepare for the journey to England. The paraphernalia I had carted out three years ago were packed away in their boxes and sent off by sea. I entered upon a course of very basic training for another sort of journey.

The USA was now in the war and its production lines were turning out war material in increasing quantities. Among this was the Catalina flying-boat, a high-wing, two-engined monoplane with a big range, ideally suited for ocean patrolling. Many of these, built in California, were destined for RAF Coastal Command, and were flown to England by civilian American pilots. The crews for these flights, which staged through Bermuda, were provided by RAF or RCAF air crews who had been training in Canada. On inquiring, I was told that I could not be carried as a passenger, but that if I liked to work my passage I would be welcome. My job would be to read the petrol gauges; not a very onerous or skilled task, but one which nevertheless required a certain amount of practice, because allowance had to be made for the tilt of the aircraft which affected the showing of the petrol levels in the tanks. Several practice flights in the skies above Bermuda gave me the rudiments of the technique.

Early one morning in November 1942, while it was still dark, I left Government House for the last time in the faithful surrey which had carried me safely about the island for the last three years. Clip-clop to Hamilton and the quayside, chug-chug to the seaplane base where the

Catalina, its outlines increasingly visible in the growing dawn, was moored. Before long we were lumbering across the water under full power, our take-off weight increased by the extra fuel tanks that had been fitted for the long flight home. And it was a long flight. The Catalina had a cruising speed of about 130 knots, and we had nearly 3500 miles to go. There was a story that if you looked down from the porthole of a Catalina you would see the same piece of seaweed that you had passed fifteen minutes earlier. Apocryphal, no doubt, but she certainly did go very slowly. After twelve hours and a consistently unfavourable head-wind, we were less than half-way across. I fervently read and re-read the petrol gauges. The result showed that the plane was in fact approaching the so-called point of no return, when there was just enough fuel to get us back to Montreal. The alternative was to fly on in the hope of picking up a tail-wind.

I can remember a total absence of panic or even anxiety. The young trainee navigator said, not particularly confidently, that he believed that a following wind lay somewhere ahead. The issue was solved, to everyone's apparent satisfaction, by the civilian American captain. Coming aft from his cockpit, still blear-eyed from the over-indulgence he had allowed himself the previous evening in Bermuda, he produced a coin from his trouser-pocket and tossed it: heads we go on, tails we go back. It came down heads. We wallowed on through the darkness, my eyes glued to the gauges. Today, having flown millions of miles all over the world, I would be scared out of my wits by such a situation (assuming it could ever arise). In 1942, ensconced on the uncomfortable little seat in front of the gauges, munching excellent sandwiches provided by the Government House cook and after some hours surprised by the first rays of the rising sun glinting on the ocean beneath, I regarded it as entirely and unworryingly in the order of things that we should be doing what we were doing.

After a certain amount of trouble making landfall off the west coast of Ireland, we finally floated down on to the waters of the Clyde at Greenock. Twenty-six hours had elapsed since we left Bermuda. It was just as well we had arrived; fuel for only about thirty minutes flying time remained in the tanks.

3

Temporary Diplomat

Reflection about the shape of this book showed that the thematic approach, though it might avoid the heavy footsteps of the timetable or calendar, was not really practicable. It can be no fluke or coincidence that the finest autobiographers who ever wrote – Cellini, Gibbon, Chateaubriand, Trollope – did not spurn the discipline and architecture afforded by chronology. Chateaubriand,* indeed, of whose childhood memories of wanderings through the deserted forests and marshes of his native Brittany one cannot have enough, carries the method to its ultimate conclusion: at the end of six large volumes, he signs off with not only a 'recapitulation of my life', but as well a 'résumé of the global changes occurring during my lifetime'. This ends with the noble passage in which he describes finishing the *Memoires* in Paris at 6 a.m. on November 16, 1841, with the moon setting behind the spire of the Invalides, itself hardly visible in the first gilded rays from the East; 'you could say that the old world is ending and the new beginning . . . I am seeing the reflections of a dawn whose sunrise I shall not see.'

So chronology shall rule, which means I must get myself from the womb-like interior of the Catalina, riding at her moorings on the Clyde, on to the next cycle of experience. Although wearing my Crosse & Blackwell uniform, I had at the time no form of military identity card, no leave papers, no unit, no commanding officer, no base or depot. I might quite possibly have been taken as a German spy and shot. Instead, within about three weeks I had been given a job as General Staff Officer Grade III at the War Office, within the Directorate of Military Operations. Here I remained until the end of the war in Europe, concerned principally, once the allies had invaded Italy in 1943, with the war in Southern Europe. It was hard but often interest-

* *Memoires d'outre-tombe*

ing work, involving, for so junior and inexperienced an officer, an alarming degree of responsibility.

At times, this could lead even such a small unit in the chain of command as myself into the presence of its ultimate and greatest link, General Sir Alan Brooke, Chief of the Imperial General Staff.* To keep him informed about everything everywhere and all the time was one of the principal functions of the General Staff. Usually his contacts were only with senior officers, but it could and did happen that, if the Brigadier was on leave, the Colonel ill, the Major called away by a family crisis, then it fell to the humble captain, or GSO III, to brief the great man about overnight developments in the particular theatre of war for which the officer's section was responsible.

The first time this happened to me I was apprehensive, to say the least. By this time, some of my military ignorance had been replaced with a tolerably firm grasp (thanks to a good memory) of the formations and units on the ground (in this case, the Italian front), the names of their commanders, the correct way of describing their activities. This newly acquired expertise was, however, no guarantee against a sudden black-out or simply a dearth of knowledge when confronted with an unforeseen demand from the CIGS for further information. In the event, I need not have worried: not about my possible ignorance, for which there were plenty of openings, but about the demeanour of Alan Brooke.

Possibly the finest staff officer of any of the allied forces, himself subject to the often near-intolerable strains of serving so demanding and capricious a master as Winston Churchill, he never appeared to be anything but calm, courteous and appreciative. If he did, at those morning briefings, ask a question to which the answer was lacking, no sign of impatience, still less rebuke, was ever, as I remember, forthcoming. It was a great example, never to be forgotten, of the tonic effect of good manners in everyday dealings. There are those – my final employer, Rupert Murdoch, was one – who believe that subordinates are best spurred on to action by a scarcely remitting hail of critical sticks and stones. This has certainly never been my belief, whether I was at the bottom, half-way up or at the top of the pile. Sheer incompetence must obviously be penalised and either transformed into efficiency or got rid of altogether. But the beneficial effects of encouragement for even quite a moderate talent can never be underestimated. Those early

* Later, Field-Marshal Lord Alanbrooke

morning briefings at the War Office, when the future Field-Marshal pored over the Captain's map and listened quietly to his report, were an object lesson in civilised behaviour.

In wartime Whitehall, the aura of Churchill permeated all departments even if he was known and visible to only the highest echelons. Sometimes, however, and in the most unexpected ways, he would make himself known to lesser mortals. This practice led to, in my case, an unforgettable experience. One night when I was on duty in my section at the War Office, having worked till about 2 or 3 a.m. on the incoming reports from the Italian front, I took advantage of a lull to lie down on the camp-bed supplied for such purposes. Immediate, profound sleep of the kind that follows on exhaustion ensued. The ringing of the green scrambler telephone at my elbow soon woke me. Dazed and disoriented, but impelled by reflex action, I took it up and said, "Duty Officer MO4 here." An unmistakable, fruity, slightly lisping voice spoke: "Thish ish the Prime Minister. What ish your latest telegram from General Alexander?" it said. Not yet sufficiently in this world to be able to reply to the question, I was conscious enough to know that I must very soon return to a full mental state. Meanwhile, it seemed best to play for time.

"I would just like to fetch the telegram and a pencil, Sir," I said. "Well, don't dally, boy," came a growl from the other end. (How did he know I was a boy?) There followed a curious conversation in which I, on the basis of the information I had, described what I believed the state of the Italian battle to be, while the Prime Minister, who had with him, as he explained down the telephone, Sir Stuart Menzies, or 'C', the Head of the Secret Service, challenged my account of things; it did not accord, he said, with his information.

I do not remember how this terrifying conversation ended. Like everything else it did have an end, though further sleep was manifestly impossible. In the morning I reported to my Colonel what had happened and before long was sent for by the Director of Military Intelligence, a Major-General who gave the appearance of having suffered a severe shock. He impressed upon me with all the vehemence at his command the need to forget the whole experience and never, never to talk about it to anyone. Looking back with the gift of today's knowledge, I am nearly certain that what must have happened was that Churchill had been reading the reports from Ultra, the extraordinary process, then known only to a few, by which we succeeded in deciphering intercepted German communications in such a way that it was possible to read their battlefield orders soon after they had been issued. Ultra told a different story from the one outlined in the telegrams from Alexander's headquarters: hence Churchill's nocturnal curiosity and annoyance.

If these War Office years were more humdrum, less star-spangled, than some of the Bermuda experience had been, if they had their moments of frustration and weariness, punctuated by intervals of real alarm as the V–1 and V–2 pilotless missiles crashed down upon the sleeping capital, they also had their consolations, especially in retrospect. Chief among these was the sense, if it does not sound too sentimental, of comradeship between individuals sharing the same tasks and responsibilities. Groups of people in the same profession, whether it be peace or wartime, will tend to develop certain feelings and attitudes in common. Somehow the melting-pot of wartime service made such a development the more remarkable and welcome. My brother officers at the War Office represented, as might be expected, a broad spectrum of humanity. Very few were regular soldiers. Some, though not many at the earlier stages, had seen active service. Yet we managed to work as a team and to achieve a fair degree of tolerance, mutual respect and, when the pressures were not too great, humour and horseplay. I can remember no single instance of criticism or reprehension, even of an unspoken nature, about my highly unorthodox way of entering the army. This wartime camaraderie, which so many temporary soldiers (or sailors or airmen) have noticed and written about, would, I suppose, be present in still larger quantities in the mess of a regiment or the wardroom of a ship. But it was enough for me to discover and benefit from it within the distinctly non-martial context of the world of the Whitehall warrior.

As the war in Europe drew to a close, my kindly superiors at the War Office were instrumental in trying to arrange that, after demobilisation, I transferred to the Foreign Office. As a result of working in the Military Operations Directorate, I was becoming familiar with the shifting geo-political patterns in the Mediterranean theatre and beginning generally to develop an interest in foreign politics, so much so that I decided to make diplomacy my chosen career. This would mean in the end passing the examination for the Foreign Office; in the meantime a spell at the coal-face, so to speak, would be all to the good.

Accordingly, after demobilisation in July 1945, I reported to the Foreign Office and was appointed, as a temporary public servant, to the post of Private Secretary to the Foreign Secretary, the most junior of a team of four. Immediately superior to me, and also a temporary diplomat although he had been there for some time, was Nikko Henderson;* above him was Valentine (commonly known as Nicholas) Lawford, a terrifyingly sophisticated man who seemed to spend much of his time on protracted private telephone conversations with titled ladies. At the top of the tree, in the highly responsible post of Principal Private Secretary, stood the kind and sagacious Bob Dixon,† who perpetually overworked without ever losing his imperturbability. From the Private Secretaries' room a door opened into the great corner office where Foreign Secretaries work. It was from the darkening windows of this ornate room that Sir Edward Grey looked out on a summer evening in August 1914 and made his remark about the lights going out all over Europe.

Though everyone was helpful and understanding, this transfer across Whitehall marked an immense and rather alarming change in my environment and pattern of work (humble enough, consisting to begin with of not much more than opening the Foreign Secretary's mail). But a bigger change was soon to come. I entered the Foreign Office in the service of Anthony Eden. After only a few days, the delayed counting of the service vote in the 1945 General Election was completed, Winston Churchill and the Conservative Government were turned out of office and in waddled the massive figure of Ernest Bevin and sat down in Eden's chair. It was rumoured at the time that the new Prime Minister, Clement Attlee, had at first intended to appoint Hugh Dalton to the Foreign Office, but was dissuaded from doing so by King George VI. Not long after the new Government had been formed, Bevin summoned a ministerial meeting in his office. Dalton, by then Chancellor of the Exchequer, was among those attending and not only arrived first but also found the room empty, Bevin having disappeared into the private loo adjoining. Shortly after Dalton's arrival I took some papers through to Bevin, to find the Chancellor alone and seated at the Foreign Secretary's desk, where he was going through a series of motions – fiddling with the inkpot, playing with the paper knife, stretching his long legs through the knee-hole – which could only be described as trying it out for size. He seemed startled at being discovered and from his fleshy features shot a look of unmistakable malevolence in my direction.

* Later Sir Nicholas Henderson, successively British Ambassador in Warsaw, Bonn, Paris and Washington
† Later Sir Pierson Dixon, Ambassador in Prague and Paris

4 Bermuda 1939: F.G. greets Mr Joseph Kennedy, U.S. Ambassador in London and father of the future President, at the marine airport

5 London 1945: in the Foreign Secretary's room at the Foreign Office:
Ernest Bevin and F.G.

The brief spell with Eden could not and did not leave any lasting impression. A month later, I wrote to someone: 'I gather I am well out of Anthony – to work for he was hell – moody, prima donna-ish and inconsiderate of others' feelings.' This vicarious judgement was obviously based on what I had picked up around the office. But to the best of my memory Eden, so far as I had any personal contact with him in the short time before he handed over to Bevin, was extremely kind and affable. I came to know him quite well in later life, when he had retired, stricken with ill-health, from active politics, and he was invariably courteous and congenial; indeed, by some trick or lapse of memory, he always referred with warmth to our fleeting connection, as though I had served him through long and arduous years. He was psychologically a curious but not unique mixture, notably temperamental and with an undisguised effeminate streak to his nature. If he were standing talking to you, for example, he would more often than not lay a demonstrative hand on your arm. (It is often said, and plausibly said, that during the Suez crisis his tendency to address the dour John Foster Dulles as "my dear" – a form of greeting often on his lips – widened considerably the gulf of mistrust that already existed between these two disparate personalities.)

Ernest Bevin provided the strongest possible contrast. So much has been written about him that there is not much to add save anecdotage. But even that, if it is the fruit of personal experience, can serve further to delineate the portrait of this remarkable man. I have met various professional 'characters' in my life but no one who surpassed or even equalled Ernie. Common sense combined with idealism, intense patriotism, a capacity to cut through the outer layers of a difficult problem in order to get to its real heart, a strong sense of humour and a rambling, sometimes incoherent but more frequently effective way of talking, with a strong West-country burr: the sum of these qualities made him not only a most unusual statesman but an unforgettable companion.

It was his habit, when the long day's work at the Foreign Office was over – say, about 8 p.m. – to relax at his desk by having a few drinks (he drank too much to be good for him). The late-duty private secretary was expected to share these sessions, which could last for at least an hour. In the Private Office, it was our view that his reluctance to go home – he lived with his wife in a flat on the top floors of the Foreign Office – was bound up with the character of Mrs Bevin. She was a tiresome old body if ever there was one, endlessly bothering Ernie, at his busiest moments, with minutiae of domestic or social life, or complaining to us about where she had been placed at an official lunch or dinner. Despite their long years of life together, she cannot have been any help to him – rather the reverse – at this momentous stage of his career. Ernie did not want an interlocutor so much as an audience for his ceaseless flow of story-telling, trade union reminiscences and, sometimes, rehearsals of his inner thinking about current problems. It was at one of these lopsided conversations, if such they can be called, that I first heard him explain the real motive of his Middle East policy, which was not to defend the position of Arab kings and pashas, even though British interests might seem to require that, but, in his own words, to "improve the lot of the fella'een". I knew little or nothing about the misfortunes of the downtrodden Egyptian masses. But he genuinely cared, because they were the common people, with a greater claim to compassion and concern than their generally inefficient and frequently corrupt governments.

'Ernie-isms' – weird ways of pronouncing words and names, especially foreign ones – were a source of constant surprise and often puzzlement. "That fellow Beans" (Benes) was the designation of the then President of Czechoslovakia. "Why don't we order some newts with our dinner?" meant that he wanted a bottle (bottles) of Nuits St Georges. Count Sforza, the Italian Foreign Minister (whom Ernie held in low regard), was "that man Storzer". Guatemala became "Gutemelia". Of somebody's speech in the House of Commons, of which Ernie did not think much: "nothing but clitch after clitch".

When the Foreign Secretary spoke in the House of Commons, a private secretary accompanied him to check his remarks. If he was speaking what he always called "ex tempor", this could be a delicate task. I was with him when he was winding up for the Government in the important debate in December 1945 on the post-war American loan and the arrangements which led to the establishment of the International Monetary Fund. This was necessarily a prepared speech, but towards the end of it he abandoned not only his text but his self-control as well. He was talking of the imminent nationalisation of various industries "which ought to have been nationalised long ago". Someone on the Conservative Opposition benches shouted "Cables" (a reference to the forthcoming nationalisation of Cable and Wireless). Ernie, by now thoroughly worked up, shouted back, "The cables is a swindle." I had later to go to the Hansard Office to put his sentence – which, whatever else it lacked, conveyed its meaning with painful clarity – into some sort of shape. Hansard very properly forbids post-facto tinkering with speeches or remarks, but I nonetheless managed, in what turned out to be my first-ever attempt at sub-editing, to re-order their shorthand record in such a way that it read, still not very grammatically, 'The cables were the biggest scandal ever carried out.'

It was on either this or a similar occasion that Ernie needed to relieve himself before going into the Chamber and I accompanied him to do likewise. As we stood side by side in front of the urinal, Ernie vigorously shaking his penis so as to rid it of the last drops, he turned to me and said, with only the trace of a smile: "This is it, Giles, this is the Socialist dream – the means of production in the hands of the people." It may be an old crack but, having never heard it before and never since, I prefer to regard it as a typical piece of Ernie's humour: undeniably coarse, indisputably witty and laced with mockery. Not that his robust socialism ever wavered, but he had little time for theory or theoreti-cians. 'Left-wing intellectual' was a term, on his lips, of blackest opprobrium, and he applied it above all to people on the left wing of the Labour Party, such as Harold Laski or Dick Crossman.

These stories may suggest that life was one long series of high-level contacts and fascinating experiences. Naturally, this was not so; it never is. Many of the days were routine, the duties menial. They could also be mildly unpleasant. This was the time when the Labour Govern-ment found itself at odds with the Soviet Union, first over Poland and then over the Greek civil war. Ernie stood for no nonsense from the Russians, an attitude which endeared him to many of his countrymen but equally made him a figure for abuse and hatred by left-wing opinion. In the pile of mail placed upon my desk every morning, addressed to the Foreign Secretary or to Bevin personally, there began to be an increasing number of envelopes which contained no letter but simply an unaccompanied, dried-up, brown, sausage-like object. I think it was Nicholas Lawford who, with his worldly wisdom, kindly informed me that these were human turds, a frequent method in some circles of expressing wordless disapproval of a public figure and his policies.

But this was nothing compared with the other shock of that autumn. In August, I took the examination for permanent entry into the Foreign Service. A month later, I was told I had failed. It was little consolation that the same fate had befallen Nikko Henderson (he took it again, passed and went on to reach the highest ranks of the public service). Instead of the glowing prospects which I had supposed to lie ahead, suddenly there was nothing. In terms of a diplomatic career, I could, like Matthew Arnold listening to the sea on Dover beach, 'only hear its melancholy, long, withdrawing roar'. What had gone wrong?

There had been no general entry to the Foreign Office since the war, and the earlier, written, and extremely competitive examination was not thought suitable. Instead, a form of test based upon the selection process used for candidates for wartime army commissions was employed, consisting of a couple of short, written sessions, followed by three or four days at a house in the country not far from London. Here, under the watchful eyes of the examining staff, which included a full range of psychiatrists, the candidates pretended, according to a prepared scenario, to be responsible for the rehabilitation and administration of an imaginary British overseas possession, recently vacated by the occupying enemy.

A knowledge of road-building, food supplies, drainage and emergency courts could just conceivably have come in handy at the Home Office, the Ministry of Education or even the Customs and Excise (the tests were for entry into the civil service as a whole). Such expertise could rather more obviously have been useful in the Sudan Civil Service, or if you were aiming to be a District Officer in Tanganyka. But what all this business had to do with diplomacy, and the gifts likely to be appropriate for the task of upholding British interests in a foreign country, was far from clear.

However, at the time these three days at the country house, with a fair sprinkling of agreeable companions, seemed better than actually working. Some of the tests consisted of written work, but others involved imaginary committees, public speaking and letter writing. One particular episode could have been my undoing. The forty or so candidates divided themselves into two syndicates which, when opportunity offered, competed against one another. One wet August afternoon this competition assumed physical and outdoor form. In the garden of the country house were two heaps of steel piping, covered with tarpaulins. The staff explained their purpose: they were the raw material for a water tank, or rather two water tanks which, when assembled, would provide reservoirs for the needs of the imaginary islanders. Two teams, one to each heap, were to race against the clock and against each other in assembling these things. I knew instantly that I would not be good at this. Thoroughly undexterous, I would be more likely to impede and slow down the progress of my team than contribute to their success. I therefore sat down under the dripping laurels and pensively smoked a cigarette while watching the frenetic efforts of my colleagues to put the tank together. If it was not an heroic gesture, it was certainly not meant to be a piece of histrionics. It was simply a display of realism, an example of honesty which denoted (or should have denoted) to the examiners a proper knowledge or recognition of one's own limitations.

The next day the would-be public servants bade each other a distrustful farewell and I returned to my duties at the Foreign Office. Whether it was the incident of the water tank or my sessions with the psychiatrist I never knew. What was beyond doubt was a letter from the Chief Civil Service Commissioner informing me that I had failed; why not try journalism, he wrote?

I contemplated returning to Oxford to resume my pre-war studies. But too much had happened, too many new vistas had opened up, to make a return to Academe seem realistic or likely to afford satisfaction. Besides, I had fallen in love; impecunious undergraduates do not make promising potential bridegrooms. Beset with worry and depression, I took to going on long solitary walks on Sundays through the City and East End, where the autumnal damps and empty bomb-sites provided a fitting accompaniment to my mood. Further to pile on the agony, I quoted aloud, while striding along, the line from *Lycidas*: 'Scatter your leaves before the mellowing year', substituting, in a welter of self-pity, the word 'hopes' for 'leaves'.

For want of anything else to do, I decided for the time being to remain at the Foreign Office where, despite the lack of any settled future, at least my colleagues were sympathetic and Ernie avuncular. There was plenty to do. The peace-making process was beginning, and this brought to London the Foreign Ministers of the United States, the Soviet Union, China and France to discuss the peace treaties with Italy and the East European countries. My diary of the time reveals that already the wartime partnership with the Russians was breaking up in an atmosphere of mutual suspicion. Quite early on in the negotiations over the Italian peace treaty, the wily Molotov, leading the Soviet delegation, staked out a claim for a Soviet mandate over Tripolitania. 'This is obviously a fundamental issue for us,' I noted: 'is Russia to get a foothold in the Mediterranean, are our vital strategic interests becoming second to the rather doubtful benefits of Russian co-operation? Bevin says he must have a Cabinet meeting tomorrow morning to thrash this out. He will also have to consult the Dominion representatives. Bevin asks Bob Dixon whether he, Bob, will talk to Eden – a highly unconstitutional step, but obviously a wise one in the circumstances.

Bob has a long conversation with Eden who is all for us hanging on to Tripolitania, even at the cost of becoming branded as an international dog-in-the-manger.'*

The other notable feature of this first of the peace conferences was the delicacy of the French position. Despite valiant, even extravagant, efforts to assert her rights, France, under de Gaulle, had not yet been fully accepted as a subscription-paying and benefit-receiving member of the Great Powers club. In particular, she had not attended, because she had not been invited to attend, the American-Russian-British Conference at Potsdam the previous month, where important post-war decisions had been taken. Any reference to Potsdam or any suggestion whatever of action or discussion taking place without France or behind her back was a sure invitation for a display of petulance on the part of Georges Bidault, the French Foreign Minister. A gallant figure from the Resistance, he contrived frequently to give the appearance (and possibly on occasion the reality) of being in an advanced state of intoxication. The Chinese were in a very different category, living in a world of their own and showing very little interest in the process of peacemaking in Europe.

This French touchiness led me into what at the time seemed a spectacular act of folly; the memory of it, still, after all these years, intermittently returns in the form of a nightmare. One dark November night, I accompanied Bevin to Lancaster House, where the conference was being held. Up the great, vulgar, gilded staircase, adorned with Government Hospitality Fund chrysanthemums, went Bevin, bound not for the main Conference Chamber, but for a small committee room. A major obstacle had arisen in the negotiations, and the three 'Great Powers' (there was then no disposition to question Britain's place in this category) decided to try between them to remove it. Hence this preliminary meeting that night, which was intended to make more fruitful a plenary session of the Conference, with France and China present, at 9.30 p.m.

The Chinese delegation had already arrived at Lancaster House and without a word to anyone had withdrawn, detached and uninterested, to the rooms set aside for their offices. They knew nothing, or cared to know nothing, of the inner meeting then in progress. The attitude of

---

* In fact, there is a well-established tradition for the Government of the day, of whatever complexion, consulting confidentially with the Opposition when matters of national interest are involved. For a Labour Foreign Secretary to make touch with his 'shadow' on the Conservative Opposition benches was quite normal.

the French was different. Led by Georges Bidault, they arrived in force at about 9.15, marched up the staircase, and took their places at the empty conference table in the big room. The minutes ticked by, 9.30 came and went, and still the inner meeting went on. It seemed impossible that M. Bidault did not know what was afoot: drumming his fingers on his briefcase, he looked about him, alert, touchy. Watching him – for my services were not required in the smaller meeting – I had my great, my totally innocent, idea; I would tell him what was happening and invite him, with all the courtesy required of a host country, to retire and wait in the greater comfort of the set of offices allotted to the French delegation.

I did so. The effect was startling. *"On m'a insulté,"* he screamed, jumping to his feet and glaring at me; and with that he strode from the room, followed by his delegation, down the double staircase, across the huge hall and out into the night, leaving, as it were, a gaping hole in the heart of Europe. From the top of the staircase I watched them go. None of the numerous people hanging about seemed to pay much attention. I alone had done this thing, and must now not only own up to it, but seek some way out. With death in the soul, I stole into the small committee room where Molotov, blinking behind his pince-nez, was stuttering his way through some unhelpful speech. In a whisper, I explained to Bob Dixon what had happened. As always, he was kind and understanding: "Go after them, extend the Foreign Secretary's apologies and persuade them to return," he said.

Outside, a light but drenching rain was falling. I told the driver of a Foreign Office car to take me to Claridges, where the French delegation was staying. On the way I asked him whether he had seen the French party leave. "They sent their cars away and had to walk," he replied, with obvious satisfaction. I arrived, anxious but at least dry, at Claridges. After some ten minutes the swing door of the hotel began to revolve at unusual speed, ejecting into the light and warmth one wet and angry Frenchman after another. Most of them dashed into the lifts and were borne aloft, but Hervé Alphand (later to be French Ambassador in Washington) remained in the hall, and I approached him, with no very clear idea in mind except of making a start somewhere. M. Alphand was a distinguished and patriotic Frenchman, but he was not helpful; he was, in fact, positively unhelpful. I retired, more than ever convinced that I must soon stop dreaming this dream and wake up to a world that might perhaps be harsh, but nothing like this.

Then I saw the robust figure of René Massigli striding across the lobby. I knew him slightly, as the French Ambassador in London, and he may have known my face, but no more. Nonetheless, this kind, good and ever-to-be-esteemed man, whom so many British people have cause to respect, had pity on me, took me upstairs to M. Bidault's room, explained like a genial herald the purpose of my coming and left me to deliver my – or rather Mr Bevin's – apologies and entreaties. They were, understandably, received without much enthusiasm, but they were enough for the purpose. The French delegation returned later that night to the plenary session at Lancaster House, and the concert of Europe was saved. I do not know to this day whether Bevin ever learnt of this episode; he would in any case have been magnanimous, for that was his way.

Somewhere towards the end of 1945, a red-faced, solidly built man with grizzled hair and an indefinable air of distinction came into the Private Secretaries' room and talked to me at length. 'Pleasant and not filled with ideas of his own importance as most of the people in this place seem to be,' my diary reads. He was Archie Clark Kerr, British Ambassador in Moscow, shortly to be created a peer (Lord Inverchapel) and appointed Ambassador in Washington. But before assuming his new post, the Government had asked him to go to Batavia (today the capital of Indonesia; then, in that still colonial era, the capital of the Dutch East Indies) and lend London's good offices in the dispute which had arisen between the Dutch colonial power and the Indonesian nationalists, intent on independence. Clark Kerr, or Archie as he was known to his intimates and, behind his back, to his subordinates, asked whether I would care to become his temporary Private Secretary? It would mean accompanying him to Moscow, where he had to pack up and make his farewells, and then to Batavia. The whole business might last three to four months.

I accepted. But before leaving London, it was essential to make some provision for the future. Just before Christmas, I had become engaged and my future in-laws would have been less than human if they had not wanted some sort of assurance of prospective earning-power (the future bride, with the insouciance of youth, gave no thought to such earthly calculations). The Civil Service Commissioner's words about journalism came back to me. I consulted the head of the Foreign Office news department, who reported that *The Times* (rather like the Foreign Office itself) was embarking on a process of post-war recruitment. Why not ring their front doorbell?

It seemed good advice. But *The Times*, traditionally loath to commit itself, would not give a positive answer. Come and see us when you return from the Far East and we may be able to employ you on a trial basis, was the utmost limit to which they would go. It was at least something to put on the scales. Armed with this half-assurance, I took leave of my fiancée, of Ernie (who thoroughly disapproved of *The Times* idea – "You'll never succeed in anything unless you begin at the bottom," he said, mindful of his own humble beginnings) and of my colleagues at the Foreign Office, and set off with Archie, in late January 1946, on a journey that was to take us half-way round the world and back.

First stop was Berlin, where we were whisked off to the house of Sir William Strang, Political Advisor to the British Commander-in-Chief. 'Large luxurious house, very comfortable,' the diary reads; 'extensive and very fully licensed dinner-party – excellent hock, claret, and champagne – five courses – cigars and liqueurs – no shortages here.' This was also true of the Strang household, liberally staffed with British soldier servants. It put one in mind of Keynes's brilliant description of another post-war scene, when in 1919 he stayed with the British General on the allied armistice commission at Spa: '*The Times* arrived regularly and in good time; and the sporting ADC had clubbed together with his brother subalterns to import a pack of hounds and was hunting the country as usual eight weeks after his arrival there. But outside on the terrace, I could hear Ludendorff unbuckling his bright breast-plate . . . Miss Bates had vanquished Brünnhilde, and Mr Weston's foot was firmly planted on the neck of Wotan.'*

There was obviously no pack of hounds in Berlin. But Wotan, for the second time in twenty-five years, had equally obviously met his match. In the city there was hardly a building that was not an empty, gutted shell. The diary runs: 'The streets are full of people looking surprisingly well-fed and well-clad. Where they are all going, I cannot imagine, as there are no shops, no offices. One of the principal occupations seems to be to drag a little cart to the Tiergarten and there hack away at one of the trees until enough firewood has been gathered for warming purposes, when it is loaded upon the cart and pulled home again. The Tiergarten is consequently beginning to look as though an armoured division had driven through it. Words cannot describe the desolation. All is rubble and death. Never can defeat have been inflicted so completely and convincingly upon a proud people.'

* *Two Memoirs* (Rupert Hart-Davis, 1949)

Two days later we flew on to Moscow and for the inside of a week I lived in the Embassy, a large early nineteenth-century house built by a rich merchant on the river exactly opposite the Kremlin. According to the diary, 'Its interior decoration is a cross between Marcel Proust and Northanger Abbey – great high rooms, massive chandeliers, heavy dark woodwork and a general air of un-live-in-able-ness.' My rooms faced the Kremlin and every night, on going to bed, I pulled back the curtains and gazed forth upon the gilt-topped cupolas of St Basil's Cathedral and the Kremlin churches, the great wall surrounding the whole, and the huge, illuminated red stars which gleamed at night-time from the summit of the four towers at each corner of the wall.

The Moscow episode was a considerable strain upon my limited linguistic powers. Within the space of a few days I had to discuss the contents of the linen cupboard with the housemaid, in fractured German; take an inventory of the store-room in Russian, which con-sisted merely of my saying "Skolka?" (how many?), when one of the servants would hold up the requisite number of fingers; and carry on a virtually ceaseless conversation with Timoleon, the pint-sized Greek butler, in lurid French. Timoleon was a remarkable character. Because of his skills as a procurer of rare or difficult items of food and drink, he had built up a position of international standing in the diplomatic community of wartime Moscow. I came upon him once, talking on the telephone to the French Ambassadress; he was using the familiar *tu* form of address. On another occasion, he revealed one of the secrets of his success. Leading me up to the top storey of the rambling Embassy building, he threw open one of the bedroom doors and invited an inspection of the contents. The room was shuttered and pitch dark. A distinct smell seemed familiar. Timoleon rattled the doorknob. As if at a signal, a mighty squawking arose. He had about forty laying hens there, protected against the Moscow winter, and providing a plentiful supply of eggs for the Ambassador's table as well as for Timoleon's other diplomatic clients.

However fascinating these glimpses into another world, the really memorable experience of those few days in Moscow was the affair of Stalin's farewell present to Archie. About midnight on the day before we were due to leave for Batavia, the front doorbell of the Embassy rang. Outside two men who had just stepped from a large black chauffeur-driven car on to the frozen snow stood waiting. One was Pavlov, principal interpreter for Stalin. The other, his arms full of packages, was a Kremlin messenger. For them, the hour was not late at all. Stalin habitually worked through the night. His staff perforce did likewise. The Embassy, on the other hand, had closed down. It was some time before a guard went to open the door, while I hurriedly put on a dressing-gown and ran down the great staircase to see what the commotion was about.*

The midnight visitors were bringing presents on behalf of their master to the departing Ambassador. They consisted of a panther-skin rug, a huge pot of caviar, two bottles of brandy and a signed photograph of Stalin ('To the friend of the Soviet Union, Lord Kerr'). But the most unusual present of all was not handed through the Embassy door by the Kremlin emissaries that night. Though the present had indeed been promised, we saw it only the next morning on departure. It was a passport and an exit visa for a Soviet citizen, a thing far rarer, in Stalin's Moscow, than caviar or a panther-skin rug.

As Archie's personality is central to this weird story, it is appropriate to explore it a little. To me he was a comparative stranger, although I had seen enough of him to know that he was unorthodox. Despite his distinguished life in diplomacy, he regarded the career and its practitioners with scarcely concealed mockery. His first ambassadorial posting had been in Guatemala. He told me that there, supervising the erection of a marquee in the Legation gardens for the annual King's Birthday reception, he had been asked by some urchins looking over the hedge and supposing that a circus was in the offing, when *los animalos* were going to arrive. From that day on, Archie intermittently, and when out of their hearing, referred to his diplomatic colleagues as 'the zoo'.

The late Jock Balfour† worked with Archie in different embassies over a number of years and left some lively notes. 'With features which in profile closely resembled those of a Red Indian Chief, Archie Inverchapel had many traits of character associated with a Renaissance *condottiere* – outstanding courage, immense and obstinate self-assurance, opportunism, and a resolve to succeed. Normally well

---

* As these words indicate, I was present in Moscow at the beginning of the story. Many years later, long after Archie's death, I decided to put down not only what I knew but to bring it up to date, by filling in the gaps and above all tracking down and talking to the principal survivor, if he still existed (which he did). The result of these researches was published in a long article in *The Sunday Times* in January 1980; that article forms the basis of this account. The rest of this chapter, therefore, departs at certain points from the chronological framework it has observed up to now.

† Sir John Balfour, sometime Ambassador in Madrid

dressed and elegant in appearance, he scorned convention: on a hot summer day in Moscow, he would sit with hairy chest exposed and nothing on above the waist – dictating his official correspondence to a female typist beside the open window of his study overlooking the Embassy garden. He was fonder of living in the country than in a town: I once heard him express surprise at having discovered that neither Stalin nor Molotov knew how to kill a hare. He talked in a quiet voice, often smiled, and had great personal charm.'

This perceptive observer also points out that, while posing as a left-winger, Archie enjoyed smart society: Proust, a favourite author of his, would have approved of his choice of friends. On the other hand his literary style – plain, unvarnished, and stripped of verbiage – was far from Proustian. Anyone who worked with him remembers his habit of using a quill pen for his more confidential reports and for correcting the drafts of others. This produced some distinguished handwriting, of which he was justly proud.

'It remains to add', concludes this former colleague, 'that for most of the time when I served with him in the Soviet Union and in the USA Archie Inverchapel was separated from his young and attractive Chilean-born wife. She left him when he was in China [he was Ambassador in Chungking from 1938 to 1942] – the most arduous of his difficult posts, and probably the one which was the finest hour of his daunting career. For all the period when they were parted he might be described as an essentially lone wolf who at times must have been acutely unhappy.'

Because of the nature of this story, there is one other aspect of Archie's life which is relevant. During his life and after, the allegation, even the assertion, was often made that he was a homosexual. He certainly liked the company and presence of good-looking young men. After all these years, what one senior member of Archie's staff in the Washington days remembers is the farm boys from Iowa who were the Ambassador's house-guests from time to time. But how far he went in these relationships is anyone's guess. Despite my youth, in four months of proximity he never made any sort of sexual approach, tactile or verbal. The same is true of another young man who later went with Archie to Washington as his private secretary. Archie equally relished the company of good-looking young women. Someone who knew him well once said of him that he was a 'sex maniac' . . . a phrase that often trips off the tongue rather too easily to be taken literally.

He very kindly lent me his house in Scotland for my honeymoon in

1946, after his departure for Washington. It was not the baronial seat he had led me to expect, but a modest bungalow overlooking a loch in Argyllshire. It had nonetheless some good things in it, including a fine, glassed-in Chippendale bookcase. Within, the spine titles temptingly visible through the glass, was a notable collection of rare and limited editions of erotica. The titles were all it was possible to read, for the doors were locked and no one knew where the key was. Collecting erotica does not, of course, make someone a sex maniac. But it does suggest certain tastes and proclivities.

Whatever these tastes, however, there is no room for doubt that Archie was a highly distinguished and successful, if somewhat unusual, diplomat. His very unorthodoxy, which included a lack of pomposity, his grasp of the priorities of political issues, his capacity for trying to understand why other people (and governments) held the opinions they did, made him an admirable reporter and analyst and an eloquent advocate. As Balfour noted, probably his greatest achievement was when he was in China, but he was a strikingly effective ambassador in wartime Moscow. The circumstances of war made Britain and the USSR allies, but it was often an uneasy alliance, shot through with mutual mistrust and, on Stalin's part, periodic outbursts of ill-will. Despite this, Archie succeeded in winning the confidence of the Soviet leaders to an extraordinary degree, especially that of Stalin. Whatever Archie's later inadequacies in Washington, it is easy to see why Ernie Bevin, when he first met him, was so impressed that he decided he was the man for that all-important post.

Archie had two farewell meetings with Stalin. One was at a small dinner in the Kremlin, attended by other members of the Embassy staff, at least one of whom was able to recall it thirty-five years later. At the dinner, Stalin was in an outgoing mood. He often was with foreigners. At the Kremlin dinner-table he turned to the mottle-faced Ambassador and said: "Lord Kerr," (Stalin could not be expected to wait for the new peer's choice of title) "you have done a lot for us, we should like to give you something to remember Russia by." Archie, solemn-faced, replied that he was thinking of becoming a Muslim and would therefore like four wives. Not surprisingly, this quip had to be explained to Stalin. It was a reference to the four Soviet girls who had married members of the British Military Mission and who had been unable to get exit visas to accompany their husbands back to England. Stalin said he would have the matter looked into. He was as good as his word. Before long, three of the four visas were forthcoming.

The second farewell to Stalin took place on January 25, just two days before Archie was due to leave Moscow for good. It consisted of a private audience, attended only (apart from the two protagonists) by Molotov, the Foreign Minister, and Pavlov, the interpreter. There is no knowing why Archie went alone to this interview. He did not speak good enough Russian to sustain a conversation without interpretation; and though Pavlov was there, it is not in diplomacy a usually recommended procedure to put total trust in your interlocutor's interpreter, however proficient. In the absence of any available report by Archie of what took place, therefore, the conversation can only be reconstructed on the basis of my recollection of what he recounted when he returned to the Embassy.

Apparently Stalin again said that he would like to give the departing Ambassador something to remember Russia by. This time Archie forsook joking and asked for what he really wanted: "Would you be willing to part with one Soviet citizen out of two hundred million?" Stalin asked what he meant by the question. Archie explained that he wanted to take Evgeni Yost with him when he left Moscow in two days' time. The name meant nothing to Stalin. Archie identified him: he was a young man employed at the British Embassy as a servant. Archie said he would like Yost to work permanently for him as a valet and later, after retirement, as a member of his staff at his Scottish home. Stalin asked Molotov to look into the matter and take the necessary action. When we left Moscow by special RAF flight two mornings later, Evgeni, with a new passport containing an exit visa, went with us.

During the few days I stayed at the Embassy I was only vaguely aware of Evgeni. He was twenty-four, of Volga German extraction, with a large, round, expressionless face, and fluent in German, which enabled me to converse haltingly with him. He was Archie's valet and masseur, and had a sister working in the Embassy as a housemaid.* He was, I gathered, in some sort of trouble with the authorities: I described it, in a letter I wrote home at the time, as 'hooliganism'.

His family were descendants of those Germans originally encouraged to emigrate to Russia by Catherine the Great. Because many of them elected to settle on the Volga Steppe, they were known as Volga Germans. After 1917, the Communist regime mercilessly harried and persecuted the rich Kulaks among them. Evgeni Yost's family certainly fell within the latter category. Either lack of curiosity or difficulties of

---

* It was with her that I checked the laundry.

communication kept me, in 1946, from learning his history. But when I talked to him in his Scottish home, thirty-three years later, he readily supplied the missing details.

His grandfather, he said, (he did not seem to remember further back than that) lived in the Ukraine and was a rich man, trading in wheat and agricultural machinery. He died in 1914 leaving five sons of whom Evgeni's father was the youngest. He too was prosperous, dealing in grain and farm machinery – a prototype Kulak. Then, in 1917, the first blow fell. Most of the family's assets were confiscated. Seven or eight years later, the authorities struck again: Evgeni's father, together with the elder children, was sentenced to a hard-labour camp 'beyond the Urals' (probably Kazakhstan, to which a large number of Russian Germans were expelled). His mother and the young ones remained in the Ukraine in the family's country house, living a precarious existence on such land and farming activities as remained.

In 1929, when Evgeni was eight, these last possessions were confiscated and the family sent to live in a nearby village, under surveillance. This was bad enough, but in 1932 came the cruellest cut of all. The mother was given the choice of accompanying the elder children beyond the Urals, or of remaining in the Ukraine with the younger ones. She chose to stay, and Evgeni stayed with her. But his sister Marguerite managed to write a new and more cheerful page in this catalogue of woes. Somehow she had succeeded in getting an introduction to a German diplomat in Moscow. As a result, she went to work for him as a maid, transferring, in 1935 or 1936, to the British Embassy. This was the time of the Great Depression and famine, brought about by forced collectivisation of peasant holdings. Marguerite was instrumental in getting her mother and younger siblings moved to the Caucasus, where conditions were somewhat easier.

She did more than that. She suggested to her employer Lady Seeds, the wife of the British Ambassador in Moscow, Sir William Seeds, that Evgeni, now rising eighteen, would suit them very well as a footman. The result was that, in 1938, Evgeni Yost began his lifetime's connection with Britain by joining the domestic staff of the British Embassy. Evgeni was never to see his mother again. Nor was he for long to enjoy the ample meals and free atmosphere of the Embassy. Seeds was succeeded by Sir Stafford Cripps in 1940. Evgeni served Cripps for only a few months before receiving his call-up papers. He was then sent to Lithuania to be trained as a sniper. In the confusion and disorder which followed the German invasion of June 1941, instructions were issued that soldiers should make their way back to Moscow as best they could. Evgeni and some of his comrades somehow found space on the over-crowded trains, and eventually arrived back in the capital. Still in uniform, he went to the Embassy ("It was my only home," he explains), now occupied only by a caretaker; like other diplomats, the British Ambassador and his staff had been evacuated to Kuibyshev. From the Embassy, Evgeni was summoned to report to a military headquarters in Moscow.

Here, after formal and routine inquiries about his identity and domicile, he found himself up against some hostile questioning. An officer with a lawyer-like manner seemed to be accusing him of something. "What are you doing at the British Embassy?" "It has been my home since I arrived in Moscow from the Ukraine." The answer did not satisfy. He was given a statement to sign, declaring he was a deserter. He refused to sign, on the grounds that the statement was not true. He was then thrown into jail where he remained for about a month, during which time various efforts were made, stopping short of torture, but certainly adding up to physical duress, to make him sign the self-incriminating document. He managed, via the Embassy, to alert Marguerite, who was with Cripps's household in Kuibyshev, but nothing came of this.

Finally, he was taken before a military court where, without being allowed to say a word or make any submission in his own defence, he was sentenced to seven years' hard labour in a camp east of the Urals. When I saw him in 1979, he could not remember accurately the charges, except that they were based on two clauses of the military code: the first implied alleged desertion, the second had to do with his connection with the British Embassy.

Evgeni advanced the unprovable theory that it was Cripps who got him put away, or at least did nothing to prevent him being put away. He recalled a conversation at the Embassy with Cripps before he was called up, when the Ambassador asked him (in German): "How do you like your country?" This question, said Evgeni, got him on the raw. He thought of the sufferings of his own and countless other families at the hands of the regime, and blurted out an angry answer. "Cripps gave me a dirty look." To deduce from this, as Evgeni did, that Cripps could later have been the begetter of his misfortune seems far-fetched. It would not have been in keeping with Cripps's character to have be-haved thus. Austere, sea-green, incorruptible are all adjectives which could have been applied to him; but not cruel or vindictive.

Even more far-fetched was Evgeni's contention that Cripps was a paid-up member of the British Communist Party. He was certainly a prominent left-wing figure, and as such was picked out by the Churchill Government in 1940 to go as Ambassador to Moscow in order to breathe some life into Anglo–Soviet relations. But as Churchill comments ruefully in his war memoirs: 'we did not at that time realise sufficiently that Soviet Communists hate extreme left-wing politicians even more than they do Tories or Liberals. The nearer a man is to Communism in sentiment the more obnoxious he is to the Soviets unless he joins the party.'

It would not seem, from this, that Cripps could have wielded sufficient influence with the Soviet military authorities to cause or encourage them to punish an individual, even if he had wished to do so. One thing is certain: the wretched Evgeni went off to a labour camp and spent the next three years, until his sentence was remitted in 1945 by the armistice amnesty, as a member of the work-force building an armaments factory. Once again, the enterprising and watchful Marguerite proved invaluable: by means of food and clothes parcels, she enabled him to survive. Seventy-five thousand were in the camp; only twelve thousand lived to benefit by the amnesty.

Evgeni's turn for the better came in the late summer of 1945. He was released, forbidden for the next five years to go anywhere near Moscow, and given a travel warrant for Kazakhstan. He decided to make a bid for Moscow and the Embassy. Aboard a train of cattle trucks bound for the capital, he and two comrades, packed together like sardines in a tin, managed by legerdemain to delude the supervising NCO into thinking they all had Moscow passes, whereas only one of them had. Arrived in Moscow, he made straight for the Embassy and Marguerite, to whom he revealed his true predicament: an amnestied deportee, without papers, who had been forbidden to be in Moscow at all. Marguerite spoke to Archie, to whom Evgeni was no more than a name. The Ambassador's immediate response was to tell him to stay where he was and he, Archie, would see what could be done. A week later, Evgeni was confirmed in his old job as footman, although he was still an outlaw in the eyes of the Soviet authorities.

In the weeks and months that followed, the sixty-three-year-old Ambassador obviously took a liking to his young servant. Once, he asked him to tell him the story of his experiences in the camp, and showed great interest when Evgeni did so. Another time Archie showed him photographs of the house in Argyllshire and asked him whether he would like to work there. "I think he knew I'd had a hard life," Evgeni said, "and that I'd never get on in the Soviet Union. He was very kind to me. I felt him to be like a father to me." Evgeni expressed warm interest in Archie's invitation. In 1979 he denied vehemently that there was any homosexual motive behind it, or that then, or at any other time, the relationship between Archie and himself was homosexual. "He never laid a finger on me." But the reverse could not have been exactly true, for Evgeni was massaging his master several times a week.

According to Evgeni, Archie's original intention was to take Marguerite with him when he left Moscow for good. She was an excellent servant, she knew British ways, she would be an invaluable addition to his Scottish household after Archie's retirement. But that was before Evgeni turned up. Then Marguerite persuaded the Ambassador to try to take Evgeni in her place. He was younger, his life lay before him, he had had the gruelling experience of the labour camp. Archie, in deciding to make the switch, clearly felt sorry for the young man and wanted to give him a fresh start in life. Despite Evgeni's vigorous rejection today of the idea of any homosexual relationship, it is at least plausible, given Archie's tastes, the breakdown of his own marriage and his inner unhappiness, that the young valet gave him a sense of companionship and possession which he was keen to prolong.

Perhaps also the exhibitionist in him came to the fore; if his plan succeeded, no one else in the Western world, let alone a British Ambassador in Washington, could equal the achievement of having a real life Soviet citizen as a personal servant. When Archie set out for the Washington Embassy later that year, he took with him not only Evgeni but a young Scottish piper, who in the mornings walked up and down outside the great Lutyens mansion on Massachusetts Avenue, playing his pipes: another piece of one-upmanship. Pipers from Scotland were one thing; to seek to include in one's retinue a Soviet citizen on the run was something quite different. Archie must have realised it was a tall order. No wonder he was quick with his response when Stalin gave him the perfect opening by asking what he wanted as a present. Which raises the still more speculative question of Stalin's motives. It is tempting, and certainly makes a good story, to argue that Stalin and his KGB advisers saw a golden opportunity to plant a man within the very heart of the British diplomatic establishment. The servants and drivers employed in Moscow by foreigners – diplomats, correspondents, businessmen – are often KGB informers. Why not go one better and have an agent at a major foreign embassy abroad?

Against this was Evgeni's angry denial that he was ever an informer or worked for the KGB. On the contrary, he described himself – and the story of his early life lends strength to his claim – as an unrelenting opponent of the regime who would not only not help it but do anything possible to encompass its downfall. Volga Germans are not, by reason of their history, ideal KGB material. Moreover, if the Russians really had decided to 'plant' someone, they would have had only two days – between the Friday of Archie's interview with Stalin and the following Sunday of his departure – to brief Evgeni about the duties and procedures of a spy. Such instructions and training would have been virtually impossible within the time limits.

To Stalin, the name and record of Evgeni Yost could have meant nothing at all. The probability is that he took the eccentric request of his friend 'Lord Kerr' at its face value. As Archie himself had put it, what was one Soviet citizen among 200 million? Stalin had nothing to lose in 'giving away' Evgeni, as though he, Evgeni, were a medieval serf and Stalin an oriental despot, which is indeed just what he was. But perhaps the KGB calculated that there was nevertheless something, however modest, to be gained. Although Archie was now bound for Batavia, his nomination to Washington had already been publicly announced, and would have been known to the Russians. Enabling a Soviet citizen to take up residence in the Washington Embassy could help to create confusion, even discredit, with consequent harm to the Anglo–American relationship.

Returning to the Embassy after the momentous interview, Archie apparently did not tell Evgeni any of the details. He merely indicated that the way was clear for him to leave the Soviet Union if he so wished; the choice was his. Evgeni had no trouble deciding. The next day, Saturday, the Embassy chauffeur drove him to the Moscow equivalent of the Passport Office, where an official plied him with awkward questions. Why did he want to leave? "I would like to see the world," replied Evgeni. "How long are you going for, and do you intend to come back?" This was difficult. Ignorant of the fact that the passport official's instructions had come from the highest level, Evgeni was fearful of revealing that his dearest wish and intention was never to return. He therefore temporised: "About three years." The official made out a passport for that period, renewable annually, added an exit visa, and the strangest parting present of modern times was ready for delivery the next morning at the airport.

The next day, Sunday, we – the Ambassador, myself and Evgeni –

left Moscow by a special VIP RAF Dakota. Timoleon, who was an Alexandrine Greek, was supposed to come with us as far as Cairo. At the last moment, it transpired that he was proposing to bring with him all his luggage, consisting of everything he had collected, liberated, won by barter or been given in return for services rendered over the last seven years. The aircraft would never have left the ground with all this on board. Apprised of the situation, Timoleon announced gloomily: *"C'est toute ma fortune – je l'apporterai avec moi ou j'y resterai."* And stay he did, reaching Cairo later (I believe by train). I can remember as though it were yesterday Evgeni's appearance at the airport. In a long overcoat and a cap with a little button on top, looking quite unmoved at this extraordinary turn in his fortunes, he stamped about in the freezing air as the plane was loaded. His sister Marguerite was there to see him off. Even the parting with her, which both must have known was for ever, produced no emotion. Presently we boarded the plane, the RAF pilot asked permission to take off, and we were away on a journey that was to take us via Cairo, New Delhi and Singapore to Batavia.

It was principally because I had no Russian and only a few words of German that I did not at the time ask the expressionless Evgeni for a description of his feelings. More than thirty years later I put the question unasked earlier. "At the airfield, I felt nothing except a terrible fear that even at this last moment I should be stopped from going, that the authorities would intervene and I would be left behind, I had no regrets whatever at leaving." He said he was equally unsurprised at a bizarre incident on the journey.

We spent twenty-four hours in New Delhi where, because Indian troops were deployed in Java, Archie wished to discuss the Indonesian issue with the Viceroy, Lord Wavell. We were to stay at the Viceroy's House, that vast and luxurious symbol of the Raj, and I had sent a telegram to the Viceregal comptroller, setting out the composition of the party. At Cairo, where we abandoned the DC3 for a larger plane, we had been joined by a number of Foreign Office people from London – secretaries, cipher clerks and others needed to staff the mission in Batavia. In my telegram, the names must have got jumbled up, because Evgeni, instead of being listed as the Ambassador's valet, appeared with Archie and myself among the officers rather than the other ranks.

The result was that, arrived at Delhi airport, Evgeni was whisked off with the rest of us by the Viceregal staff and installed in the Minto suite at Viceroy's House: bedroom, sitting-room, bathroom, and a posse of bowing turbaned Sikhs, in the scarlet-and-gold Viceregal livery, to attend to his slightest needs. This was indeed a far cry from a labour camp in the eastern Soviet Union, where Evgeni had been less than twelve months before.

The Clark-Kerr mission to Batavia was not a success. For three months we tried, unavailingly, to establish a basis of compromise between the Dutch colonial authorities and the Indonesian nationalists and their claims. Laurens van der Post, later to become celebrated as author, traveller and sage, was the British Army intelligence officer responsible for liaison between our mission and the Indonesians. Neither the unhelpful stolidity of the Dutch colonial authorities nor the difficulty of pinning the Indonesians down to any consistent position seemed to affect him. His deep-set blue eyes and quiet, almost dream-like way of speaking showed no sign of the frustration and sense of impotence which weighed upon us less mystical mortals. None was so bored as Archie. One thing he did do was to draft, in his best quill-pen script, a letter of thanks to Stalin for the gifts of caviar, brandy, panther skin and 'the young Soviet masseur'. For the rest he spent most of the day, in the extremely uncomfortable house where we were lodged, reading French novels and Trevelyan's recently published *English Social History*. Evgeni looked after him and gave him massage, as he had done in Moscow. If he had been 'Stalin's spy', he would have found little or nothing to spy on. 'A great deal of our day is spent in talking to people who drop in here to gossip,' I wrote in a letter home. 'We frequently learn more about the negotiations which we are supposed to be conducting from news reports than from ourselves.'

Evgeni recalled, slightly shamefacedly, that he was busy in one respect. He became very friendly with a Russian lady married to a Dutch banker. She was much younger than her husband, and assured Evgeni that he did not mind. This proved to be untrue, so the friendship came to an end. But it afforded Evgeni many glimpses into the social life of Batavia, such as it was, and thus into some of the ways of the West.

Sometime in April, the abortive mission was recalled and we flew home, stopping for a couple of days at The Hague to report to the Netherlands Government. I then left Archie and my temporary position in the Foreign Office and joined the staff of *The Times*. Versions of the rest of the Evgeni story came through to me during the next three or four years, in dribs and drabs: how he accompanied Archie to Washington in 1946 and then, after Archie's retirement in 1948, served him for some time as general factotum at his house in Argyllshire. At that point,

I lost touch completely and only resumed it when I began in 1979 to talk to some of the people subsequently involved in the Evgeni story.

Even before Archie left London for Washington, senior officials in the Foreign Office had misgivings about Evgeni going with him. Their preoccupation was not surprising. Whatever his own history, he was a fully fledged Soviet citizen in most unusual circumstances. Moreover, though peace had come to the world, the international sky was darkening. In September 1945, Igor Gouzenko, a young cipher clerk at the Soviet Embassy in Ottawa, had defected and revealed that atomic information was reaching the Russians. Six months later, Dr Alan Nunn May, who had been employed during the war on highly secret nuclear research, was arrested and charged with passing on information about the Canadian Government's refined uranium plant.

The alarm felt in Canada soon spread to the USA. Suspicion of Soviet motives and Soviet acts was now the common coin of Western Intelligence. The nature and scope of US–British collaboration on nuclear explosives was such as to make the Washington Embassy a highly sensitive place. It must have seemed, and did seem, to the authorities in London that transplanting Evgeni to Washington was asking for trouble. Archie however did not see things that way; he persisted and he carried the day. By June, he and Evgeni (and the young piper) were installed in Washington.

All might still have passed off quietly had it not been for Archie's exhibitionism. He was given to pricking balloons and challenging other people's values. Though generally kindly and considerate, he liked shocking people by some extravagant or outrageous statement which he himself did not necessarily believe. Moreover he found the Washington post, which should have been the crowning glory of a long and distinguished career, strangely unsatisfying. Though he had many good American friends around the world, particularly among American newspaper correspondents, the hot-house atmosphere of Washington, the earnestness which runs through so much conversation there, left him moody and often uninterested. He also seemed to lack the most rudimentary knowledge of savoir-faire, as defined by American usage. His appointment was, in fact, a serious error in judgement on the part of Ernest Bevin. All this was the background to his habit of dropping the fairly astounding remark that "I have a Russian slave at the Embassy given to me by Stalin."

Even before the joke began to circulate widely (and to receive publicity in the American press), other protests were beginning to be heard. It is perhaps the most ironic and amazing part of the whole Evgeni story that the person within the Embassy who first complained about his presence was Donald Maclean, at the time acting Head of Chancery. This is a post roughly equivalent, in commercial life, to office manager. It was therefore well within Maclean's rights, it was indeed his duty, to draw the attention of his superiors to what he believed might be a weak link in the Embassy's security arrangements. According to Sir John Balfour, then the No. 2 in the mission after the Ambassador, Maclean came to him not long after Evgeni's arrival and said something like: "This is a bad business, the Ambassador has a Russian servant here." Balfour was inclined to agree. He and Maclean confronted Archie with their fears. But he sent them packing and Evgeni's position remained unchanged.

Why did Maclean act as he did? Because he lived for years in seclusion in Moscow, seeing no British people, and is now dead, it is impossible to give his version. One is forced therefore to speculate, and very fascinating speculation it is. There is no need here to rehearse the Maclean part of the Burgess-and-Maclean saga. No suspicion existed at this time that Maclean was a Soviet informer. Though he tended to drink too much, his work in Washington appeared satisfactory, and the private life of his wife and himself called for no special comment. Yet in fact Maclean was the spy code-named 'Homer', whose activities were later revealed through intercepts of messages from the Soviet Consulate-General in New York. These told Western Intelligence circles that from 1945 onwards 'Homer' was delivering high-grade secret material from the British Embassy in Washington to a Soviet contact. Kim Philby, the double agent, says in his book that in 1949, before leaving London to take up his appointment as Head of the British Secret Intelligence Services in Washington, he was told of strong suspicions that there had been a leakage through the Embassy there four years previously.

In objecting to Evgeni's presence within the Embassy, Maclean could have had at least three motives. He might have feared that his Soviet masters had set a watchdog over him to monitor, perhaps even to take over, his work. If so, he must have felt uncomfortable, indeed alarmed. Or he may have feared that Evgeni's presence, and Archie's boasting of it, would result in British and American security surveillance in and around the Embassy being intensified. Again grounds for disquiet. Or, finally, he might have been reacting according to some form of Pavlovian reflex. Though himself working for Moscow, his

Foreign Office training and almost subconscious instinct may have led him, when he heard Archie showing off about his Russian 'slave', to protest against what by any accepted standard was an irregularity, much as someone who regularly cheats the Inland Revenue can be outraged by a crime such as the Great Train Robbery.

Evgeni remembers meeting Maclean only once, when the latter paid an unexpected visit to the servants' hall at the Embassy residence. He looked intently at Evgeni and asked him how he liked America and how the life compared with Russia. Evgeni made some comparisons highly unfavourable to the Soviet Union. Maclean's face dropped and he quickly left the room. When I talked to Evgeni in Scotland he claimed that Maclean made it his business to get rid of him because of his anti-Soviet views. This seems to me no worse and no better than any other guess about the nature of the game Maclean was playing.

Meanwhile a certain tension was building up within the Embassy itself. Balfour remembered an occasion when Hugh Dalton (Chancellor of the Exchequer) and Lord Catto, Governor of the Bank of England, were staying in the house. At dinner, there was a scene. Archie did his bragging – "I have a Russian valet whom Stalin let me take out" – but added, in his provocative and teasing way, "There are some reactionaries on my staff here who don't like it at all." Balfour burst out, "Yes I'm one of them." Archie was genuinely furious: "How dare you!" There was general embarrassment, the visitors becoming abnormally interested in the contents of their plates. But Archie's wrath soon subsided.

Evgeni all this time was carrying out his normal duties, looking after Archie, waiting at table, helping Maddox the butler with the silver. He seems to have been, as I remember him in Moscow and Batavia, remarkably self-possessed. Another member of Archie's personal staff recalls how surprised he was, soon after their arrival, to find Evgeni splashing happily about in the Embassy pool, which was supposed to be reserved for the senior staff.

If he had wanted to be an informer, he had plenty of opportunity. Archie, unorthodox as ever, would spend long periods lying in his bath, reading telegrams and official papers. When he had finished with them, he handed them over to Evgeni to give to the private secretary, who replaced them in the safe. Like the famous German agent Cicero, valet to the British Ambassador in Turkey during the war, Evgeni could, other things being equal, have made use of these documents for espionage purposes.

But other things were not equal. At the time, Evgeni still barely understood and could not read English. He was quite unaware of the controversy building up around him and his position. On the contrary, he was something of a star turn with visitors to the Embassy: Mr Anthony Eden, as he then was, and the Duke of Windsor were among those who wanted, as Archie had wanted back in Moscow, to hear from Evgeni's own lips (in German) his account of life in a Soviet forced-labour camp. As for his leisure activities, he made friends with some Washington White Russians ("like myself") and had an American girl-friend whom he brought back to the house and introduced to the Ambassador. He was also keen on one of the housemaids. When the time came for his passport to be extended, a messenger took it round to the Soviet Embassy; Evgeni did not go himself.

At this distance of time, it is difficult to assess the extent of the public or official outcry in Washington about Evgeni. Archie, evidently sensing that the 'Russian slave' remark caused too many eyebrows to be raised, had a new line: "No need to worry, he's a German." But it is difficult to believe, amid the massing clouds of the Cold War, that this was particularly reassuring, even to people with a working knowledge of the history of ethnic minorities in Russia. Both the State Department and the Federal Bureau of Investigation became interested and critical. Evgeni was, after all, still a Soviet citizen, with a passport issued to him in Moscow. If he had not been a member of Archie's staff and travelled with him from London to Washington, it is inconceivable that the Americans would ever have given him a visa.

After about a year in Washington, Archie returned on leave to Inverchapel, his Scottish home in Argyllshire, taking Evgeni with him. When the leave was up, the Ambassador told his valet that he, Evgeni, would not be returning to Washington. The Americans, he explained, did not like Evgeni's presence at the Embassy. So Evgeni remained at Inverchapel, working in the house and garden on maintenance jobs. The following year, 1948, Archie retired from the Washington Embassy and from the public service. He had been there only two years but, apart from his lack of success, he was by this time sixty-six, long past retiring age, his heart was giving him trouble, and with the launching of the Marshall plan an ambassador was needed in Washington with a broad basis of economic knowledge lacking to Archie.

For another two years at Inverchapel, Evgeni continued to serve Archie and Tita, the doll-like Chilean wife whom Archie had re-married in Washington. There was a bad motor accident outside

Glasgow, from which Evgeni, at the wheel, emerged unscathed but in which Archie and Tita were badly hurt. After that Evgeni worked at the Inverchapel farm, breeding hens and making money for Archie by selling eggs. At last, in 1950, armed with a loan of £1,000 from Archie, he struck out on his own, buying a fish-and-chip business in Rothesay, on the Isle of Bute. Archie died rather suddenly in 1951, but by this time Evgeni was well launched into a business career. Today, he still lives in Rothesay, which he rarely leaves.

He and his Scottish wife, whom he married in 1956 and from whom he is now divorced, have had nine children, now grown up. He speaks fluent English with a strong Glaswegian accent. He has twice unsuccessfully applied for British citizenship and is thus officially stateless. He has no wish to return, even on a visit, to the Soviet Union: "I'd finish up behind the Urals" – in a labour camp. Every few years, he says, he receives a visit from someone he describes as a Home Office official, who asks whether he has had any unusual visitors or been approached by the Russians (which he has not).

Though he receives letters intermittently from his sister Marguerite, he does not reply. This was the arrangement they made when he left Moscow. Sometime not long after that, about 1948, the Soviet authorities told her she must leave her job as housemaid in the British Embassy and go back to her mother's home in the Ukraine. Evgeni thinks this was because of "the publicity about me", but an equally likely explanation is to be found in the new campaign mounted by the Soviet authorities in 1948 against Volga Germans.

In 1979, when I twice went to see him, Evgeni seemed quite content with the mild prosperity he has achieved amidst the scenic beauties of the Firth of Clyde. "When I first came here," he said, "everyone wanted to know my story, and I told them all of the enormities of the Soviet system, the lack of freedom, the low standard of living, the labour camps . . . Journalists used to come from Glasgow to ask me questions, but I turned them all away because I was scared of any publicity, I was still frightened of being kidnapped or bumped off by Soviet agents."

As the years went by, he lost these fears. Also, he was too busy to over-indulge in introspection. He bought a second fish-and-chip shop, then went into juke boxes, which he installed in shops in the Clydeside town. A restaurant in Rothesay was added to the growing Yost empire and later still he moved into the ice-cream business as wholesaler and manufacturer; "at one time I was supplying the whole of Rothesay with ice-cream."

He made no bones about his political views. "I am a staunch Conservative and voted for Mrs Thatcher [he has had the vote since 1974]. I encourage all my family to vote Conservative. You've got to have opportunity and reward. Socialism simply drives money away. So long as there are rich people about, there's nothing much to worry about." He also talked, in a quasi-visionary way, about probable developments within the Soviet Union. "In twenty or thirty years' time, the Soviet system will have collapsed in favour of a parliamentary electoral regime. It is unthinkable that a few party bosses can oppress tens of millions of people for ever." He professed unbounded admiration and affection for the British way of life. Allegations that British Intelligence made him work for them under threat of being returned to the Soviet Union met with his indignant denial. "But if they had asked me," he added, "no pressure would have been needed because I would have done it for nothing."

4

The Times – London and Paris

On May 13, 1946, my diplomatic career, such as it was, behind me, I began work as a probationary foreign sub-editor at *The Times*. Among my new colleagues, there were, as far as I can recall, none of those Fellows-of-All-Souls or world-expert-on-Sanskrit characters who figure in various nostalgic accounts of *The Times*' sub-editor's room in the twenties and thirties. The experience was not agreeable. Not only did the hours – 4 p.m. to midnight – distort the day out of all recognition, but the work itself was uninspiring. Composing or re-writing what someone else has written is the reverse of creative effort. Not that it is unskilled: a good sub-editor, with a knowledge of the subject he is dealing with and a proper appreciation of style, can work wonders, without ever changing the sense, on a message from a correspondent who has quite possibly written it away from reference books and against the clock. Headline-writing also calls for a certain nimbleness of mind: not only should the headline accurately convey the essence of the piece beneath it, it must also, and obviously, fit the space allotted to it. I was hopeless at this. My choice of words tended either to fall short or, more often, to over-run. Indeed the main reason for the distastefulness of the work was my incompetence; not many people enjoy doing what they are bad at, even if a great host of bungling golfers, dim-witted bridge-players and amateur pianists exist to disprove the point.

I cannot recall being unduly awed by joining *The Times*, a newspaper which Abraham Lincoln declared to be one of the greatest powers in the world – "In fact," he told William Howard Russell, the war correspondent, "I don't know of anything which has more power, except perhaps the Mississippi." Its shabby old buildings opposite Blackfriars Station, within sight and sound of the Thames as it flows towards the sea, seemed, at least at first, to lack atmosphere, let alone romance. But this early impression was a mistaken one. In fact, those draughty, cramped, fusty surroundings (swept away in the early sixties and replaced by a singularly repulsive exercise in glass and concrete) were a perfect setting for the old-fashioned scene which lay behind the sombre brick façade and for the earnest, self-important people who supplied its human element.

The tone was set immediately by the printed notice in the antiquated lift which, clanking ominously, propelled one upwards to the editorial floors. 'Messengers are forbidden, under pain of dismissal, to use this lift except when accompanying a visitor' it ran. Today, such a diktat on the part of the management would risk bringing out the chapel, or office branch, of the relevant print union in an instant protest strike. In 1946, the spirit and wording of this dire warning, itself the relic of an earlier age, were unremarkable.

Having arrived at the editorial level, the newly joined recruit, if destined for the foreign side of the paper, would report to an executive with the title of foreign news editor (for a long time, the post of foreign editor had been in abeyance). In his youth, this man, called Ralph Deakin, had been an English teacher in Vienna. There, according to legend, the Emperor Franz Josef, driving in his carriage, had once replied to Deakin's pavement reverence by taking off his hat to him. It was an experience from which Deakin never really recovered. From then on, he increasingly assumed the mantle of a statesman-journalist, one who is, or rather one who would like to be thought, privy to the secrets of chancelries and cabinets, himself consulted discreetly from time to time by the ruling few. This posturing was all the more ridiculous because in fact Deakin enjoyed, and everyone knew it, no power whatever within the office over public policy-making. But despite his frustrations, he was a passionate, indeed romantic, upholder of the standards and status of *The Times*. He held and would readily express the view that, among the British community in a foreign capital, the Ambassador naturally came first and equally naturally the *Times* correspondent came second. He also had the rather disconcerting habit of assuring new boys that while *Times* salaries were admittedly on the low side (I started on £400 a year), anyone killed on the paper's business could be sure of generous treatment in the obituary columns.

Some time later on, the recruit would be ushered into the presence of the Editor himself, sitting in a pool of light cast by a green-shaded lamp in a dingy room which looked on to a dark courtyard. In the courtyard the editorial Rolls, an immensely high, Queen-Mary-like affair, stood waiting to bear him off to the House of Commons or No. 10 Downing

Street or even Buckingham Palace, where he really would become privy to confidences and asked for his views. My first Editor was Robin Barrington-Ward, a man of infinite courtesy with a startling resemblance to that master of farce, the late Robertson Hare. He gave the continuous impression of bearing, none too easily, the cares of nearly all the world upon his modestly proportioned shoulders. 'No man is more in need of a holiday than he who has just returned from one' was one of his kindly aphorisms.

Immediately below him in the hierarchy, and his successor when he died of Parkinson's disease and overwork in 1948, was William Casey, who never ran any risk of the latter. An indolent and charming Irishman, who had written two plays for the Abbey Theatre in Dublin, of which he had been manager for a short time, he was endowed with shrewd judgement and a profound reluctance to take things too seriously. Above all he liked long and vinous meals at the Garrick Club or the long since defunct Apéritif in Jermyn Street. His closest and strangest ally in conviviality, as well as in other things, was the unpredictable Stanley Morrison, the great typographer and historian of the paper. No one was more responsible than he for defining, with passionate eloquence, *The Times*' role as the gazette of the ruling class. His black-suited, somewhat sinister figure and piercing hyena-like laugh were familiar sights and sounds in the grimy passages of Printing House Square.

As well as Barrington-Ward, another prodigious worker was Donald Tyerman, then Assistant Editor. Severely handicapped by the effects of poliomyelitis, he nonetheless hobbled about the office on his crutches, involving himself in almost every branch of the paper's activities and writing most of the political and economic leaders. Talented and courageous though he was, Donald had some of the defects of a man who has had to fight against adversity. He would not readily admit that anyone could know more than he and could be abrasive in his personal relationships. By any test of merit, he should have succeeded Barrington-Ward. But he was not always in control of his drinking habits, and there was a widely-held belief that people who wished him no good on one occasion encouraged him, in the crucial period in 1948 during which the next editorship was being decided, to get drunk and make a spectacle of himself within the office, a fact which was duly noted on high. He later became a distinguished editor of *The Economist*.

'On high' meant, in Printing House Square terms, the co-proprietors, Colonel John Astor* and Mr John Walter, the representative and descendant of the family which originally founded *The Times* in 1785. The latter, though in 1946 an elderly man, took a lively interest in the paper's staff and activities. Through him a line of continuity stretched back directly to some of the great *Times* personalities of the nineteenth century. As a young man he had gone to Paris to learn French under the wing of Henri de Blowitz, the fabulous Paris correspondent of the paper whom *Punch* once referred to as Blowitz-own-Tromp.† John Astor, the chief proprietor, was shy and diffident and so not easy to talk to. Under Barrington-Ward, *The Times* adopted in these post-war years a generally left-of-centre attitude on social and economic issues. The result was that Astor was frequently the recipient of complaints from his grand Tory friends about something *The Times* had said or failed to say. Despite this, he scrupulously observed the rules which he himself had helped to draw up, namely that, while the proprietors could appoint, and in theory dismiss, an editor, that editor should be left free from interference in all matters concerning editorial policy. Astor appeared to regard his ownership of and responsibilities towards *The Times* in much the same way as a conscientious and paternalist nineteenth-century landowner might regard the possession of his estate. Everyone on the staff was seen as a member of a great family – it was indeed officially designated a Companionship – and the paucity of the pay was presumably supposed to be offset by periodic staff outings to Hever Castle, the Astor seat in Kent, where tea and a tour of the Italian garden were provided. The formula, for all its paternalism, worked surprisingly well. There really was, at all levels, a sense of corporate loyalty, of pride and job-satisfaction which would be difficult, if not impossible, to find in any newspaper office today.

From my lowly place at the sub-editor's table I naturally had no contact with these gods. But as time went on, I began to soften the impact of the nightly drudgery by offering, and having accepted, contributions to the space in the leader columns occupied by the 'light' or fourth leader. Called into being by Northcliffe in 1914, these miniature essays about some bizarre or piquant item of news followed the more portentous articles in the columns alongside, and have thus been compared to 'an urchin clinging to the back of a dray'. They were

---

* Later First Lord Astor of Hever
† I was later to write a biography of Blowitz, *A Prince of Journalists* (Faber & Faber, 1962), when John Walter's reminiscences were invaluable.

in the *belles lettres* tradition, somewhat arch and self-conscious by today's standards but evidently affording much pleasure to readers. Most of them were written by Peter Fleming,* who had a deft pen for that sort of thing, and my occasional efforts were little more than a pastiche of his. Their appearance in the paper nonetheless provided the first opportunity of seeing one's own stuff in print. To any non-journalist or non-writer it is impossible to convey the never failing excitement and satisfaction of the experience. Nearly forty years and millions of words later, I still, with quickened pulse, turn first to the page of any publication on which I expect to find printed a specimen of my own prose and read and re-read it with an undiminished sense of awe and pleasure, occasionally diluted with rage at the damage that has been inflicted by some moronic sub-editor.

Lest anyone should find this fanciful, he has only to refer to Marcel Proust for confirmation. In *Contre Sainte Beuve*† he describes opening *Le Figaro* every day in search of an article he has written for the paper. Finally it appears. 'I begin to read. Every phrase conveys the image I meant to call up . . . more abundant, more detailed, enriched – since I, the author, am for the time being the reader . . . I feel it really impossible that the ten thousand who at this moment are engaged in reading my article should not be feeling as much admiration for me as I feel myself.' He imagines for a moment the reaction of those who are unable to understand the article and therefore find it an inferior product. He tries, but is unable, to read the article with their eyes. 'As soon as I begin to read, the entrancing pictures come to life; I marvel at them impartially, one after another . . .' Proust's sense of self-esteem, as described in this passage, is no doubt in dubious taste, bordering on narcissism. But his account of his sensations as he searches the newspaper for his favourite author sounds a chord in many a writer's heart.

The diary entry for Saturday June 29, 1946, the Feast of St Peter and St Paul, consists of only two words: 'Get married'. Anthony Trollope, in his autobiography, declared that 'my marriage was like the marriage of other people, and of no special interest to any one except my wife and me'. There is much to be said for such discretion. But my marriage has meant so much to me, the support and companionship of my wife through the years been so important, that something more must be said.

---

* Traveller and author, whose best-known works are *Brazilian Adventure* and *News from Tartary*.
† English edition, translated by Sylvia Townsend Warner (Chatto and Windus, 1958)

6 Florence 1952:
Bernard Berenson

7 France 1955: Pierre Poujade
harangues the crowd

8 Paris 1954: Pierre Mendès-France, 'a star of great brilliance'

Kitty was only nineteen when we became engaged, the previous winter, and not much over twenty when we married. She was and is vivacious, interested in almost everything and absolutely everybody, extremely practical, and capable, like her mother, of evoking affection and loyalty in others. Her own loyalty – to her parents, her husband, and later on, her children – was and is boundless. When, nearly forty years on, I retired from *The Sunday Times*, there was a reference, among the kind things said, to the fact that I was 'through all these years supported, encouraged, often no doubt consoled, by his formidable wife . . .' Formidable when applied to a woman conjures up visions of Lady Catherine de Bourgh or Betsy Trotwood. But the dictionary defines it as meaning, among other things, 'tending to inspire awe or admiration because of . . . strength, excellence etc.', and it was obviously in this sense that the tribute was cast, and justifiably cast.

Support and encouragement are exactly what I have had from Kitty throughout our life together. She would often accompany me on journalistic forays, when her unstoppable capacity for making friends greatly enlarged the pool of information, as men and women poured out to her their thoughts or spoke of their aspirations. Later on, she developed her own interests and part-time career, becoming a London lay magistrate and serving for some years on the national Parole Board. This latter job gave rise to fierce altercation, whenever they met, between her and Frank Longford,* who appeared to think, even long after her term on the Parole Board was over, that she was personally responsible for keeping in prison some of the criminals whom he favoured, especially the Moors murderess Myra Hyndley. There can be little doubt that if she had chosen to make a full career in the law, instead of putting the duties of wife and mother first, her quick mind and natural intelligence would have led her far.

Back in 1946, the material prospects were far from certain. *The Times* had not yet accepted me as a permanent member of the staff. Yet we had absolutely no doubts. If her parents had any, they generously concealed them. My future father-in-law Buck De La Warr, himself only forty-six, was the head of an ancient family who had succeeded to his title as a boy and then joined the Labour Party. He was of course accused of betraying his class. As a young man he had held office in the Labour Governments of the twenties and the National Government in the thirties. Now, with the post-war Labour Government in power with a

* Lord Longford, penal reformer and prisoner's friend

huge majority, he had left the Labour Party and moved over to the Conservatives. Whatever his motives, nobody could accuse him of place-seeking or of leaving a sinking ship; he had indeed done just the reverse. My mother-in-law was a saint-like woman who adored her only daughter, as she was later to adore, and be adored by, our children. Though essentially non-political, she had been loyally through the heady Labour days, but the experience did not stop her, gentle and unassuming as she usually was, from exuding from time to time what was known in the family (the reference was to the decoration of an Earl's coronet) as the smell of crushed strawberry leaves: that is, letting people know who she was.

And speaking of such things, this is the place to tell a story which, though it belongs to a later date, has caught up with us through most of our married life. When some years later I was made *Times* correspondent in Rome, I went ahead of Kitty, who had just had our first child, to find a flat and put down some roots. The week before she was due to join me, a new friend at the American Embassy telephoned to invite me to dinner at some future date. I explained that my wife would be here by then. "But of course," he said hospitably, "we shall expect Mrs Giles too." I thought quickly. Kitty, as an Earl's daughter, had the courtesy title of Lady Kitty, and was generally known as such. We were probably going to be in Rome for some years. Would it not be better to avoid possible future embarrassments by getting things straight from the start? Yes, it would, I decided, so I said to my friend, "You won't mind my mentioning it, I hope, but actually she's not Mrs Giles . . .' Before I had had time to complete the sentence, he had burst out, "But of course I quite understand, that makes no difference, you must bring her all the same." The story crops up in varying versions, but that is the only true one. How it became widely known is a mystery, unless the American – to whom I finally explained the true state of affairs – dined off it. If he did, I certainly do not hold it against him.

After the honeymoon at Archie's house in Argyllshire, our first home together was in a mews. It was conveniently placed, a few hundred yards from Hyde Park Corner, just behind St George's Hospital. What was less convenient was that its ground floor, over which the flat extended, was a stable for horses. This of course was the whole idea of a mews, but there could not have been many left in their original state by 1946. At all times a powerful smell of dung and ammonia, bringing back memories of Bermuda, permeated the place. At night, in our bedroom, we could hear the horses stamping, running the rope of their

head-collars through the tethering rings, and occasionally whinnying.
By day, the courtyard below was thronged with riders waiting to board
their mounts and proceed to Rotten Row. Apart from the undeniably
picturesque aspect of the scene, one positive benefit was that the heat
generated by the horses, above all at night, helped to keep the flat warm
– or, more accurately, prevented it from becoming glacial – in the
cruelly bitter winter of 1946/47.

But we were not destined to live there long. I had finally broken away
from the detested sub-editors' table and become a fully fledged and
permanently employed writing journalist. The job was that of assistant
diplomatic correspondent, which involved keeping in touch with the
Foreign Office, the Colonial Office and various embassies in order to
gather the material for the reporting of foreign affairs. *Times* journalism
was anonymous in those days, as it was to remain for many years. But
one night I had the personal satisfaction, even if my name did not
appear, of supplying five separate pieces for the paper. If this was not
investigative journalism of the modern type, striking fear into the
hearts of tyrannical bureaucrats or shady directors of companies, it was
reasonably competent and painstaking work and appeared to give
satisfaction to my employers. Soon after the turn of the year
Barrington-Ward appointed me assistant correspondent in Paris. It was
May before we made the move. One fine evening towards the end of the
month, having driven from London, we made our way uncertainly into
the city, its chestnut trees weighed down by their white candles, its
streets and boulevards redolent with the unforgettable smell of under-
refined petrol.

Distance, we all know, lends enchantment; this is true of time as well
as of space. Looking back, down the perspective of the years, it seems
that Paris in that unusually hot summer of 1947 was a spellbinding
place. Traffic was a trickle, compared with the flood-tide of later years;
parking no problem. As the chestnuts shed their candles and the leaves
lost their youthful green, an air of delicious lassitude crept over
everything. In the evening, the rays of the setting sun burnished the
gold on the dome of the Invalides and threw long, purple shadows
across the *allées* of the Tuileries gardens. Sometimes the heat was
almost unbearable. For years I have been telling the story of how,
wishing on a day when the temperature stood at 104° in the shade to
walk from the Rue Royale to the Chambre des Deputés, I was compelled by the glare and burning sensation coming off the *pavé* to cross the
Place de la Concorde with eyes closed. It cannot really be true, yet so

light was the traffic that it is just possible.

The only blemish on this idyllic picture was the food. While a flourishing black market for luxuries was available for anyone willing to pay the price, ordinary fare in restaurants or private homes was austere. Because of my pre-war gastronomic adventures with the dons of Brasenose, I liked to think of myself as a gourmet and *amateur des vins*. After the food rationing of London, the prospect of some succulent meals was keenly awaited. In the event, dinner on the night of our arrival at the hotel where we stayed until we found an apartment consisted of some thin and tasteless soup, an omelette and salad, and twelve cherries, the whole washed down with a remarkably acidulous bottle of claret. The bread was not only rationed but bright yellow and heavily indigestible. This was the result, so it was said, of a recent visit to the United States by M. Léon Blum, the veteran Socialist leader, when on behalf of his Government he asked the Americans to supply bread-hungry France with wheat. Uncertain in English, he apparently used the word 'corn', whereupon large quantities of maize were shipped over which, when ground and milled, yielded the yellow peril which we and millions of French people ate that night and throughout the months to come.

A few nights after this disappointing meal, we sat under the scented lime trees of a garden just outside Paris and listened to Gaston Palewski* talk about how inevitable it was that de Gaulle would return to power and lead France back to her rightful place among the great nations. The house and garden belonged to some friends of friends to whom we had an introduction, and Gaston (the love of Nancy Mitford's† life, who appears in her novels heavily and romantically disguised as Fabrice, Duc de Sauveterre) was among the dinner guests. Then in his middle forties, a brave and patriotic Frenchman, he had spent some of the war years in London as one of de Gaulle's most trusted and loyal lieutenants (Lord Halifax is alleged to have asked, "Who is that Polish officer who seems to know so much about France?"). In 1947, eighteen months after the General had resigned in dudgeon as head of the provisional Government because he could not get his way over the shaping of the new constitution, Gaston was as fanatically devoted to and confident in de Gaulle as he was to remain throughout the succeeding years. His

* General de Gaulle's Directeur de Cabinet just after the war
† The eldest of the celebrated Mitford sisters. Her married name was Mrs Peter Rodd, and she lived in or near Paris from 1946 onwards (see p. 85).

loyalty was beyond reproach, his sense of timing less so. Almost exactly eleven years were to elapse before his confident prophecies came true.

Paris in that broiling summer may on the surface and in retrospect have seemed enchanting, but in fact the social and political scene was lit with flashes of lightning and shaken by rumblings of thunder. The Communist party, the largest in France, had recently ended its increasingly uncomfortable membership of the coalition Government, moving into a position which was to become, as the year went on, all but insurrectionary. The other, right-hand side of the stage was occupied by de Gaulle and his newly founded Rassemblement du Peuple Français (RPF), a vaguely populist movement devoted to anti-Communism and the (peaceful and legal) ending of the existing party system. "We want to change the regime," said the General in early June. This would be done by re-establishing democracy, "the system under which power flows directly from the people and not through various combinations of parties". To many ears, this sounded like the language of an ambitious populist.

By midsummer, the country was afflicted with a series of crippling strikes. The railways stopped running, the Paris stations stood silent and deserted, stranded tourists, many of them British, besieged the air terminal at the Invalides in the largely vain hope of finding a passage home. The strike movement spread to other nationalised industries. The economy itself seemed endangered. The unions' demand for higher wages to meet the increased cost of living was certainly justified. But there were other less professional influences at work. As the Prime Minister, M. Ramadier, put it in Parliament, was not their (the strikers') "spontaneity" surprising when one considered that all these strikes had been directed against the State and nationalised industry? The theory that the Communists, through their hold on the unions, were seeking a trial of strength with the regime was reinforced by international developments. Earlier in the summer, General Marshall, the US Secretary of State, had made his historic offer of American help in the reconstruction of Europe. Ernest Bevin had come rumbling over to Paris to discuss the proper response with the exciteable Georges Bidault. They invited Molotov to join them, but within a few days the latter had rejected out of hand any idea of a common European economic programme. It was a turning point in post-war Europe. From now on, the iron curtain would be more than a Churchillian phrase; it had become a geographical reality. The effect of this division upon French politics was real and immediate. As the Communists warmed to their wrecking tactics, so political tension and labour unrest increased. This was the crisis for which General de Gaulle was preparing, whose dénouement Palewski had so confidently foretold under the lime trees that May evening.

For a newcomer, the situation provided both advantages and drawbacks. It was, for anyone remotely interested in public affairs, constantly fascinating. On the other hand, to understand and describe it called for special gifts. In these I was badly lacking. Though familiar with a wide range of French literature, my spoken French was not much more than the fruit of an ordinary public school education: in other words, it was shamefully inadequate. Nor could my knowledge of French politics be said to be in any way special. Some preparatory reading in London and a laborious study of the French newspapers could do no more than provide a rough and ready framework. Luckily the No. 1 man in *The Times*' Paris office, Gerald Norman, more than compensated for these deficiencies. His mother was French, he was bilingual, and, his Harrow education notwithstanding, he possessed that particular gift for logical analysis and attention to minute detail that is generally associated with the higher reaches of French schooling. The late Louis Spears, in his brilliant book* about the fall of France in 1940, wrote of a certain Frenchman who had turned up in Bordeaux during the last stages of the drama as 'sallow, ascetic, the product of hot rooms and difficult examinations'. The description could be made to fit Gerald.

It must have been no fun for him at such a time to have a novice appointed as his subordinate. But he showed no signs of irritation or impatience (although he is said to have remarked to someone before our arrival that he supposed 'he would now have to take over the trade union scene entirely' – a reference, apparently, to Kitty's noble origins, though how they could be thought to handicap my reporting efforts is not clear). On the contrary, acting on the sensible premiss that the best way to teach a beginner to swim is to throw him in at the deep end, Gerald despatched me, as the political and industrial crisis deepened, to cover every aspect of it. I became an habitué of the Assemblée Nationale, the parliament building at the southern end of the Pont de la Concorde, whose unbroken walls, together with the self-centred nature of much of its deliberations, has caused the Paris wits and cynics to call it the *maison sans fenêtres*. In the surrounding streets and across the river, in the Tuileries gardens, large numbers of police and Gardes

* *Assignment to Catastrophe* (Heinemann, 1954)

Républicains, sweating in the afternoon heat, were often deployed as a discouragement to left-wing demonstrators. Within, into the tiny and stifling Press gallery which looked down upon the semicircular Chamber beneath, swept great cascades of rhetoric and insult, elegantly formed French phrases alternating with short and earthy expressions, correctly calculated to enrage those for whom they were intended. Just as, in the years to come, I became eloquent in Italian through listening to sermons in Roman churches, so now this French parliamentary experience did wonders for my grasp, or rather lack of grasp, of the language.

If the summer of 1947 was a time of unrest, the autumn brought a marked deepening of the tension. In October, the RPF enjoyed sweeping successes in the municipal elections. Only six months after its formation, the group (it could hardly be called, nor would it wish to be called, a party) emerged as the most strongly supported body in France. But the Communists' strength was largely undiminished, so that they alone remained as the formidable opponents, in size and spirit, of the RPF. General de Gaulle had succeeded in polarising French opinion. He was not slow to follow up his success. Very soon after the elections, he was calling peremptorily for an early dissolution of the Assemblée Nationale, to be followed by new elections on the basis of majority voting on the British model. His scorn for the existing party system was almost as strong as it was for *"les séparatistes"*, his invariable word for the Communists. Was it possible that his moment had come, that Palewski had been right? Compared with the harassed and fumbling efforts of the Prime Minister to govern – with his white beard and elastic-sided boots, Remadier could wrongly be seen as a left-over from the discredited Third Republic – de Gaulle's lofty call to "end the regime of confusion and division which reduces the State to impotence" seemed at once mandatory and prophetic.

In fact, it was not. Out of the drama of that amazing autumn came the revelation that the young Fourth Republic, with all its defects, was better able to defend itself than its enemies expected. The challenge from both ends of the spectrum was certainly strident. By mid-November, public service strikes were spreading fast. Water-workers, sewage men, dustmen, undertakers withdrew their labour and reduced the Paris streets to a state of insanitary disorder. Troops had to be deployed in Marseilles to control left-wing disorders. De Gaulle called a press conference. It was my first sight of him. Churchill is credited, rightly or wrongly, with having said of him that he resembled a female llama surprised while bathing. There was not much of the llama, a sad-eyed beast, about the man who, in the ballroom of a Paris hotel in front of hundreds of journalists, castigated the regime, scornfully and with expressive gestures comparing the political parties to Kipling's chattering Bandar-log (the monkey people), who claimed to be Kings of the jungle. The birth of the RPF, he said, his voice in its vehemence rising almost to the pitch of falsetto, was as important an event as the birth of the Resistance on June 18, 1940 – the date of de Gaulle's London broadcast to stricken France. The RPF, he immodestly declared, was "an elemental force which corresponds exactly to French people's promptings and instinct".

It was a star performance. But were his claims borne out by the facts? The surprising thing, in Paris at least, as the railway strikes began to affect food supplies, gas pressure fell, the telephone service became fragmentary and shortage of newsprint reduced newspapers to a single sheet, was the way in which life went on as normally as possible. It might have been London in the blitz. Even the resignation of the Ramadier Government and its replacement with another – in fact, much the same – team headed by Robert Schuman, failed to evoke much public reaction, one way or another. On November 21, in what seemed to be a touching gesture of goodwill, electricity cuts, which had been keeping us all in partial darkness, were suspended long enough to allow millions of people to listen to the broadcast of Princess Elizabeth's wedding in Westminster Abbey.

The new Minister of the Interior in the Schuman Government was Jules Moch, a tough right-wing Socialist Jew who had lost a son in the Resistance. He met the growing threat of sabotage on the railways – one night the Paris–Lille express was derailed with a loss of twenty lives – with courageous energy. Eighty thousand reservists were recalled to the colours. Hundreds of saboteurs were arrested, special editions of L'Humanité, the Communist paper, seized. There was by this time no doubt about what was at stake. The Communist leadership, with its control of the biggest union, was trying to bring the country to a standstill. Up to a point, but not beyond that point, they were able to hide their political motives beneath the cloak of inadequate wage levels. In the Assemblée Nationale, where the new Government was trying to get a right-to-work bill passed, there were scenes of unparalleled ferocity. One evening, a Communist member refused to leave the tribune after he had finished speaking. M. Edouard Herriot, the gigantic and splendid President or Speaker (he was said to eat three dozen oysters and an entire roast chicken for his dinner, and when he paid a visit to austerity-struck London, wisely brought hampers of food for his own consumption) suspended the sitting. The defiant Communist remained *in situ* until towards dawn he was escorted out of the Chamber by an unarmed military guard. The streets outside bristled with troops, the bridges across the river were forbidden to traffic.

By mid-December, the struggle was over. The right-to-work bill passed the Chamber, the Communist call to strike began to fall on deaf ears. The Communist-dominated trade union ordered its members back to work. "The battle is won," said Jules Moch, "I am master of the situation." It was true. Though it had undeniably disrupted the life of the country, the Communist Party's attempt to exert despotic control over the working class had failed. At one point 1.5 million workers had been on strike. But despite the discomforts and shortages, the tempo of life, although sometimes slowed, had never really wavered. The satisfaction and interest of witnessing and describing for the readers of *The Times* this French saga surpassed by an immeasurable degree the writing of elegant little fourth leaders. I felt I had become a proper journalist.

Politics, in the widest sense, remained a constant professional preoccupation. Looking through the relevant files of *The Times* today, it takes the breath away to see how frequently political and economic news from Paris dominated the pages. The struggles of successive French governments to remain afloat and to master (they never did) the perennial problem of wages and prices form the subject of innumerable despatches from Gerald Norman and myself which were more often than not given pride of place on the main news page. It is inconceivable that the great mass of the British public had the faintest interest in these febrile goings on, described with such minute care and accuracy by the Paris office of *The Times*; equally inconceivable that French news would be given the same prominence today. The truth is that *The Times* of those days was written and edited for a tiny, informed minority who really did want to read in detail about the shifting patterns of French politics or indeed any other comparable developments in the world. In many ways, it was a readership, for all its elitism, more genuinely international in outlook than anything that could be found today, despite Britain's membership of the European Community. It was moreover a readership able to take in its stride such products of old-fashioned journalism as the following: 'M. Queunille [the then Prime Minister] who in recent months has so often applied a cold towel to the heated head of the body politic . . .' However ponderous and contrived my style then was, at least the metaphor has the merit of being unmixed.

Though the House without Windows continued to be the centre of political activity and confusion, much of the real and lasting work of reconstructing France and pulling her into the twentieth century went on in a much less known building nearby. This was the Commissariat du Plan in the Place Sainte Clothilde, where Jean Monnet and his team of brilliant young men and women laid down the lines along which post-war France was to adapt to new world conditions. The rise and fall of governments, the assaults of the Communists upon the functioning of the State, the sneers and jeers of de Gaulle and his men about the inadequacies of the regime seemed to have no impact at all upon this remarkable institution. Helped by the fact that in France the State traditionally plays a major part in the organisation and direction of the economy, Monnet's team not only laid the foundations but built much of the structure which in future years was to contribute so significantly to French prosperity. I only got to know Monnet himself later on, when he had transferred all his massive but controlled energies to the construction of Europe. In 1948 and 1949, I kept in close touch with his young subordinates, often taking them to lunch in the nearby Mont Blanc restaurant. There, on the flower-surrounded terrace in summer, or in winter inside, in the delicious, food-scented fug of a good French bistro, they would talk eloquently, and without any ideological bias, about their work and about the future of France. These conversations seemed to me far more important and interesting than that of the intellectual *coteries* of the existentialist cafés in the Boulevard St Germain.

Was it this sustained contact with a central planning agency, operating within the limits of a democratic State, which first inclined me politically leftwards? I have never been a member of any political party, but in British elections between 1945 and 1970 I voted consistently for Labour. This was partly because the smash-and-grab, devil-take-the-hindmost aspect of the operations of a free economy ('market forces') has always seemed to me crude and divisive. But another force which inclined me leftwards during these first Paris years had nothing to do with French politics or French people. It was the attitude of British Tories – some of them at least – in this period of their political opposition.

Westminster MPs were often in Paris on parliamentary visits or missions. They would drop into the *Times* office, conveniently placed as it was in the Place de l'Opéra, for a chat. In particular, the memory of David Eccles endures. Very different from the gentle, Christian elder statesman and philosopher he later became, he seemed in those days, in his expensively made suit with its double-breasted waistcoat, the embodiment of cocksure Toryism. Seated in the office armchair, he would dilate with amused condescension upon the follies of the Labour Government and its utter unsuitability for office. If this performance had been just an example of political cut-and-thrust, a rehearsal of some such well-hallowed formula as get-the-rascals-out, it would not have been offensive. But it seemed to be more than this. His attitude reflected the born-to-rule belief which permeated much of Conservative thinking at the time. According to this, despite the magnitude of the Labour victory in the 1945 election, the Labour Government somehow had no right to be where it was. That right belonged, as though by divine dispensation, to the Tories.

It may be unfair to attribute too exactly these ideas to David Eccles. But certainly this was the effect he had on me at that time. Even stronger and more disagreeable was the impression left by periodic visits to Kitty's parents' home in Sussex. Tory though my father-in-law had become, he would have been incapable of descending to such levels of arrogance and complacency. But this was not true of some of his friends whom we met there. Rob Hudson* was an outstanding offender. A big bruiser of a man, ruthless in his ambitions but with considerable natural charm, his scorn for the Labour Government – not just its alleged incompetence but its sheer audacity for existing – knew no bounds. To hear him talk, you would think it was the patriotic duty of every true Englishman and woman to cheat and defraud and generally sabotage any enterprise or operation which derived from the Government. And indeed there were gleeful accounts over the brandy of how so-and-so, Rob's neighbour in Wiltshire, kept a pack of fox-hounds to be set off as a loss on the farm accounts. A truly rational mind would no doubt have remained unaffected by such petulant talk, which did not deserve serious consideration. But it was impossible not to be repelled and influenced by it, in a way that left, for better or for worse, certain effects upon me. I was not the only person. Duff Cooper, a staunch Tory and former Minister, described sitting next to Lady Salisbury at a Buckingham Palace banquet in early 1950. She com-

---

* R.H. Hudson, later 1st Viscount Hudson, Minister of Agriculture in the wartime coalition Government

plained loudly about the number of Labour representatives present. "I tried to explain to her", he told someone later, "that the King's Ministers are Socialists, but it was no good – like trying to explain the hydrogen bomb to a Chinese of the Ming dynasty." (A curious mirror-image occurred many years later, when François Mitterrand's election as President and the installation of a Socialist Government in Paris led the French *haute bourgeoisie* to assume somewhat similar attitudes: smarting from the higher taxation and other indignities imposed upon them, some of them adopted the pretence that Mitterrand had no right to be President and could not be said to be the true representative of France.)

Being a correspondent in Paris involved more than following French affairs. Intermittent diplomatic conferences and meetings – Ernie Bevin's generous silhouette became a familiar sight as he was driven from the British Embassy to the Quai d'Orsay or elsewhere – needed covering. Paris was also the permanent seat of the Organization for European Economic Co-operation, the sixteen-country body that was established to co-ordinate the economic development of Western Europe and specifically to divide up Marshall Aid. Its proceedings were at once important and heavy-going. Gerald Norman bore the brunt of reporting them, but I also played my part, hanging about the Château de la Muette, in Passy, the seat of the organisation, at all hours of the night while finance and economic ministers prolonged their counsels. Plans for freer trade in Europe, I pointed out with a burst of candour to the readers of *The Times*, are 'difficult to understand and still harder to explain'. Occasionally this forbidding scene was illumined by a little human drama: as when the tall and broad Paul Hoffman, the American administrator of the Marshall Plan, driven to distraction by the inability of European Governments to agree, seized the small and slim Georges Bidault by the lapels and, almost lifting him off the ground, shouted, "Integrate, damn you, integrate."

The Gaullist movement, above all its leader, was a never-ending source of fascination and sometimes repugnance. Despite the charges of Bonapartism levelled against him, nothing could stain the honour or impugn the motives of the General himself. But the methods of some of his followers were a good deal more open to question. At RPF meetings and rallies, the stewards tended to deal vigorously, too vigorously, with any hecklers. At the General's so-called press conferences, the questions from the floor were nearly all prearranged. Sometimes, if the Minister of the Interior, the redoubtable Jules Moch, was to be believed, the Gaullist heavy men resorted to near-lethal methods. Communist demonstrators in Grenoble in September 1948 clashed with Gaullists; some of the latter were injured by stones or blows but Communist casualties included those caused by bullets which subsequent investigation showed could not have come from the police or the Communists. The finger pointed to the shock formations which followed the General around in his progresses. These revelations had no noticeable impact upon public opinion. As the country continued to be disturbed by largely political strikes, as weak coalition governments collapsed and were replaced by scarcely distinguishable other weak coalition governments, so the General's populist appeal to sweep all this away received enthusiastic response wherever he made it. But his trouble was that, having forsworn a *coup d'état* or any other non-constitutional way of winning his way back to power, he was blocked in. While the wheels of the Fourth Republic continued to turn, however sluggishly, there was nothing he could do save keep up a constant barrage of verbal scorn and ridicule. Not surprisingly, the political parties who were the objects of these attacks showed no readiness to leave the stage.

France was and is a highly centralised country. Almost anything of any importance tends or promises to happen in Paris. The result, for a correspondent, is not only that he feels he cannot, because of the burden of work, tear himself away from the capital, but also that, even if he were to do so, he would be imbued with the sense (only partially true) that whatever is going on in the provinces does not matter. Certainly I rarely left Paris, save on holiday. But there were exceptions, two of them for ever memorable. The first was when, in the autumn of 1947, escaping for a long weekend, we drove south-west to stay with French friends in the department of La Sarthe. They lived near the great Benedictine abbey at Solesmes and took us to Mass there on Sunday morning. As the Gregorian plain chant for which the Abbey is famous soared upwards and outwards from the choir, as one of the monks, after the Consecration, came down from the chancel into the nave to bestow the Kiss of Peace upon the members of the congregation, so the vision was revealed of another France, far removed from angry rivalries in the Assemblée Nationale or the pretensions of the unions, a vision which had its natural counterpart in the unchanged countryside without, its autumn colours reflected in the streams and rivers, its small, unremarkable villages grouped around their parish churches.

The second outing was in May 1949, when we accepted an invitation from the Jurade of St Émilion, the modern re-creation of the medieval town council, to attend a great wine junket. Wine judging, archery and banqueting filled up two or three supremely happy days. One banquet lasted from noon until six in the evening. It was not a moment too long, seeing that there were eighty-six different vintage wines to be tasted. My neighbour at the feast was a well-known St Émilion *vigneron*, who had been making and tasting wine all his life. As the precious wines, including Château Cheval Blanc 1928 and Château Figeac 1926, were poured, I noticed two things about him. Except to light another one, he never removed the Gauloise *mégot*, or cigarette butt, from his lips, whence its acrid smoke curled up into his eyes or billowed out into the glass he was tasting from. And he evidently found nothing wrong about receiving a dollop of, say, a 1934 wine on top of a quantity of the 1929 still in his glass. Mindful of the fastidious ritual of wine-tasting at Oxford, I asked him how he could justify these two practices. Courteously but with noticeable strength of language, he said that the English, for all their appreciation of fine claret, were much too pernickety; smoking made no difference whatever to the palate, if anything improved it, while anyone with a real knowledge of wine should be able to distinguish one vintage from another in the same glass. To this day, I do not know whether he was pulling my leg. His approach to wine, though certainly original and perhaps suitable for him, is not to be recommended.

Most big cities of any antiquity are a series of villages or quarters, each with well-defined and individual characteristics. This is above all true of Paris. We began our life there, once we had got out of the hotel, in a tiny rented apartment in a modern block in the Rue Barbet de Jouy, in the 7th *arrondissement*. Its windows gave on to the playground of a *lycée* and framed, deeper in the perspective, the dome of the Invalides, the sight of which, at any time of the day or night, never failed to have a heart-stopping effect. The street was quiet and leafy. With its remaining private houses, including the residence of the Archbishop of Paris, its ambience was distinctly Proustian; here was the heart of the Faubourg St Germain itself and it would have been no great surprise, in that hot and nearly car-less summer, to see Madame de Guermantes, seated in a victoria drawn by two handsome bays, on her round of afternoon calls. She would probably have stopped at the big white house opposite our block. It was the home of the Comtesse Jean de Polignac, whose musical parties Proust himself may have attended.

This flat was no more than a staging post. Its owners reclaimed it after the summer and we began again the search for accommodation. Innumerable gloomy apartments off the Boulevard St Germain, near the Eiffel Tower, in Passy, in Auteuil, behind the Gare St Lazare, at the wrong end of the Avenue Hoche, giving on to the Boulevard Haussman, bordering the Parc Monceau, a stone's throw from the Porte Maillot, were inspected. Their shabby *salons*, filled with reproduction Louis Quinze chairs and sofas and smelling of hot cat, seemed an entirely appropriate setting for their equally shabby but nonetheless grasping owners, mostly widows of uncertain temper who had seen their *rentes* eroded by war and inflation. Finally, near to despair, we struck gold: a tiny three-room mezzanine apartment on the south side of the Ile St Louis, whose full-length windows gave on to the river and the apse of Notre Dame. By day, the tramps sunned themselves on the cobbled slipway just opposite, their immobility broken from time to time by the need to take a swig from an ever-present dark bottle. A colourful island character, M. Dansonville, would amble into view, bestowing greetings and invariably followed or preceded by his pet tame duck. Great barges, their engines churning up the water, set up vibrations which shook the windows of the quayside houses. At night, looking diagonally across the river one could see the brilliantly lit sixth-floor windows of the Tour d'Argent restaurant, behind which the clients would be paying through the nose for the privilege of eating the famous *canard pressé*. Here we lived for more than two years, though the rent was more than we could truly afford. Once John Astor and his wife, on a visit to Paris, came to lunch. We hatched a plan designed to show as dramatically as possible the need for more money. They would be given – standards must be preserved – an excellent meal in the tiny dining-room and then, returning to the sitting-room, would find it bare of furniture, the debt collectors having distrained it while we ate. Needless to say, while the first part – the good lunch – was achieved, the second part was never carried out.

One of the apartments we looked at was not far from the Rue Barbet de Jouy. It consisted of the ground floor of an old mansion in the Rue Monsieur, *entre cour et jardin*, like all classic French houses. For various reasons we did not take it, but Nancy Mitford did. She always referred to the neighbourhood as "Mr Street", and could be seen any day, a tall slim woman dressed in very expensive French *haute couture* clothes, striding along on one of her countless pedestrian expeditions to discover some new gem of French architecture or taste. Nancy's lunch parties in

No. 7 Mr Street became famous. Never more than six, they brought together an invariably amusing mixture of French and expatriate guests, who babbled away in the two languages, the conversation punctuated and sometimes nearly drowned out by the high-pitched giggling of the hostess.

We often entertained Nancy and were entertained by her. I loved her wit and intelligence but was not deluded – any more than most French were – by her exaggerated Francophilia. She certainly knew, or taught herself, a lot about French art and literature, but remained resolutely, almost comically, English herself. She adored Gaston Palewski to the point of idolatry and he was clearly amused by her. But he was a famous ladies' man,* despite the affliction of permanent acne, and for all her romantic treatment of him in her novels, her physical relationship with him must have been intermittent. She had some tiresome characteristics. One of them was a rabid anti-Americanism, which could have been inspired by her great friend Evelyn Waugh. She had never been to the USA and had good American friends in Paris, notably Susan-Mary Patten,† with whom she shared a love for the historic quarters of Paris. This did not prevent her, in her novel *Don't Tell Alfred*, from cruelly caricaturing Susan-Mary as an earnest bore with the unappealing name of Mildred Jungfleisch.

Kitty was not taken by Nancy nearly as much as I was. She found her habit of turning everything into a joke especially tiresome. One day there was an example of this which went beyond all bounds. During the German occupation, an exceptionally brave member of the Resistance from the upper reaches of French society had a girl-friend from the same milieu who had fallen for one of the most senior German officials. She agreed to betray her first, unsuspecting lover and did so by kissing him in the Metro, thus tipping the wink to the Gestapo. He was arrested, imprisoned, tortured. Nancy's comment on this repellant story, uttered in her exaggerated Mitford drawl and accompanied by a cascade of silvery laughter, was: "But all's fair in love and war, isn't it?" (It is only right to record that when, many years later, Nancy lay dying of an agonising cancer, she made jokes about that as well. Gaston Palewski was her last visitor, a few hours before she died, though she was too near the end to be aware of his presence.)

* Later on, when French Ambassador in Rome, he was known as 'M. l'Embrassadeur'.
† Later Mrs Joseph Alsop. She and her first husband became two of our closest friends. She has left a lively account of these Paris years in her book *To Marietta from Paris* (Weidenfeld & Nicolson, 1976).

9 Paris 1947: Duff and Diana Cooper in the Embassy with Mr and Mrs
   Bevin

10 Rome 1951: Mgr. Montini (the future Pope Paul VI) looking characteristically Hamlet-like

When we arrived, and until the end of 1947, the British Ambassador was Duff Cooper. His and Diana Cooper's occupancy of the Embassy is legendary. Everything about it had a magic quality, in which *luxe* and *volupté* (though Diana's influence made sure that there was not too much *calme*) were dominant ingredients. The farewell ball they gave just before Christmas assumed the proportions and generated the atmosphere of an historic occasion. Everyone wore orders and decorations and the centre of attention was Winston Churchill, a hero figure to the French. He stood receiving homage in one of the downstairs drawing-rooms, the lovely Odette Pol Roger, in a red satin dress, on his arm. Despite the disparity of their ages, they enjoyed a long-lasting romantic attachment which included, in Churchill's case, the consumption of large quantities of excellent Pol Roger champagne and the bestowal of the name Pol Roger upon one of his race horses. A few days after the ball, the Coopers steamed away in the Golden Arrow, the farewell scene at the Gare du Nord being taken over by the extraordinarily tiresome (and gifted) Louise de Vilmorin, poet, novelist and Duff's mistress, who insisted on jumping into the train and travelling with them to Calais and Dover. She was a monologist to beat all monologists. Many people believed she rehearsed the stories – they could hardly be called anecdotes, running on occasion to the length of a short novella – with which she expected (woe betide the interrupter) to keep a large dinner-table spellbound. On first hearing, they were amusing and elegantly told; but naturally enough they palled at the second and third repetition.

Duff and Diana were extremely good to us and we grew very fond of them both. In his tastes and activities, his profound knowledge of English and French literature, his love of good conversation and of wine – 'writing in my sixty-fourth year', he confesses in his autobiography,[*] 'I can truthfully say that since I reached the age of discretion I have consistently drunk more than most people would say was good for me' – his marital infidelities, his extravagance and generosity, his tendency to flare up and then flare down again, Duff seemed a figure who would have been more at home in the eighteenth than in the twentieth century. He was kind and encouraging to the young, and the more I got to know him the more valued his praise and friendly counsel became.

After leaving the Embassy, the Coopers decided to settle in France, which they did at the pretty, small château of St Firmin, just outside

[*]*Old Men Forget* (Rupert Hart-Davis, 1953)

Chantilly, leased to them by the Institut de France. There they entertained extensively and brilliantly. A record of those Chantilly years and a roll-call of those who stayed or ate or drank there would read today like the annals of Holland House, or of Garsington in Lady Otteline Morrell's time. Not that there was anything specifically political or blue-stocking about these gatherings; the inclusion of some of Duff's White's club friends tended to keep the intellectual level on an even keel, though Duff himself was apt, at the least excuse and sometimes with no excuse at all, to break into lengthy and accurate quotation in English or French. (Strangely, the White's club types, though no social democrats, were not as offensively arrogant about the British scene as the Eccleses and Hudsons of the political world; the treasures of Duff's cellar, liberally made available, may have softened their passions, or perhaps they did not have those sort of passions.)

Duff's famous temper could be a pitfall for the unwary. In this immediately post-war period, his anti-German sentiments were ferociously strong: a united Germany, he accurately contended, had three times in eighty years imposed the horrors of war upon Europe, and this must never be allowed to happen again. One night, a large dinner-party at St Firmin was short of one man. An SOS went out to the Embassy in Paris. A young Third Secretary called Teddy Jackson, a total stranger to the house, responded to it. Large and fair-haired, he seemed even younger than he was, suggesting the animal image of a St Bernard puppy, all bounce and good nature. After the ladies had withdrawn from the dining-room, the talk turned to European politics and Duff did one of his anti-German turns. "But with great respect wouldn't you agree", said the daring – too daring – Jackson, "that we have to learn to live with the Germans – we should be looking to the future, not the past." One of the early signs of Duff's rages was the swelling of the veins in his prominent forehead; his face would turn purple and the enlarged vein begin to throb. Jackson's remark evoked just these symptoms, their intensity greater than I can ever remember. At the top of his voice he pulverised Jackson, tore him verbally limb from limb, casting the bitterest aspersions not just upon him personally but upon the entire British Foreign Office. When the performance ceased, the wretched Jackson seemed – though this cannot really be true – to be no longer there. It was as though he had been blown to pieces, or at least had slipped, propelled by the onslaught, from his chair and taken refuge beneath the ample folds of the white damask tablecloth. When the men joined the ladies, Jackson was not among them. He had, not surprisingly, surmised that his presence was no longer welcome and slunk off back to Paris. The next day, Duff could remember nothing whatever about the episode. When reminded, he expressed astonishment that an after-dinner discussion could cause anyone to react in such a way. Being not only mercurial but essentially good-natured, it would be surprising if he did not write a note or send a message to Jackson, assuring him that it was all good clean fun, with no offence meant and none to be taken.

The Coopers were succeeded by a very different ménage. The Harveys, Oliver and Maudie, though good hosts and certainly familiar, through previous incarnations, with the Paris scene, lacked altogether the Bohemian and raffish element which made the Coopers' reign so appealing. Although an experienced diplomatist with a mind of his own, he was a dry stick, apparently unsure of himself, while she, though a much more attractive personality, seemed subdued in or by his presence. Such a change in mood and pace was almost inevitable after the Cooper regime. It certainly did not justify the spoiling operation mounted, with the maximum of glee and malice, by Diana Cooper against everything the hapless Harveys said and did. Vicars who retire but go on living in the parish have a special duty not to embarrass or make more difficult the existence of their successors. Duff, from the distance of Chantilly or the Travellers' club in the Champs Elysées, observed this convention, but Diana did not. Her anti-Harvey campaign became sufficiently notorious for Nancy Mitford to make it one of the themes of her novel *Don't Tell Alfred*: thinly disguised as Lady Leone, Diana is made by Nancy's pen to return to the Embassy after leaving it, where in a disused set of rooms she sets up a rival establishment to her successors and is visited there by everyone who is anyone in Paris.

Sometime towards the end of 1949, Casey, who had become Editor of *The Times*, asked me if I would like to go to Rome as correspondent. There was no doubt about the answer. I would be the chief correspondent with an assistant. There would be ample opportunity, indeed it would be imperative, to travel, for unlike France, Italy was and is a country whose unity, not a century old at that date, is a fragile affair, compounded by strong regional loyalties, dialects and traditions. But excitement at the prospect was tempered by regrets at leaving Paris. So many friendships, French and non-French, had been made, so many stirring times lived through that it was difficult to imagine another world. In particular, the Ile St Louis, with its authentic and largely unspoilt seventeenth-century architecture and atmosphere, would be hard to leave. There was, as well, something about those Paris years which had a special place in the long and troubled story of Anglo–French relations. To a degree that has never been equalled since, many French people admired the British role in the war, cherished the memory of British and French co-operation in the Resistance, revered the person and achievements of Winston Churchill. The stereotype French image of an Englishman – well-cut suit, bowler-hat, furled umbrella, stiff upper lip, *Times* under arm – was, it is true, irritatingly inflexible and unobservant. But it is more agreeable to be liked than otherwise and there was certainly a lot of liking in France at that time for British ideals, real or imagined.

When I had a fracas with a lorry-driver about parking on the island – he felled me with a single blow and was nearly felled in his turn by Kitty, who had witnessed the affair from the windows of the apartment and came rushing down into the street, arms flailing – the man was made by his employer and the police to come and apologise. This was handsome, as I had undoubtedly taunted him. Still suffering from concussion, I received the apology gravely and assured him that it was my earnest hope that our reconciliation would "*resserrer les liens entre nos deux pays*". It is difficult to think of this ludicrous and rather touching scene occurring today.

We spent Christmas 1949 at St Firmin with the Coopers (thirty to dinner, sixty in afterwards). This was the occasion when the bonds of friendship with Nancy Mitford were strained to breaking point. The conversation, with her present, had turned to a discussion of French classical drama. I stated my dislike of the alexandrine, the iambic line of six feet favoured in French heroic verse. This was *not*, as Nancy herself would put it, a tease. I really did and still do find tiresome the relentless rhythm – like drums in the jungle – of the six foot line, as declaimed by French classical actors. This insult to Racine and Corneille was too much for Nancy's Francophilia. Speechless with rage, she slammed out of the room and refused to say a word to me for the rest of the visit.

As the forties gave way to the fifties, we drove to London in our latest acquisition: a shiny black Citroen *onze legère*, of the type in which gangsters in French thriller films of the period invariably made their getaway. It was very smart, with special additions of Scotch tartan loose covers and a white steering wheel. Although slow and noisy, its *traction avant* (front-wheel drive) pulled you round the corners as though the car were on rails. It seemed the very embodiment of the everlasting and wholly admirable French effort to be different.

5

Roma Immortalis

Victorian travellers, arriving in Rome from the north by way of the Via Cassia, were invariably moved, sometimes to the point of deep emotion, by their first sight of the city. 'How pleasing', wrote Cardinal Wiseman, the first Archbishop of Westminster since the Reformation, 'was the usual indication to early travellers, by voice and outstretched whip, embodied in the well-known exclamation of every *vetturino*, "Ecco Roma".' Niebuhr, the German scholar and historian of Rome, had the same sensations: 'it was with solemn feelings that this morning, from the barren heights of the moor-like Campagna, I first caught sight of the cupola of St Peter's and then of the city from the [Milvian] bridge, where all the majesty of her buildings and her history seemed to lie spread out before the eye of the stranger.'

Although I arrived not by aid of *vetturino* but in the faithful Citroen, the experience was much the same. It had been a long and lonely drive from London, 'peeling off the kilometres, sizzling down the long black liquid reaches of Nationale Sept, the plane trees going sha-sha-sha through the open window, the windscreen yellowing with crushed midges . . .' (Cyril Connolly on driving south through France). Once into Italy, though the spring sunshine lent a honey colour to the dusty brick walls of Siena and accentuated the greenness of the young wheat in the fields, the way seemed longer than ever. Then, just as those earlier travellers had described, Rome finally came into sight, with the Alban hills and the line of the sea beyond.

English – British – people who spend any time in Italy have always had a tendency to regard it not so much as a country as a huge and splendidly furnished indoor and outdoor museum, its human inhabitants diverting specimens of an exuberant race. Such an attitude is obviously untenable for a newspaper correspondent, sent to report on contemporary events and problems. But though in the next three years I did do a great deal of such reporting, travelling the length and breadth of Italy to do so, and trying always to remember that after twenty years of Fascism and the destruction of much of the economy by war, Italy's democratic leaders needed from abroad understanding and encouragement in their task, it would be useless to deny that much of the joy of this time came from the associations and aesthetic satisfaction of the past. How could it be otherwise? Soon after arriving in Rome, I looked up a French friend who was a member of the French Embassy. This involved going to the Palazzo Farnese, which the French Government rents from the Italian Government for an annual peppercorn rent. The most magnificent and majestic of all Roman palaces, it was built by Michelangelo (responsible for the vast external cornice) and Sangallo. My friend worked in an office about the size of a tennis court, its ceiling paintings the work of Carracci. The sound of splashing water as it fell from fountains into huge granite basins in the piazza outside the Embassy provided a continuous obbligato to our conversation. It is very difficult, indeed it is pointless to try, to resist the influence of this kind of setting.

Nor were these influences always urban. The spell of the Campagna, the countryside which used to begin just outside the walls of Rome (it is today increasingly the victim of hideous urban sprawl) proved just as strong as it did for the innumerable poets, writers and painters who in previous centuries had immortalised it in their work. 'The champaign with its endless fleece of feathery grasses everywhere', wrote Browning. In the 1950s, in a way that would be much more difficult today, you could easily find unlimited expanses of these feathery grasses, their silence broken only by the song of the larks above or, on occasion, by the thin but insistent piping of a shepherd boy rounding up his sheep. These shepherds, wild of appearance and always carrying a large umbrella, are almost a race apart. A friend of mine lost his way while riding in the Campagna, and made inquiries of a shepherd, who was lying on the grass, reading a book. From his total ignorance of his surroundings, he seemed to be mentally deficient. Yet his book was *Orlando Innamorato*, by the chivalric poet Boiardo: the English equivalent would be to find a farm worker reading *The Faerie Queen*.

The apartment where we lived throughout our Roman experience was modern and without much charm in itself. But it had a large southwards-facing terrace, to which would be wafted, on warm evenings in early summer, the smell, unsullied as it would be now by the stench of petrol fumes, of hay in the Campagna. Beneath swirled the muddy brown waters of the Tiber from whose opposite bank rose the

Aventine, the highest and, with its coronet of convents, the most picturesque of all the Roman hills. The back of the apartment looked out over the roofs of Trastevere, the most genuinely Roman of all districts, where a form of dialect is spoken and where the changeless pattern of Italian life prevailed – sunshine and raucous morning voices, long afternoon siestas, still longer talkative evenings, the whole time-table punctuated by the intermittent sound of church-bells.

Italy was governed by a coalition in which the Christian Democrats played the principal role. Their leader and the Prime Minister was Alcide de Gaspari, one of the great heroes of post-war Europe. For eight years, from December 1945 to July 1953, this quiet, modest, devout man controlled the destinies of Italy, whose people owe him a debt less only in degree than that which the first Italy owed to Cavour. He had a most unusual career. Born an Austrian, in the then Austrian province of Trento, he sat as a young politician in the Imperial Diet in Vienna as one of the deputies for the Trento. His native language was thus German, as it was (with significant consequences) for two others of the architects of modern Europe: Robert Schuman (born in German Alsace) and Konrad Adenauer. After the 1914–18 war, when the Trento passed to Italy, de Gaspari found himself, by now an Italian citizen, representing the same district in the Parliament in Rome. His anti-Fascist record was impeccable. After four years in the twenties in prison, he was rescued by the Vatican, in whose library he worked, poor but at least un-molested, until the fall of Mussolini. Following the liberation of Italy, he became first a Minister and before long Prime Minister. It was an unenviable task. The hopes of national unity and cohesion, indulged in so freely immediately after the liberation, had soon been dissipated. The economy, shattered by war and beset by chronic unemployment, was chaotic; and over the recovery of Trieste and its hinterland, occupied jointly by allied and Yugoslav forces, neo-Fascists and right-wing nostalgics made an unholy alliance, repeatedly accusing the Government of failing to stand up for Italian rights.

By the time I got to Rome, de Gaspari was in a more comfortable position, the Christian Democrats and their allies having soundly defeated the Communists in the 1948 general election, a turning point for Italy and Western Europe. All the other difficulties remained, however, and when I sought an interview with the Prime Minister it was not surprising that I should have been kept waiting several weeks. Finally the appointment was made and after a long wait in the ante-room I was shown into de Gaspari's office. He was writing at his desk and without looking up bade me sit down. When he had finished what he was doing, he pushed his reading glasses on to the top of his head and surveyed his visitor. He obviously could not believe what he saw. *"Non e il corrispondente del* Times, *e troppo giovane,"** he declared, and it took me ten minutes of the next precious hour to convince him not only of my identity but of my seriousness of purpose. It is a nice point whether looking young (which, at thirty-one, I undoubtedly did) is an advantage or a disadvantage when dealing with what Italians call *i pezzi grossi* (big noises).

De Gaspari was obviously a very big noise. But once reassured, he was both courteous and forthcoming. He had no doubt about who in Italy were the enemies of progress: on the one hand, the conservative interests, the landowners, the propertied classes, on the other, the Communists. He equally had no doubt about which was the more fearsome of the two. The Communists, he argued (this was not the Communist party of later years, which developed into a form of Euro-Communism with specifically Italian characteristics) were not a national opposition but the agents and supporters of a foreign power, who took their opposition into the streets. The more he talked – and I was to see him many times in the succeeding years – the more convincing and reasonable he sounded. Sometimes he, the resolute anti-Fascist, allowed himself the luxury of wishing that he could govern by decree of personal authority. The post-war constitution, in a natural reaction to Mussolini's system, had created two parliamentary chambers of equal powers. The result was that de Gaspari and his ministers had to spend much more of their time than they could spare in these two chambers, making the same speech twice over.

But having deplored these defects, de Gaspari was always quick to add that progress had to be made through democratic means, however cumbersome these might be. He was no despot. The more I saw him the more I liked and admired him. He combined in one person patriotism without bombast, political skill without demagogy and a strong sense of public duty without any apparent trace of personal aggrandisement. Something of the same respect, though hardly the same affection, was evoked by Sforza, the Foreign Minister – Ernie Bevin's despised Storzer. Inordinately vain and immensely talkative, he was nonetheless a brave and high-minded man who had spent twenty years in exile rather than live under Fascism. Despite his rather affectedly old-world

---

* "You are not *The Times* correspondent, you're too·young"

way of talking, he could voice some strong opinions, often reflecting his dislike of the Fascist years. Once he said something to me about "that filthy beastly little King [Victor Emmanuel III, who had accepted without demur Mussolini's regime] whom Winston Churchill supported". Now he was engaged, together with de Gaspari, in working towards the reinstatement of the new, democratic Italy in the framework of international, and specifically Western, relations. It was ungrateful and largely unspectacular work, the very reverse of Mussolini's ridiculous – but acclaimed – posturing on the balcony overlooking the Piazza Venezia.

It cannot have been easy to govern Italy of that time. (It is probably not easy at any time to govern Italy.) Though the country had decisively rejected Fascism and (a good deal less decisively) the monarchy, a great unsatisfied mass of opinion remained, longing in an unformulated way for glory or recognition or esteem. Bernard Berenson,* who knew as much as any foreigner about his adopted country, once described Italy to me, in a particularly harsh comparison, as being like "an elderly and failing whore – always a grievance about something or someone". There was a good deal in this, of course, yet this national sense of discontent, of readiness to blame someone else, usually foreign influences, for real or supposed ills was and is by no means confined to Italy. The *nous sommes trahis* attitude of mind is far too prevalent to be associated with any particular country. It may not be admirable but it is essentially human, an observation which would also cover the intermittent Italian hysteria of these years over Trieste. In 1948, in a ploy designed to ensure a victory for the anti-Communist parties in that year's general elections, the British, French and American Governments had issued a declaration of support for the return of the territory to Italy. Any subsequent apparent or suspected weakening of that support could be guaranteed to bring on hostile questions in the Rome Parliament and sometimes violent demonstrations in the big cities. The position of the three allied powers was naturally complicated by the defection of Tito from the Soviet bloc; from then on, it was necessary to encourage Tito without reneging on Italy, a diplomatic conjuring trick which predictably turned out to be almost impossible to perform. No wonder that de Gaspari said to me at one of our meetings that while the question of Trieste might look small in London or Washington, in Italy it was everything: pious aspirations from Britain or the USA (there were

* See footnote, p. 98.

plenty of those) that Rome and Belgrade should settle the Trieste problem between them were not, he said with unusual asperity, good enough.

Most of these high-level conversations which the youthful *corrispondente del Times* (pronounced Teemez) had in Rome or elsewhere, were recorded by him in a series of letters to Printing House Square, in whose archives they are preserved today. They read like despatches from ambassadors. Perhaps Deakin really was right and the *Times* man of that period was a kind of deputy Ambassador. The letters were circulated to interested parties at Printing House Square and contributed, one must hope, (though there was very little sign of this) to leading articles written in London. The practice was a general one. Every *Times* correspondent in a foreign capital was expected and encouraged to indulge in it, though how many did so was a matter of personal zeal. In the 1980s this would be nearly inconceivable. Then it was simply a continuation of the belief, adumbrated by the nineteenth-century panjandrums of Printing House Square, that in terms of foreign news and 'intelligence', what did not go into the paper was almost, if not entirely, as important as that which did. Mackenzie Wallace, who became Foreign Editor in 1890 and who was more of a statesman and scholar than a journalist in anything like the sense that the word conveys today, once explained to the irrepressible Blowitz in Paris why *The Times* had not published one of his despatches. It reported, quite accurately as events proved, the secret *entente* reached between France and Russia. Wallace told Blowitz that further corroboration was needed before such a startling piece of news could be published. But, he added, presumably as a note of consolation but one which must have infuriated Blowitz, "such an experienced journalist as you are must be aware that the *un*published information is often the most valuable."

Hanging about in ministerial ante-rooms in Rome for appointments with ministers was one part of the job. But another was getting about the country to see things for oneself. In the summer of 1950, now able to speak reasonable Italian, I toured first the north, then the south. From the great industrial centres of Milan and Turin, the superbly sited port of Genoa, the rich farmlands of the Po Valley, the arcaded streets of Bologna, dominated by their leaning medieval towers, two facts stood out: that there were only two political forces in Italy, the Communists and their friends and the Christian Democrats and theirs; and that the industrialists and landowners, almost to a man, conveniently blamed everything on the Communists. Yet even these sharp and apparently inflexible divisions could become blurred. In Tuscany, the peasants tended, with commendable perspicacity, to have it both ways. They voted Communist, but took care to have their marriages solemnised, their children baptised and themselves buried according to the rites of the Church. In Genoa, I met a formal naval officer, by now employed by the management of the shipyard. One day he came upon a workman in the yard whom he recognised as having served as a sailor under him. They greeted each other warmly and the ex-officer said, in a bantering tone, that he supposed the man was a Communist. "Naturally," was the reply, "but of course I remain a monarchist because I was in the Navy."

The trip to the south took longer and left more lasting, indeed indelible, impressions. Ever since the Bourbon Kingdom of Naples was joined with the Piedmontese monarchy to make a united Italy in 1860, the 'southern question' had been the staple diet of Italian politicians. It had remained a question without an answer. In Calabria (the toe), Lucania (the instep) and Apulia (the heel) the problems were (and still to a large degree are) chronic: over-population and massive under-employment, large under-cultivated estates and absentee landlords, small-holdings incapable of providing a living, an acute lack of communications and housing, and an almost universal shortage of water. By way of preparation, I read Carlo Levi's fine novel *Cristo si è fermato a Eboli* (*Christ stopped at Eboli*), but nothing could give adequate warning of the poverty-stricken villages where hope itself seemed to have died in the squalor and resignation. In the Fascist period, mass emigration and military and colonial adventures had done something to relieve the unremitting pressure of a growing population upon inadequate resources. Now those outlets were closed, and the 'southern question' was there in all its horrendous reality. In some of the remoter villages in Calabria it was difficult to find an Italian speaker, and I would take someone from the neighbouring town to interpret the local dialect, based upon Greek or Albanian. Among the many obstacles to land reform was the age-old reluctance of peasants to live on their land. A constant sight was that of peasants walking or on donkeys, either on the way to or returning from work – assuming they were lucky enough to have found work as *braccianti* or casual labourers. Yet as is so often true in very poor places, an innate sense prevailed of courtesy and hospitality towards the stranger with whom bread and wine, if there were any, would always be shared. Sometimes there were unexpected patches of prosperity, as in the province of Bari, where the *trulli* houses, curious little beehive-shaped, white-washed buildings, with double walls for warmth in winter and coolness in summer, had apparently infected their inhabitants with a desire for cleanliness and good order, contrasting strongly with the squalor elsewhere. As so often in Italy, strange exceptions occurred to challenge or disturb general patterns. Although the big absentee landlords had rightly earned themselves a bad reputation, there were in the province of Potenza vast estates administered by their owner, the head of one of the great families of Italy, on principles that bordered on the quixotic. The result was that peasants who had at last attained the longed-for status of proprietor by buying land on favourable terms from the Prince later were disgusted at finding that the State was not ready to forgive them their taxes in a bad year, as the Prince used to do with the rents.

Much has changed in the thirty-five years that have elapsed since this journey so full of splendours and miseries, so rewarding in memorable Byzantine and baroque monuments and vistas of mountain and sea, so studded with impressions of human hopelessness. Roads have been built, irrigation provided, houses constructed, tourism introduced, some of the excess manpower drawn away to the industrial north, consumer purchasing power increased. Yet Southern Italy remains at least in part much as I saw it, almost another country, a constant challenge to the spirit of man and the enterprise of governments, as I described in the long articles I wrote for *The Times*.

Bernard Berenson (BB)* first came into our lives – or we into his – through a common friend. We met in Rome and thereafter paid many happy visits to I Tatti, the great villa at Settignano, outside Florence – 'a library with living rooms attached' was BB's own description of it, though it is only accurate to record that there were a large number of living rooms – where he had made his home at the beginning of the century. Though close to ninety, BB had retained all his curiosity, all his appetite for new people to whom he would display his gifts for learned disquisition mixed with outrageous generalisation and a taste for worldly gossip. He could be very nice to the young, provided he liked them, and fortunately we seemed to come within that category. *Unsereiner*, it was called in the jargon of I Tatti, meaning one of us. He would sit for long periods on the sofa in the drawing-room at I Tatti

---

* Berenson, of Lithuanian-Jewish origins, naturalised American, art historian, author, diarist. For many years dominated the field of Italian Renaissance art, for which he was adviser to Joseph Duveen, the dealer. Died 1959, aged ninety-four.

holding Kitty's hand in his own, while he talked about everything except art, a subject he would rarely broach. Nonetheless it was his library, his own collection of paintings – including a fine Cima da Conegliano – and his writings which first implanted in me an undying love of Italian renaissance art, above all the Venetian and Florentine painters.

Staying at I Tatti, at least to begin with, could be something of an ordeal. The life there had much in common with those ducal and princely courts whose rulers had often commissioned the very pictures which it was BB's life's work to identify and authenticate. You never knew whom you were going to meet there. The company could range from the King of Sweden – a fellow scholar and archaeologist – to a group of Americans who had come up the hill from Florence to 'do' their famous compatriot, in the same way that they had 'done' the Sistine Chapel in Rome or St Mark's in Venice. Nicky Mariano, BB's friend, companion and hostess, one of the most delightful women ever to draw breath, who after Mrs Berenson's death ran I Tatti and ran BB, was a polyglot who sometimes contrived to mix up her languages. On one occasion, so the legend tells, she was dealing on the telephone with an American who wanted to pay respects to BB. Nicky, ever attentive to his comfort and wishes, did not think he would be amused, and sought to deter them. "I'm not sure," she said doubtfully in her charmingly accented English, "he's not too well today – nothing serious, but he's a little *giu*" (Italian for 'down'). Mindful of BB's modest stature and his ethnic origins, the American at the other end was not at all surprised by this statement of the obvious. "Yes of course we know that, but can't we see him all the same?"

The guests, those staying in the house and those who had come to lunch or dinner, would assemble before the meal in the drawing-room under the gaze of two huge Sassetta panels of St Francis which, affected by the near-tropical temperatures of the central heating at full blast, would intermittently make ominous cracking noises. Then the door would open and in came a small, neat figure, with tiny feet and hands, immaculately dressed in a handmade suit with a flower in the button-hole, his Van Dyck beard perfectly trimmed. He would go round the circle of guests, by now all standing, greeting each one with a word and a sad little smile. After this royal performance, the party proceeded to the dining-room, where the conversation would flow on in three or four languages, with BB always dominating it but also showing a capacity, rare in a person of his strength of opinion, to listen to the views of others. Since his death in 1959, various biographers and memoir-writers have not always treated him kindly. He is described as an exhibitionist, selfish, bad-tempered, a snob, intolerant and lacking in compassion. He may have had all these characteristics, especially in earlier life. All I can set down is that I never saw any of them. He was always courteous, attentive and completely fascinating, with as well stocked a mind as anyone I have ever met and a simplicity of taste which complemented his aesthetic sophistication.* In the afternoons at I Tatti, the unchanging routine was to accompany BB when he was driven by his alarmingly incompetent Welsh chauffeur Parry up the mountain above Settignano for his daily walk. There, on the woodland paths and rides, he would frequently stop to marvel at some ordinary manifestation such as a butterfly on the wing or a tuft of grasses blowing in the wind. For him, nature was the greatest artist of all. It was on one of these walks that BB, aged nearly ninety but bounding like a mountain goat down a boulder-strewn slope, looked back and saw me picking my way over the unfamiliar ground with care and uncertainty: "Are you all right, my dear boy?" he said. "Here, take my stick."

A very different expatriate in Italy whom we came to know well was Percy Lubbock, man of letters and friend of Henry James and Edith Wharton. By now elderly and nearly blind, he lived in a beautiful house on the sea at Lerici, near La Spezia, left to him by his late wife, Lady Sybil, who by all accounts must have been a tartar, albeit a rich one. There was a very different atmosphere from I Tatti. Percy was not fastidious – no button-holes and neat beards for him – and had let his person (though not his mind) deteriorate. It was a widely held and largely justified belief that he drank a good deal more than was good for him of the remarkably nasty local white wine. An ever-changing guard of young Englishmen lived in the house, their main, indeed their only duty being to read to Percy, who listened expressionless, his hands clasped around his enormous stomach and looking not unlike a Japanese bonze. He had some lively memories of Henry James, including a fine description of his conversational manner of pausing until he

---

* BB's political judgements were not always on the level of his artistic and literary ones. We kept up a correspondence after I left Italy, and in one letter written in December 1956, in the aftermath of the Suez fiasco, he was prophesying that unless 'the West' looked quickly and efficiently to its laurels, it would be pushed out of everywhere and 'Russia would meet Spain at the Pyrenees and join hands heartily with Franco'. He claimed to have inside information that secret negotiations to this effect were already under way.

had found precisely the right word to convey his meaning – "He cast around over the whole vast field of human utterance." Percy also had a story about James and Edith Wharton being driven in the latter's new car. She explained that she had bought it with the proceeds of her latest novel. James for a while digested this in silence and then said, with no trace of self-pity but simply as a statement of fact, that *his* last novel had yielded sufficient to enable him to buy his gardener a wheelbarrow.

Social life in Rome was largely what you wanted to make it. Some of the great Roman families, helped by judicious marriages with rich foreigners, continued to entertain in their vast palaces on a lavish scale. This was not our world, though it was always worth pausing, perhaps on the way home from the office, before a palace or an embassy at which a dinner-party was being given for a cardinal. Protocol demanded that princes of the Church should be greeted at the street door and accompanied up the grand staircase to meet their hosts by two, perhaps four, liveried servants bearing long, lighted candles; a fine sight for an onlooker. I sometimes wondered what would have happened if the cardinal's hosts lived, as many people in Rome do live, in a fourth-floor flat approachable only by way of a rickety lift. The answer must be that such a person would not invite a cardinal or, if he did so, the cardinal would not accept. Our only comparable Roman experience with candles, though the setting was very different, was when the present Queen, then Princess Elizabeth and living in Malta while Prince Philip was serving in his ship there, paid a visit to Rome. In the course of it she celebrated her twenty-fifth birthday. John Russell,* first secretary of the Embassy, gave a party in her honour when a birthday cake with twenty-five blazing candles was borne into the dining-room on the back of a diminutive Sicilian donkey, who almost inevitably made a large and audible mess on the carpet.

One Roman friend in particular posed a difficult social problem. He was Mario Praz, for many years Professor of Italian Studies at Manchester University. In the 1950s, he held the chair of English Literature at the University of Rome and lived in Via Giulia in what was more of a museum than an apartment, filled with the precious furniture, much of it English Regency and French *Empire*, which he spent a lifetime collecting. A learned and amusing conversationalist, he ought, despite a somewhat forbidding appearance, to have been an addition to any party. The snag was that it was sometimes difficult to get Italians to

* Later Sir John Russell and Ambassador to Ethiopia, Brazil and Spain (see also p. 182)

meet him. He was a *jetattura*, a possessor of the *mal'occhio* (evil eye). To
speak to him, to touch him, even to speak *of* him could have the direst
consequences. How he had gained this reputation or whether it was
deserved or not, I never discovered. He certainly brought no harm to
me or my family. But there was no denying the evidence of one's eyes as
people pressed back against the wall to avoid contact with poor Mario,
the index and little finger of their right hands discreetly extended,
horn-like, in a desperate attempt to ward off possible evil. (Men have a
more powerful and less visible remedy against such dangers: plunge the
right hand into the trouser pocket and get a firm grip on the testicles.)

On May 26, 1951, the diary entry reads 'To Abruzzi with Silone'.
This was a memorable experience. Ignazio Silone, for many years
under-valued in his own country as a writer, is in fact one of the
foremost writers and thinkers Italy has produced this century. (He died
in 1978.) Iris Origo has called her fine essay* on him 'A Study in
Integrity', an entirely appropriate title. Born in the Abruzzo village of
Pescina de' Marsi, on the barren hillside above the dried-up lake of
Fucino, he was educated in Church schools, joined the Communist
party, was imprisoned in Spain, lived in Paris and Switzerland in exile
from the Fascist regime in Italy, abandoned the Communists, wrote
many novels and, by the time I knew him, sat in the Italian Parliament
as a Socialist deputy for his region. His experiences had left him deeply
preoccupied with the problem of man's suffering and his need for
brotherhood and freedom. As Iris Origo points out, he looked, with his
big, dark, melancholy eyes, more a Spaniard than an Italian. He was
reserved and slow to express himself and we only got to know him
through his attractive Irish wife Darina. 'A Socialist without a Party, a
Christian without a Church' (his own self-description), he was in fact
very close to being a mystic.

Fontamara, probably his best-known novel, is a thinly disguised
story about Pescina, his native village, where the peasants suffered so
harshly at the hands of the landowners. 'For twenty years [the quotation is from the novel] the same earth, the same rain, wind, the same
feast days, the same food, the same poverty – a poverty inherited from
our fathers, who received it from their grandfathers and against which
honest work was of no avail . . . The life of men and beasts, and of the
land itself, revolved in a close circle . . . There has never been a way
out. At that time, a man could perhaps save twenty or thirty soldi a

* In *A Need to Testify* (John Murray, 1984)

month, and in summer perhaps even a hundred, so that by the autumn he had thirty lire. They disappeared at once – an interest on some loan, or to the doctor, the chemist or the priest. And so one began again, the next day . . .' When Silone was only fourteen, a severe earthquake destroyed the greater part of Pescina, killing his mother. So the 'Fontamara' he took us to see was not the town of his early childhood but a mostly modern reconstruction. In the warm May weather, with the spring flowers colouring the hillsides and a great circle of mountains, some of them still snow-capped, dominating the plain below, the place did not look like the well of desolation so graphically depicted in the novel. When I remarked on this to Silone, he said nothing but smiled his slow, sad smile. Perhaps he was thinking of the last words of the book: 'after so much suffering and despair, what is to be done?'

If Southern Italy had provided a subject of recurring fascination, two other fields of inquiry or discovery proved equally rewarding. The first was archaeology, hitherto a totally closed book to me. Encouraged by BB and by the general environment, I began to take an interest in the ancient world which lay so close to hand. Among other results were some special contributions to *The Times*, 'scoops' in their own way, describing recent discoveries of great importance. One of them concerned the remarkable excavations at Palestrina, twenty-three miles east of Rome, where wartime bombing had laid bare the outlines of the great Temple of Fortuna, one of the most important Roman shrines of the pre-Christian era. Cicero describes the fame of the oracle at Palestrina, or Praeneste, whose original temple was reconstructed and enlarged under Sulla. What the modern excavations had done was to reveal the full extent of the immense construction, laid out along a series of terraces conforming to the steeply sloping ground and linked by steps and ramps. The design was a subject of irresistible interest to the architects of the Renaissance. Sangallo, Palladio and others all produced plans, some of them rather fantastic, of what a restored Praeneste would look like. Now the bombs and the excavators had revealed the truth. The unknown architect who in the first century BC had known how to introduce into his splendid concept such a sense of space and grandeur had fully established a claim to be considered the father of Italian architecture. (Years later, when we no longer lived in Italy but were paying a return visit to Rome, we drove out to visit the scene of this earlier labour of love. It was a fine spring day, the light golden and almost tangible. We climbed up the steps and ramps from the lower temple area to the topmost terrace, above which stands the Renaissance palace of the Barberini family. Within the palace, a fine stone ceremonial staircase leads on up to the *piano nobile*. As we began to climb this, a flow of polyphonic choral sound burst forth from above. Despite the intensity of its volume, it had a strange, almost disembodied sound, as though it was floating on invisible clouds. For a moment I wondered if it was possible that death had intervened and this was the ascent to heaven. It was certainly how going to heaven ought to be. But in the big room above, a group of mortal, not immortal, singers was practising a Palestrina mass with the fervour of artists who knew they were performing in the composer's home town.)

The second archaeological scoop, in the sense that nothing had up to then appeared about the subject in a non-learned journal, came from Sicily. Travelling there in the autumn of 1951, we came upon a remarkable archaeological dig at Piazza Armerina, a small and otherwise undistinguished town in the middle of the island. There the remains of a huge and sumptuous Roman villa of the late imperial era, the chief of whose wonders was a series of marvellously preserved coloured mosaic floors, were being released from massive sand deposits which had conserved them so well over the centuries. In fact, the villa had been known about for a long time and earlier excavations had uncovered some of its glories. But these new efforts were far more thorough than anything that had gone before. In particular, they had revealed a much wider expanse of the polychrome mosaics. These, in the richness of their colourings, the variety of their style and design and their mixture of classical inspiration and Byzantine style of representation of the human form, recalled the marvels of the Ravenna churches. By far the most spectacular and unexpected was the floor of the Bikini girls, showing eight young female gymnasts, arranged in two rows, one above the other. Some are running, one is using the dumb-bells, another throwing the discus, and one is doing nothing except twirl a parasol in a somewhat affected manner.

The other area of particular interest was the Vatican. My schoolboy inclinations towards the Roman Catholic Church had long since been abandoned, but the pomp and mysteries of the headquarters of that Church, the existence within the state of Italy of Vatican City, a tiny independent sovereign territory, the connection between the Church and Italian politics, an especially sensitive link at a time when the 'confessional' Christian Democrat party ruled the roost: all these had served to whet the appetite long before I arrived in Rome.

Also by this time, I had read and re-read *Hadrian the Seventh*, the

extraordinary book by Frederick William Rolfe (Baron Corvo). It was
of this work that D.H. Lawrence wrote that 'if it is the work of a demon,
not a mere poseur . . . and if some of it is caviar, at least it came out of
the belly of a live fish.' There is little to admire in Rolfe himself: a
spoiled priest and paranoic pervert who, after biting nearly every hand
that fed him, died in Venice in 1913, friendless, penniless and in-
famous. But Hadrian is in its weird way a masterpiece, a tale to leave
Walter Mitty and Baron Munchausen standing at the post. The hero,
George Arthur Rose – a transparent disguise for the impoverished and
embittered Rolfe – is elected to the Papacy, after a series of extraordinary developments, by the Conclave of Cardinals in Rome. (The splendidly authentic details of Conclave ritual show that Rolfe was well-
informed about and drew upon the details of the actual Conclave of
1903, which elected Sarto, the Patriarch of Venice, as Pius X.) After a
whirlwind and unconventional reign, this English Pope is murdered by
a crazed and jealous Protestant socialist, in the course of what today
would be called a summit meeting. In his usual unorthodox way,
Hadrian is walking instead of driving through the streets of Rome, the
Kaiser on his right and the King of Italy on his left accompanying the
Supreme Pontiff on this unusual stroll. 'On the way, carriages met them
and disgorged sovereigns; state coaches met them and emitted cardinals; courtiers alighted from horseback and emerged from cars.' Then
comes the shot. 'The slim white figure stopped, wavered, and sank
down. The whole world seemed to stand still, while the human race
gasped once.' This splendid and improbable flight of Corvine fancy
never fails, however many times re-read. Or was it so fanciful? In our
time we have seen the white-clad figure of a Pope shot down in cold
blood in St Peter's Square.

Another literary source for what he called 'the mysterious glamour of
the antique organization of Rome' was Lytton Strachey, in his pre-
judiced and mocking essay on Manning. That glamour was soon to be
sampled and proved to be all that Strachey had described. Only a few
days after first getting to Rome, I went to St Peter's for Pontifical High
Mass on Easter morning. It was Holy Year and huge crowds filled the
basilica and Bernini's colonnaded piazza. Just before 10 a.m. the papal
procession entered the west door. As it did so, the huge church, already
alive with light from the April sunshine and the great red and gold
hangings on the walls, was suddenly transformed when, at the touch of
a switch, every chandelier sprang into life. The procession, led by the
Swiss Guards, who were followed by members of the papal court and

the bishops and the cardinals in their swishing vermilion robes, moved slowly up the nave, and lastly came the Pope himself, borne aloft in the *sedia gestotoria* (a kind of portable throne whose motion is said to be highly inducive of sea-sickness) and flanked by fan-bearers carrying the massive ostrich-feather fans known as *flabelli*. The whole scene could have been painted, without any changes, by Benozzo Gozzoli.

In the next three years I attended many ceremonies in St Peter's, and they never failed to provide at the least a magnificent spectacle, at the most some moments of deep religious significance. When the Pope celebrates Mass, the Swiss Guards, at the moment of elevation, kneel and lower their swords in salute, a gesture of unbelievable majesty. The reigning Pope Pacelli (Pius XII), although towards the end of his life allowing himself to wallow in Mariolatry, had a fine presence, which added to the sense of theatre. His ascetic features, the graceful movement of his benedictory hands, his air of tranquil dignity, lent a much needed extra dimension to what was often a scene of considerable disorganisation. Protocol is not the Vatican's strong point. Elderly cardinals fluff their entrances, do not know where to stand or what to do, turn up wearing the wrong liturgical colours; seating arrangements in St Peter's tend to be chaotic, the timetable collapses, photographers clamber about on the altars. But none of this seems to matter. The crowds shout their fervent greetings, the organ thunders, beneath Bernini's baldaquin the priests and prelates move about with hieratic grace. In that Holy Year, the pulling power of the Papacy could also be seen in the streets. At the end of July, the Pope went to the papal summer residence at Castle Gandolfo, in the Alban hills, whence he returned twice weekly for audiences at the Vatican. Alone in the back of a large black car, he was escorted by special units of the Italian police, their bouncing little jeeps making a rather undignified contrast with the white-clad, gesturing central figure. As the car passed through the streets, the traffic was held up and the people on the pavements cheered and waved. The Roman Question – the take-over in 1870 by the new Italian Kingdom of the papal territories and the self-chosen isolation of the Pope within the Vatican – seemed a long time buried.

Before leaving London, I had equipped myself with letters of introduction from Douglas Woodruff* and Archbishop David Mathew, author and historian and Apostolic Delegate in British Africa. It was not an easy job to get anyone in the Vatican to pay any attention.

---

* Editor of *The Tablet*, 1936–67, and a former *Times* man

Its idea of public relations was then, and still is largely today, despite some improvements, comparable to that of the Kremlin: both institutions will make known, at a time of their choosing, what they want to make known, and they will do it by official statements, not by press conferences or meetings with individual journalists. Armed with my letters, I was resolved to break through this system. One of them was to Mgr Tardini who, in the absence of a Cardinal Secretary of State, a post then unfilled, was the effective head of the Vatican's foreign office and as such very close to the Pope. The first response to the letter, once presented, was a summons by the great man's secretary who explained, with exquisite courtesy but in unmistakable language, that the Church did not have contacts with the press; all inquiries should be addressed to the *Osservatore Romano*, the Vatican's semi-official newspaper. I explained, in equally unmistakable language, that *The Times* was not quite like other newspapers (could the same argument be deployed today?) and needed to be informed on every aspect of life in Rome and Italy. Surely there was no denying that the Vatican was one of the most important of these aspects?

It worked. I was soon in the presence of a rather grumpy, elderly, Roman prelate who showed himself a worthy exponent of the *realpolitik* which generally characterises the Church's secular dealings. Tardini quickly scoffed at the idea of an alliance between the Vatican and other anti-Communist forces in the world. How could there be any understanding between Islam and Rome? How, for that matter, could there be any formal connection between the Roman Catholic and other faiths, even if they did share a common hostility to Communism? "The Church does not deal in politics, [to my delight, he talked like the Inquisitor from *St Joan*] her crusade against Communism is a crusade against anti-Christ." At the end, I asked him whether, in search of enlightenment about Vatican policy, I could come and see him again? He willingly assented and I made my way out along frescoed corridors and through courtyards alive with the music of splashing fountains.

The next target was at once easier and more important. Mgr Montini, who in later years became Pope Paul VI, was, as assistant acting Secretary of State, actually below Tardini in the hierarchy, but most people credited him with having more influence, especially with the Pope. That belief must have accounted for the number of those wanting to see him and the fevered state of his waiting-room. He had the enviable but potentially inconvenient gift of making each visitor feel that he was the person Montini had been waiting all his life to talk to.

The result was that his daily arrangements became hopelessly dislo-
cated. It was not unknown for people with appointments to wait several
hours before they were ushered in. Bishops and cardinals suffered this
treatment along with lesser mortals. The first time I went to see
Montini, a knowing friend advised taking along a packet of sandwiches
"because if your appointment is 11 a.m. or later, you'll almost certainly
miss your lunch." In fact, this did not happen, but the ante-room was
full of purple-sashed monsignori and pectorally crossed bishops, who
regarded with barely concealed dislike this lay and obviously foreign
addition to the waiting-list.

But the delay was worth it. With his deep-set eyes and expressive
gestures, Montini was an impressive talker of great subtlety, the very
opposite of the earthy and outspoken Tardini. He later became a
cardinal and Archbishop of Milan and was widely seen as the most
probable successor to John XXIII. (The latter, whose family name was
Roncalli, was by contrast an unexpected successor to the throne of St
Peter. When from the Conclave which in 1965 elected him the white
smoke was seen billowing forth, signifying that a Pope had been
chosen, the Foreign Office in London was said to have been momentarily nonplussed. Who was this Roncalli? Apparently all they had in
the files was a brief report dating back to the time when he was Papal
Nunzio in Paris. It was then, and may still be, the rule that British
embassies should provide short notes on the other Heads of Missions in
the same capital. The note from the Embassy in Paris on Mgr Roncalli,
prepared many years previously, read: 'typical, fat, soapy, Italian
priest' – a strikingly inadequate and ill-judged summing-up of the man
who turned out to be one of the best-loved and most influential Popes of
modern times.)

Though appreciative of Montini's qualities, John XXIII used to say
of him that he was "*un po' amletico*" (a bit Hamlet-like), meaning, I
suppose, that he had difficulty in making up his mind. In my many
talks with him, something of this defect (if that is what it was) made
itself felt. He no sooner said something than he proceeded to un-say it,
leaving the listener bewildered as to what it was this highly cultivated
priest did think. Once he remarked, apropos of some political discussion we had been having, where he seemed inclined both to criticise the
de Gaspari Government for inanition and to deny he was criticising it,
"In political questions the Church has to be general, just as in religious
matters she cannot afford not to be particular" – an aphorism which
recalled not so much Bernard Shaw as G.K. Chesterton. Commenting

on this in my private report to Printing House Square, I wrote that I had no doubt that if I had asked Montini whether, in the interests of getting things done, the Church would prefer more authoritarian methods for governing Italy, he would have replied: "The Church is empirical in its approach, neither condemning nor approving of regimes *per se* but according to whether they achieve that which ought to be achieved."

On one of my return visits to Rome, some years later, after Montini had become Pope, I had a private audience with him. He was affable and welcoming, but by that time, beset with the cares and responsibility of his great office, he had retreated into banal generalities which by comparison made those earlier conversations seem almost incisive. Despite this increased display of Hamletism, I think he was genuinely taken aback and distressed by the effects of his predecessor's reforming zeal and by public reactions to the second Vatican Council. He certainly spoke of John XXIII's personality having been "too often arbitrarily interpreted" – coded language, I surmise, for saying that the Vatican Council and its only begetter never intended that the door should be opened to individual interpretation of the Church's doctrines and practice. Were I a Roman Catholic, I believe that I too would regret some of the changes that have come about, particularly the substitution, in the Mass, of the vernacular for Latin. That has surely struck a near-lethal blow at the idea of the universality of the Roman Church. In the commendable interest of associating people more closely with the liturgy and procedures of the Mass, the reformers have largely destroyed the tradition by which everyone, whatever his or her language or level of intelligence and understanding, in whatever country he or she might be, used to hear the same words and share in the same responses. It is clear that something precious has been lost, less obvious that the gain offsets the loss.

The Roman experience was too good to last. Time finally ran out for us. Towards the end of 1952, the new Editor of *The Times*, Sir William Haley, told me to prepare to leave and return to Paris, as head of the office there, in succession to Gerald Norman.

The years in Rome left several abiding impressions about the nature of Italian society and the Italian political process. The first was the impact of the Roman Catholic Church at nearly every point of national life. This is less evident today than in my time; the legalisation, by Parliament and referendum, of divorce in the seventies was a striking reminder of the way in which the Vatican can no longer be sure of calling the tune. But it is still impossible to imagine an Italy in which the priesthood, ranging from the rural parish priest hurrying in soutane and biretta along the village street on the way to Mass, up to the cardinals of the Curia being driven about Rome in shiny cars with Vatican number plates, ceases to exert an ever-present influence; that influence being compounded of the triple, Dostoievskian formula of mystery, miracle and authority. It is no coincidence or fluke that Christian Democracy, though it may no longer enjoy a monopoly of power, remains, with its confessional foundations, one of the mainstays of the State. Anticlericalism certainly exists, but is a mere shadow of its vigorous French counterpart, and will surely stay that way. Whether these priestly presences should be seen as a source of good or evil depends on your viewpoint. Though the powers they confer are open to abuse, they probably do less harm than their critics pretend. And in some indefinable way Italy, despite the historic role of the Church in her midst, manages to avoid the atmosphere of a priest-ridden society associated with Ireland or Malta.

The second impression, a profound one, was of the width of the gulf separating ordinary public opinion from the feverish activities of the professional politicians. The plottings and posturings of the parties in Rome, the columns of newsprint, written in a mandarin-like language by the professional commentators, which daily fill the newspapers of all persuasions, seem to leave the general public at least indifferent or bewildered, at most contemptuous. It is as though the political game, of great complexity and fascination for those actually playing it, were being carried on in a sealed and windowless room, whose atmosphere consequently is in a permanently overheated state. It is not that Italian politicians are, in general, any more or less incompetent or wily than politicians in other countries. But something in the national temperament, as well as the earlier history of what today constitutes united Italy, induces them to regard the pressures and counter-pressures of politics as ends in themselves, related only by chance to the needs of the nation and the community. Were it not for the fact that the country seems to survive surprisingly well under the system, it would be tempting to condemn it as being bound in the end to result in alienation and instability.

Thirdly there was the impression – familiar to any observer of the Italian scene – that Italians, for all their acceptance of Mussolini's absurd and erratic leadership, normally have little respect for authority, whether central or external. Though in my Roman years, the Italian Communist Party (PCI), under Palmiro Togliatti's fiery generalship,

seemed to be in the vanguard of international Communism, its links
with Moscow cast in tempered steel, it really should have come as no
surprise that the PCI developed at one stage into one of the leading
examples of Euro-Communism. Italian Communism has a face of its
own, just as the growth of the black or parallel economy – commercial
and artisan activity carried on behind the back of the tax inspector or
the government statistician – is a particularly Italian manifestation of
disregard for the normal rules.

So is the Italian attitude towards work: seen as something (when it is
to be had) which is necessary for the sustainment of life, it does not
possess, as in the case of Protestant countries imbued with the work
ethic, a moral quality of its own. In the 1950s, when the American
Marshall Aid programme was helping Italy, with other countries of
Western Europe, along the road to economic recovery, a story went the
rounds in Rome which may or may not have been true, but which
illustrates the point perfectly. A young and eager American official,
working at the Marshall Aid office in Rome, decided to run down to
Naples to see how the programme was faring there. He took a train
which landed him there in the early afternoon of a hot summer's day. In
the streets, there was no one about, for this was siesta time. Eventually
the American came upon a man who, having no roof of his own, was
taking his nap propped up against a wall. With some difficulty the
American prodded him into consciousness and asked him why he was
not working. The man explained that he had no job and no means of
getting one. "Why don't you raise a loan and open a small shop?" asked
the American. The man of Naples was unimpressed, scarcely bothering
to keep his eyes open. "Then if you did well," persisted the visitor,
"you could increase your borrowing power and open more shops." At
last a flicker of interest: "What happens then?" The American, continuing his saga of competitive capitalism, painted a picture within
which the still recumbent figure became an entrepreneur of national
importance, went into politics, perhaps finished up as President of the
Republic. By now the Italian was standing up, visibly excited: "What
then, what then?" The American, his imagination exhausted, could
embellish no further. "Why," he said, "I suppose you'd finally retire
and take a long rest." The man slumped back against the wall: "That's
what I was doing when you woke me," he said disgustedly. The
parable, if such it be, is obviously not for universal application. If it
were, life in Italy or elsewhere would come to a halt. But as an
expression of realism and resignation, it seems to embody the common

sense and dignity which is the element of much of Italian life.

If leaving Paris three years earlier had been a wrench, saying goodbye to Italy was the spiritual equivalent of a major surgical operation. On Christmas Eve 1952 we bade farewell to the beloved Campagna by climbing to the top of Mount Soracte, the imposing mass which rises, looking like the Rock of Gibraltar, from the plain 25 miles north of Rome. It was sunny and hot, and on such a day, with the green and brown and deserted-looking countryside rolling away from the foot of the mountain as far as the eye could carry on one side, and the Tiber flowing in loops and bends, like a dirty brown ribbon, between Soracte and the mountains on the other, the unique quality of this landscape, so suffused with light and comfortable melancholy, took on added emphasis. It was easy to see how Dickens, who found it monotonous and gloomy when first he saw it, came to write later of it as 'the wild plain where nothing is now heard but the wind and where the solitary lizards gamble unmolested in the sun'.

6

Paris – Death and Rebirth
of a Republic

The man who ordered us back to Paris was to me an unknown quantity. Sir William Haley, knighted for his services as Director-General of the BBC, became Editor of *The Times* in October 1952 and remained so for fourteen years. I never got to know him well. Few did. A powerful intellect, a limitless capacity for work, a firmness of conviction amounting at times to inflexibility were accompanied by a diffidence of manner, a degree of shyness which often seemed to make human intercourse, for him, an experience so painful as to call for its avoidance wherever possible. That at least is how he appeared to most people. A few senior members of the staff at Printing House Square claimed to have pierced his armour and to have found within a warm and compassionate human being. I have kept a file of his memoranda to me – typically, he found communication easier on paper than by word of mouth – and over the years they frequently sounded a note of encouragement and understanding that meant much to a hard-worked correspondent. But when we met face to face, either in Paris or London, the shutters were usually down. In London, the rendezvous was apt to be the dining-room at his club, the Athenaeum, where to the awfulness of the food was added Haley's dislike of drink in any form. "I suppose you'll want some of *that*," he would say, indicating with a disapproving gesture a very small decanter of what proved to be very nasty red wine on its way to someone else's table.

Yet he was in many ways a great Editor, of an authoritarian kind. His rectitude was total. He once, to emphasise that for someone in his position favours should neither be received nor given, sent back to the donor a case of Jaffa oranges which the Israeli Embassy had tried to give him as a Christmas present. If a *Times* man came under criticism, however exalted, from outside, he would be steadfast in springing to the defence. Something I had written during the Suez affair in 1956 called down on my head the wrath of Selwyn Lloyd, then Foreign Secretary. I reported this fact to Printing House Square. 'I certainly should not worry', replied Haley, 'about any strictures which Selwyn Lloyd makes privately or publicly about *The Times*.' To the world, this could have seemed the sublimest arrogance. To someone under attack, it was supporting fire of the most potent and welcome kind.

A voracious reader, above all of forgotten nineteenth-century novels (George Gissing was one of his heroes), Haley took to composing a weekly column on books and authors which appeared in *The Times* over the pseudonym of Oliver Edwards. The cheeky young Bernard Levin, then at the beginning of his literary career, declared that this was so stupifyingly boring as to make a dog howl. But Haley persevered and much of his correspondence to me was in search of some detail about French books or writers which he wanted to introduce into his column. In April 1957 the Queen and Prince Philip paid a state visit to Paris, a spectacular event requiring much eye-witnessing and copious description. Haley, who needed information about the general standing of Alfred de Musset in French literary and theatrical circles, considerately waited until the royal visit was past, and then wrote a letter which began: 'I remember that when I was present at the height of the fighting on the River Sangro [during the Italian campaign in 1943/44], a telegram arrived from Broadcasting House for the BBC war correspondent, asking him to obtain immediately a recording of an Italian donkey's bray. This has always stayed in my mind and I have not, therefore, worried you with [the Musset request] during the Queen's visit.' So this outwardly stern and difficult man could indulge himself with humorous anecdote. An even more surprising example (because it was spoken, not written) became one of the heirlooms of Printing House Square. Presiding over the daily news conference, Haley was displeased to hear one day that the Cairo correspondent, instead of being at his post to report a big story which had broken there, had gone off to Petra, in Jordan. "What does he hope to achieve for us in Petra?" he asked. The foreign news editors thoughtlessly replied that the man had in mind a colour piece. "We know the colour of Petra,"* snapped the well-read Editor. "Get him back."

Soon after we returned to Paris, Duff Cooper died, aged only

* 'Match me such marvel save in Eastern clime,
  A rose-red city half as old as Time.' (Dean Burgon)

sixty-three (New Year's Day 1954). It was a bitter blow. His and Diana's kindness and hospitality to us at their house near Chantilly was unending. We seemed to spend nearly every weekend there, Duff's company and conversation being one of the principal joys. Directly I learnt the news, I filed a message to *The Times*, expressing the thought that his death would distress a very wide circle of French people 'who had known, respected and felt affection for this most Francophile of Englishmen'. I also paid a heart-felt tribute to his achievements as the first British Ambassador in Paris after the liberation. To read the *Times* obituary the next morning was like receiving a bucket of cold water in the face. I never discovered who wrote it, but he was no friend or admirer of Duff's. According to this anonymous author, Duff had failed in or made a mess of every public duty he had undertaken. Even in Paris, 'his range of contacts was perhaps too small to make him the ideal Ambassador'. As for his personality, he was 'unwilling to suffer either fools or sobersides gladly'. The obituary was a real hatchet job, not the first that *The Times* had carried out on this engaging and courageous man; in the pre-war, Munich days, when the paper was editorially appeasement-minded, it had sought to dismiss Duff's resignation speech in the House of Commons (he resigned in protest against the Munich agreement) as a 'damp squib'.

His friends sprang to his defence. Glowing tributes to Duff – some of them certainly organised and a few probably written by these or other allies – began to appear in British and French publications. Several remarked with asperity upon the *Times* obituary. I shared in the indignation and willingly co-operated in the task of showing up Printing House Square for its vindictiveness and inaccuracy, in particular persuading French parliamentarians involved in one aspect or another of Franco–British relations to write protests to *The Times* itself.*

While this was going on, Haley paid a visit to Paris. With some intensity, Kitty pointed out to him how pleased Duff would have been by the slanging given to him in a paper he had despised ever since Munich. Haley smiled, saying nothing. I also raised the Duff Cooper affair with him. Though he did not seem to mind my attitude and activities, he was in general completely unrepentant. Time would show, he said, that the paper was right. Looking back on it now, all

---

* A booklet of these protests and appreciations, including the offending *Times* piece, was subsequently produced by the *Daily Telegraph* and circulated privately to Duff's friends.

passion spent, I would say that some of what the bilious obituarist wrote holds up. It is true, as anyone who knew him would have in honesty to admit, that Duff did not find 'fools or sobersides' easy to tolerate, true also that he had not been a successful Minister of Information in 1940/41. But other parts of the piece were mistaken, particularly as regards his role as Ambassador. Despite their tendency in those immediately post-war years to welcome rather too liberally various literary or cultural figures with collaborationist reputations, the Coopers were an outstandingly successful team to re-open the Embassy. Duff's genuine affection for France and things French could not, and did not, fail to evoke corresponding reactions. Haley would have been a bigger man if he could have brought himself to admit that *The Times* was not infallible and had, in this particular case, been in partial error. But this was not his way.

I was in charge of *The Times* office in Paris from early 1953 until the end of 1960. Those eight years, for a journalist with as much editorial space at his disposal as Printing House Square usually provided for its Paris correspondence, presented an unequalled opportunity for reporting upon and analysing the gradual erosion and final collapse of the Fourth Republic, the dramatic circumstances of General de Gaulle's return to power in 1958 and his paternity of the Fifth Republic, the fiasco of the Suez affair, the ever-darkening shadows cast by the war in Algeria, and the coming and going of international statesmen for whom Paris was still (as it largely remains today) the focal point of Western Europe. During this time, there were two general elections, which were the excuse for extensive travels in the French provinces, their generally placid and practical attitudes towards politics and the life of the nation contrasting sharply with the perpetually fevered atmosphere of the capital.

As this book is not a history of France but one man's reminiscences, it is natural that personalities should linger in the memory longer than the events in which they were involved. General de Gaulle inevitably remained the most fascinating and enigmatic of all. But by the mid-fifties he had largely withdrawn from public life, as though in despair at the persistence of a political system which, according to him, was doomed to lead France further into mediocrity and worse. Indeed he freely expressed this despair to the visitors he would receive during his periodic visits to Paris from Colombey-les-deux-Eglises, his retreat in eastern France. Foreign journalists were hardly ever admitted to these sessions, but a friend of mine in the British Embassy who saw him in

May 1956 gave me a graphic description. According to this the General, so far from being ready to step back into French politics as the saviour of the nation, had moved on to a plane of aloofness and lofty, almost Spenglerian, despondence. No national revival, he said, could take place by imposition from above. It must grow up, slowly and spontaneously, from the bottom. In the meantime, it was not impossible that there might be some adventures, with the Communists posing a much greater threat than anything likely to be mounted by the extreme right (a prophecy that was to prove sensationally false within two years). As he rose to go, my friend, phasing himself (so he thought) into the General's new historic timescale, said something about hoping that the situation might be better in ten years' time. Gravely, the General replied: "Better speak of a hundred years."

But if de Gaulle had thus gloomily removed himself from the political scene, another star of great brilliance and dazzling performance began to illuminate the heavens, attracting the mingled admiration and hostility of those who watched its passage. This was Pierre Mendès-France, who became Prime Minister in June 1954. Then aged forty-seven, this sallow-skinned, dark-haired stocky Jew, who always looked as though he were in need of a shave and possessed an intellect as sharp and questing as any in France or indeed in Europe, had already had a meteoric career. He had held junior financial office in the pre-war Blum Government at the age of thirty-one. After wartime service in a Free French bomber squadron, he became Minister for National Economy in the post-liberation de Gaulle Government, characteristically resigning after failing to win acceptance for his bold plans for national recovery. Since then, he had been in opposition, voicing increasingly bitter criticism of the policies of successive governments over Indo-China and North Africa and in the economic and financial field.

No one could say that Mendès-France (invariably referred to either as 'Mendès' or 'PMF') went out of his way to charm. He had an abrasive manner, seemed actually to enjoy making enemies and was intolerant of criticism. His relentlessness in argument could drive his hearers almost to distraction. "I shall never again", said de Gaulle after one meeting with him, "allow anyone to speak to me for three hours about economics." For someone who owed much of his popular appeal to being (as he claimed) different from and more high-principled than other politicians, he was not above resorting to gimmicks and gestures of a kind to catch the headlines. An example was his campaign, as Prime Minister, to diminish the high incidence of French alcoholism by making a great show of only drinking milk himself. The objective was admirable. But as one small hotel-keeper in Louviers, the Norman town of which Mendès was mayor, put it to me when I went electioneering there the following year, "Mendès doesn't drink milk at all, he drinks wine like the rest of us – I've served him many times at banquets."

This was the man whom the National Assembly voted into power on June 18, 1954 – the anniversary of the day in 1940 when de Gaulle made his appeal from London to the French people. From the very start, his approach was unorthodox. French public affairs were, even by the standards of the Fourth Republic, in a state of formidable disarray. A few months earlier, the fortress of Dien Bien Phu, in Indo-China, had fallen to the forces of Ho Chi Minh, an event which unleashed a great wave of feeling in France that this colonial commitment, yielding no identifiable rewards, must be brought to an end. Even more disturbing, because of its international implications, was the cloud overhanging French parliamentary and political life in the shape of the plan for a six-power European Defence Community. This was a device, thought up by the French themselves, for making the rearmament of Germany, rendered necessary by the growing threat from the Soviet Union, more acceptable to French opinion. For two years previous to 1954, indeterminate discussion and dissension, reflecting fears of Germany and of a new and untried European omelette, had rumbled on. To her allies, France seemed to be in her most tiresome and difficult mood. It finally became too much for the US Secretary of State, Mr John Foster Dulles. At a celebrated press conference in Paris in December 1953, that earnest and determined representative of American evangelical tradition had declared, his fleshy jowls shaking in indignation, his eyes behind their steel-rimmed spectacles full of self-righteousness, that unless ratification of the EDC plan was forthcoming soon, the USA would be compelled to make "an agonizing reappraisal" of its basic policies. With considerable fervour but not much accuracy he said that the EDC had become a symbol throughout the world of a sincere and rational effort to end Franco–German hostility. As the main obstacle to EDC was France itself, this threat, the meaning of which was clear to no one, was naturally not well received in Paris. It appeared, to me and many others, that Dulles had quite possibly administered a lethal dose to a patient already far from well.

Faced with the Indo-Chinese and EDC problems, as well as an incipient economic crisis at home, Mendès asked the National Assembly to give him, in effect, a four-week contract. During this time he would seek to lance the Indo-Chinese boil and set about trying to solve the EDC and economic crisis. If he failed, his Government would offer its resignation. It was an extraordinary and entirely unorthodox gamble but it worked, in the sense that Mendès both got his majority from the Assembly and achieved most of his three objectives (the economic one inevitably remained unfinished, for no single man or government could overnight transform a nation's books and methods). Within a month, thanks partly to Mendès' diplomacy at the international Geneva conference, a cease-fire in Indo-China had been arranged, to the immense relief of most French people. Within another month, the EDC was dead, killed by a vote in the National Assembly (his critics maintained that Mendès had held the dagger). Mr Dulles' dire prophecies proved false. The world did not come to an end. Within another month an alternative arrangement for German rearmament, arrived at after intense international negotiation, had been approved by the National Assembly. By a whirlwind display of virtuosity and perseverance, which included a new and realistic approach to the status of the two French North African protectorates in Tunisia and Morocco, Mendès had achieved what previous governments had failed in. In doing so, and by availing himself of modern publicity techniques – his Saturday night radio fireside chats were, it is true, not so much modern as a throw-back to the Roosevelt era in the USA, but they enjoyed large audiences – he succeeded in building up a considerable body of enthusiastic support in the country as a whole. 1954 was indeed, for Mendès as for France itself, an *annus mirabilis*, and an outstanding example of what in politics one strong and determined personality can do against the highest odds.

But there is usually a price to be paid for such feats of daring, especially when they are carried out with obvious disdain for past performance. Mendès paid the price in full. By the end of the year, with the Government in trouble, I described in a despatch to *The Times* the strong, sometimes violent, personal feelings entertained against the personality and methods of the Prime Minister. 'By making himself popular with the country, by implying that until he came on the scene all was chaos and darkness whereas now he is introducing sweetness and light, by showing himself hypersensitive to criticism, he has . . . helped to create a bitterness which, combined with the unscrupulous methods employed against him by some of his opponents, has encouraged exactly the opposite of the spirit of national unity which is his admitted goal.' He also, as he felt his political life ebbing away, descended to some of the tricks – curious nominations to the Legion of Honour, appointments made not for reasons of suitability but in order to appease or buy off criticism – which he affected to despise when performed by other governments and other prime ministers.

Early in 1955, after having been Prime Minister for only eight months, he was voted out and except for a brief period in Guy Mollet's Government in 1956 never again held office. But he will always occupy a special place in French political history, if only for the charisma that he managed to spread about him, winning the admiration of millions outside the self-perpetuating circle of professional politicians and creating, in 'Mendèsism', a dream world in which the light of reason banishes the darkness of prejudice and passion. As one of his colleagues said of him, he was very intelligent but lacked common sense. He not only scorned but was normally incapable of going through the various emollient motions which are necessary to keep a shaky and disparate coalition together. That is why he brought François Mitterrand, the future President and born political fixer, into his Government; when it came to parliamentary management, he said, Mitterand was "like a pianist at the keyboard – he knows everybody and everything." My abiding memory of this remarkable man is not of the many meetings I had with him in later years, when the originality of his mind and power of his assertions remained undimmed. It is rather of the spectacle of him responding from the tribune in the National Assembly to the criticisms which, as his short Premiership wore on, swiftly mounted in range and strength. Rarely if ever did he try the soft answer as a means of turning away wrath. Instead, he usually succeeded by his sarcasm and the intellectual arrogance of his replies in creating new enemies and adding to the hostility of old ones. There was something both noble and tragic about the scene and its principal actor.

The observer of another country has two broad choices in determining his methods and activities. He can mingle with the high and mighty, peer into the minds and try and divine the motives of the nation's leaders, seek to understand their policies and the policies which they who oppose them would put into practice instead. Or he can approach his subject from the grass roots, making contact and talking with as many and varied groups and milieux as might be said to represent, in sum, public opinion, thus getting to know something of the forces and counter-forces which help to define the direction of the national will. Blowitz, the great Paris correspondent of *The Times* at the end of the nineteenth century, was unashamedly a man for the high and mighty. His despatches are full of information, some of it in the form of direct and quotable interviews, gleaned from the lips of ministers, ambassadors, even sovereigns. More than half a century later, when I succeeded to his chair – literally, if the office legend was to be believed that the ornate and imposing piece in the chief correspondent's room was where Blowitz himself placed his portly little form – there was still much to be said, in a highly centralised country like France and a city as much of an international centre as Paris, for this elitist approach. It was indeed unavoidable if the paper in London was to be kept properly informed. Besides, the other, *vox populi* method is unavoidably a hit-and-miss affair. No journalist, however industrious, can transform himself into a one-man opinion poll. It is a hazardous undertaking to purport to know what 'the French' or 'the Germans' or indeed the inhabitants of Weston-super-Mare are thinking at any particular moment.

Nevertheless, some sort of blending of the two methods is the best guarantee of all-round insight into the fears and hopes and state of mind of a nation. It was therefore, after the excitements of EDC and the Mendès period, that I began to study with enthusiasm the impact of a movement, above all the personality of its leader, which from 1953 onwards began to make itself increasingly felt among a cross-section of the French people deserving the description of grass roots. This was Poujadism and its only begetter M. Pierre Poujade. The movement was called the Union for the Defence of Tradesmen and Artisans and its constituency was that army of 'little men' – shopkeepers and self-employed craftsmen – who were and to a certain extent still are so representative of a large slice of French society.

Poujadism began in the head and in the bookshop at St Céré, in the department of the Lot, belonging to Pierre Poujade. There was no coincidence in this geography. For generations, this part of central France had seen a steady drain of population, a constant lowering in its standards of living compared with the rest of the country. Concurrently, the number of small tradesmen increased, as those who remained sought, *faute de mieux*, to gain the only livelihood that seemed possible. Many of them, once wartime inflation and shortages had abated, were having a very thin time of it. Not surprisingly, they proved a willing audience for Poujade's proposal that they should refuse to pay their taxes until Government and Parliament had promulgated a satisfactory fiscal reform. Encouraging Frenchmen to resist the tax-inspector is a platform on which it would be exceedingly difficult, even for an amateur, to make a false step. Flaubert, in his *Dictionnaire des Idées Reçues*, couples together *octroi* and *douane*, and recommends '*on doit se revolter contre et la frauder'*. There was, in the French method of imposing and collecting taxes, much that was cumbrous and unfair. Poujade was on to a good thing. It was therefore significant but not extraordinary that the simple message from St Céré had by 1955 spread to all but fifteen of the ninety departments of France, significant and bordering on the extraordinary that in March of that year Poujade and his followers were able to exert such an influence upon the deputies in the National Assembly that they nearly brought the Government down by insisting on immediate abrogation of the law which provided penalties for resistance to tax collection. By this time Poujade and his principal lieutenants were talking in high-falutin' and populist terms of the need to bring together a new 'States-General' (comparable to the body which heralded the French revolution in 1789) in which would be represented the different social and commercial interests of the country – tradesmen, civil servants, farmers, workers. What relation this was to bear to Parliament or the trade unions was imprecise. Poujadism had begun to assume the proportions of a political as well as a social phenomenon.

In the spring of 1955 there was a national newspaper strike in London which kept *The Times*, along with other papers, out of circulation for nearly a month. I took the enforced breathing space as an opportunity to visit Poujade country, to see the movement in its natural setting and talk to its leader. The black Citroen carried us through fine spring weather down to some of the most beautiful parts of France, the valleys of the Dordogne and the Lot, and so to St Céré, the Lourdes, so to speak, of Poujadism. It proved to be a small placid place of great charm, criss-crossed by streams and rich in medieval buildings. Here the statistics of the little men told their own tale. With a population of 3,200, the town had 270 shopkeepers, or one shop for every 12 consumers. The headquarters of the movement were in two small rooms, overflowing with typists and correspondence and visitors, over the famous bookshop where the then unknown Poujade used to eke out a precarious existence. He himself was not there, but we finally caught up with him in a country town not far from Toulouse, where he was to address a meeting on the town football ground. It was a scene that could have been set by Balzac.

After we had hung about for a considerable time, a line of cars drove up and stopped outside a restaurant. Out of them got Pierre Poujade, his attractive wife, his small daughter and his staff and companions. Lunch followed, attended by about fifty local members of the Poujade movement and also, by invitation, by what *Times* conventions (this was before the day of signed bye-lines) required to be described as 'this correspondent'. It was a high-spirited and convivial affair. Before lunch, Poujade was presented with a bottle of Armagnac (the local product), Madame Poujade with a bouquet of roses, while young Mlle Poujade was photographed and patted on the head so many times and became so excited that had she had an English nanny there would certainly have been menacing references to it all ending in tears. It was impossible, among these cheerful and hospitable people, to believe that this new group was a potential menace to the State, to realise that the tax strike which it was encouraging was an act of rebellion less only in degree to the refusal to do military service.

After lunch I had a session with Poujade. Then in his early thirties, he was a rubicund man in love with the sound of his own southern-accented, hoarse but strangely compelling voice. His language was peppered with words and expressions which varied from the picturesque to the near-obscene. He also talked a great deal of nonsense. "We are the strongest group of claimants in France," he said. But they had nothing against Parliament because "We are the electors." He spent a long time explaining how the tax system should be reformed, emphasising, surely insincerely, that they were not against paying taxes so much as demanding more equitable and sensible arrangements. Then he said that this fiscal issue was now a "secondary question". Where then was he heading? His answer combined obscurity with menace. "Soon we shall have millions of people . . . we shall remain vigilant for action whenever the State leaves its proper role, which is that of defence, education, police etc."

At the meeting in the afternoon, Poujade stormed and ranted but also, in a quieter passage, told a story without excessive words or gestures about his visit to Parliament which was designed (successfully) to make that body and its members appear not only dishonest but ridiculous. The thousands of Gascon faces under their floppy berets reacted with laughter and evident approval when Poujade attacked the ubiquitous and iniquitous "they" in Paris. The man obviously had a way with crowds. But how much did his tub-thumping really represent popular feeling and portend a mass movement of disobedience? Here the *vox populi* technique, for all its inadequacies, produced one memorably appropriate quotation: "You know, we're terrible grumblers," a violently anti-Semitic ironmonger in St Céré told me. "It is typical of the French to talk a lot and do nothing." At the end of this instructive journey, I reported to *The Times*, now back in circulation, that Poujade was 'a palpable demagogue, but it is difficult to see in him the qualities of any sort of national leader.'

This judgement proved to be substantially correct. The Poujadists as a political party enjoyed considerable successes in the parliamentary elections in early 1956, campaigning on the simple and epigrammatic slogan of '*Sortez les sortants*' (i.e. throw out the deputies who are standing again). But they never established any coherence as a par-liamentary group and apart from posing as the (extreme right-wing) guardians of the honour of the French Army and French Algeria, they contributed little or nothing to the political scene. Poujade himself, the despiser of parliamentarians, stood as a candidate for the National Assembly in a by-election and was soundly beaten. With General de Gaulle's return to power in 1958, Poujadism and its leader became a spent force. But the very word Poujadism has entered into the lan-guage, and not just the French language, as the symbol and reminder of the never-ending grievances of the 'little man' crushed, like a defence-less insect, beneath the massive and uncomprehending weight of the machinery of State. Wherever free speech prevails, there will always be a place, from time to time, for the populist exponent of such grievances. If he (or she) can attain to the standard of earthy oratory achieved by Pierre Poujade, he is bound to enjoy a certain measure of fleeting success.

The support of the Poujadists for French Algeria was not a random choice. As the Algerian 'rebellion' took hold – it was really a bitter and cruel war for national independence, waged by the Algerian National Liberation Front – so its impact upon the French political scene bit deeper. It became a test of patriotism to assert that Algeria was French (a contention underpinned by the constitutional fiction that it was part and parcel of metropolitan France) and would for ever remain French, even if that meant committing more and more of the French army and more and more of the taxpayers' money. This was not, nearly everyone insisted, another colonial war like the one that had trapped France in Indo-China. Pineau, the Foreign Minister in the Government formed in early 1956 by the Socialist Guy Mollet, told Nehru, the Indian Prime Minister, that if the British in India had been present there in the same proportions to the native population as French settlers were present in Algeria, there would have been 47 million of them. It was a good point. The problem of the British withdrawal from India would in such circumstances have assumed very different dimensions.

Those million-plus settlers made their feelings quite plain when Mollet, the new Prime Minister, visited Algiers early in 1956. They mobbed him, amidst scenes of unparalleled disorder. Mollet, by profession a schoolteacher (of English), decent, patriotic but unequipped with the strength of will or energy of a man like Mendès-France, lacked the stomach to stand up to this kind of thing. He quickly became, if not exactly the settler's friend at least a strong proponent of Algeria-is-and-will-remain-French. Almost any Prime Minister would probably have done the same thing. Typically it was Mendès, a member of the Radical party who had accepted ministerial office in this Socialist-led Government, who soon resigned from it in protest over its Algerian policies. It was not, he explained, the issue of sending more troops to Algeria, which he would have been ready to do; what he objected to was 'policies which ignore the feelings and the miseries of the native population'.

Thus quite early on the political and moral dilemma was defined which would increasingly affect French affairs until, two years later, the Fourth Republic collapsed under its weight. There was another element in this Algerian drama which became crucial in the light of the main event of 1956, the Suez crisis. This was the French belief, founded on a good deal of evidence, that the Algerian rebellion was being fed and fuelled from Cairo. At the Socialist Party Congress that summer, Mollet denounced what he called Nasser's megalomania and defined pan-Islamism as a threat to peace. By the time Nasser nationalised the Suez Canal, on 26 July, most French people of all persuasions were convinced, rightly or wrongly, that French fortunes could not prosper so long as Nasser flourished. Much of what ensued, including impatience with the British and rage with the Americans, must be seen in the light of this Algerian factor.

Sitting in Paris that summer and autumn, neither I nor anyone else save a handful of people knew what was going on behind the scenes, above all between London and Paris. There were some bizarre sights, such as the spectacle of a Socialist Prime Minister defending in the National Assembly the rights of private shareholders in the Suez Canal Company. There was the ever-widening contrast between a Socialist Government in Paris, determined on resolute action against Nasser, and a Socialist Opposition in London, increasingly critical of the acts and suspected intentions of the Eden Conservative Government. Eden and Selwyn Lloyd, the Foreign Secretary, came twice to Paris to confer with their French colleagues. Meeting British correspondents at the British Embassy, they were bafflingly non-committal. Eden seemed relaxed, almost languid; there was no sign whatever of the storms and troubles to come.

Enough has now been written by British, French and Israeli actors in the drama to construct virtually all of the story of the secret plan to co-ordinate an Anglo–French attack on Egypt with a prior Israeli assault. The Anglo–French operation was to be presented as a move to separate the combatants – i.e. Israelis and Egyptians. I first learnt of the execution of this plan when a Dutch journalist, a good friend and incidentally a Jew, said as we passed in the street that he had heard it on the radio. He asked incredulously whether it could possibly be true. I assured him, from the deepest inner conviction, that it could not. Whatever the French, in their obsession over Nasser and Algeria, might do, it was unthinkable that British diplomacy would, in collusion with Israel, on the backs, as it were, of the Israelis commit troops to action against an Arab country, whatever the provocation. My Dutch friend, an ardent Anglophile, seemed relieved but not surprised. He went on his way, confirmed in his belief that the practical and pragmatic British would never make a mistake of this enormity. No amount of the drinks I subsequently bought him or apologies I offered him for having unwittingly entered into mistaken judgement quite restored this excellent man's faith in the superiority of British wisdom.

In the days and weeks that followed, during which the cease-fire and withdrawal of Anglo–French forces took place, it was often difficult among French friends to explain British acts and motives. At a large dinner-party in a French house at which I was present, the British Ambassador in Paris, Gladwyn Jebb,* put it accurately and succinctly but with a lack of tact that succeeded in offending everyone, French and British, in the room: "The two nations have behaved in a manner exactly contrary to what could have been expected – the French wanted to stay, the British to run away." In *The Times*, I wrote that 'in the eyes of the French people, France, its Government and its Parliament, has stood firm and un-wavering behind the decision to intervene in Egypt; the United Kingdom, having started off just as firmly, then began to divide and dither, to behave in fact as the French Parliament and Government are said to behave when, in the face of a need for decision and action, all that occurs is the clash of opinions and factions.'

There were some compensations during this unhappy time. Because of Suez I got to know a leading exponent of 'the clash of opinions' and

---

* Later Lord Gladwyn, Liberal foreign affairs spokesman in the Lords

remained his friend and admirer until his untimely death. Just quite how Hugh Gaitskell, not long after the cease-fire, found his way to our door I cannot remember. He was in Paris on political business, which included what must surely have been a painful meeting with his fellow socialist Guy Mollet, and turned up one day at our flat just before lunch. For some reason which was never clear, he was clutching a bag of oranges. It so happened that we had some people to lunch that day, including Raymond Aron, one of the most brilliant Frenchmen of modern times, with an uncompromisingly clear and Cartesian method of arguing, however inconvenient the conclusions to which it led him. It had brought him recently to come out in favour of Algerian independence (at the time, a viewpoint so unorthodox as to be almost treasonable) and he was also highly critical of the Suez affair. We pressed Hugh Gaitskell to abandon his oranges in favour of our lunch, which he readily did. The ensuing conversation, even if it had the disadvantage of being, where Suez was concerned, between people of like mind, was profoundly stimulating.

In the few years left to him, I got to know Gaitskell well. His unexpected death in 1963 was, in my view, a national tragedy as well as the subject for personal grief. With the exception of his strongly held opposition to Britain's entry into the European Community (a view based on his belief that a rich man's club like the Community could bring few advantages and in some cases do positive harm to the Third World), I found myself agreeing for most of the time with his brand of democratic socialism, embracing as it did a highly civilised sense of human values and an unshakeable attachment to personal rights and liberties. The question of what sort of a Prime Minister Hugh would have been, and what sort of a Labour Party would have developed had he lived to lead the party to victory in 1964, must constitute one of the major guessing games of modern British political history. One quality (assuming he had continued to enjoy good health) would not have been lacking, and that was his energy and apparent tirelessness. In December 1959, during a visit to London, we went with friends to a performance of *Der Rosenkavalier* at Covent Garden. The Gaitskells were of the party and proposed that afterwards we should go to their house at Frognal, Hampstead, for drinks. Once there, and despite the fact that he had had a punishing day at Westminster, Hugh insisted on rolling back the carpet, putting some pre-war dance music on the record-player and swooping, *chassé*-ing and reversing his way round and round the room until his succession of lady partners pleaded for mercy. It was the small hours of the morning before, exhausted, we got away. He loudly deplored this early end, as it seemed to him, of the proceedings.

The Paris apartment to which Hugh had brought his oranges that November day was in the Place de la Madeleine, in the heart of the city, on the fourth floor, looking down upon the great church opposite. It was unfurnished, and by bringing our furniture from store in England and adding it to our personal possessions conveyed from Rome, we contrived to make a comfortable and convenient home for ourselves and our two, later our three, children. Certain French friends, coming for the first time, did not quite know what to make of it. Precipitating themselves towards the windows and looking at the illuminated signs of Thomas Cook's office opposite, they would say, "*Comment*, we always thought it was only tradespeople who lived here." Four floors below, at street level, were two famous restaurants, Larue (which before long folded up) and Lucas Carton; a *pâtissier* with the improbable name, conjuring up visions of demure establishments in English country towns serving scones and tea, of Penny; a long-established Paris silversmith, Odiot; and a shop selling very expensive lady's lingerie. It was called Charmereine, a fact which caused Susan Haley, William Haley's wife, to remark, when she first saw it, that it surely ought to be Charmeroi. We laughed immoderately, but the great Editor's stern features scarcely unbent.

Over the years, a great many people came to lunch and dinner in that flat. Susan-Mary Patten★ was good enough to write in her book that 'the Giles do more and give more pleasure with less money than any couple in Paris . . . I have never had a dull moment there.' That was a matter of opinion, but what was unchallengeably true about the statement was the reference to money. Working for *The Times* was still, despite my relatively senior position, an ill-paid affair, and although foreign allowances helped, it is something of a mystery how we managed. Much of this coming and going had the professional purpose of finding out what people were saying and thinking.

But there were also birds of passage who had nothing to do with the French scene. Among them was Evelyn Waugh, who often stayed with Diana Cooper at Chantilly. Despite his fearsome reputation for quarrelling and savaging people in public, with us he was never anything but gentle and good company. Emboldened by this, and seeking a little excitement, on one occasion I carefully prepared a question I wanted

★ See footnote p. 86

him to answer. After allowing the best claret time to circulate and distribute its blessings, I asked him: "When you became a Catholic, did you find yourself missing the majesty of the Prayer Book for the mumble of the Mass?" Not only was there no explosion, there was for a time no reply. Then, after a long pause, he responded simply, "Yes." It was an effective and dignified reproof for what had been a piece of impertinence. Not that he held it against me. The following year, on holiday in England, we went to see him at his home at Stinchcombe, in Gloucestershire, where he was a generous host. Showing us his possessions, he pointed out three paintings depicting travel in the eighteenth, nineteenth and twentieth centuries. The first showed a highwayman pointing his pistol through the window of a stage-coach and demanding the passengers' valuables. The second depicted an early railway carriage, with a kindly guard at the window, asking for tickets. The third was a scene in a big airliner, whose two port engines were on fire; as the plane plunged earthwards out of control, a hostess was vainly trying to comfort the terrified passengers. "I had that specially painted to match the other two," explained Evelyn with relish, "but I'm going to get the artist back to touch it up – he hasn't put enough flames in."

From about 1955 onwards, the diary has frequent references to the Giscard d'Estaings lunching or dining in Place de la Madeleine, and also to us being entertained by them. This was Valéry, the future President of the Republic, and his pretty, shy wife Anne-Aymone. I had got to know him when, as an exceptionally promising young civil servant, he was in the private office of one of the Fourth Republic's Prime Ministers. In 1956 he decided to enter politics and was elected to Parliament, being returned for the same seat two years later in the elections that followed General de Gaulle's return to power. On that occasion, with his consent, I followed him on his electoral campaign. In his constituency in the Massif Central, he patted babies and bullocks with a practised touch, made effective little speeches to small crowds in market places and town halls, listened to grievances while skilfully avoiding firm commitments to remove them. In the evening, the day's work done, he and I would repair to his family château, most of it closed down for the winter, and over a simple meal cooked by the caretaker discuss the problems of France and the world.

I liked and admired him very much. He had a brilliant analytical mind, with an apparent answer to everything and considerable ease and charm of manner. Later, when he became a junior Minister in the first Government of the Fifth Republic, he blossomed into a formidable orator, capable of making long speeches on difficult financial and technical matters without a note. *The Times* was by then running an open-ended series of articles under the general title of 'People to Watch'. I contributed a piece about Valéry. It ended with the cautious but certainly successful prophecy that in the years to come, he would be well placed to lead or influence a respectable right-wing party which would have a part to play in the post-Gaullist era.

Later on, after I had left Paris but still retained a lively interest in French affairs, I kept in touch with him. After he became President in 1974, he would receive me in his surprisingly modest office in the Elysée Palace and talk with all his youthful brilliance. He invariably referred with pleasure to the 'People to Watch' article. On another occasion, dining privately with him and Anne-Aymone at the house of some friends in Paris, he unfolded a fascinating scenario, according to which, under his Presidency, the extremes in French politics – the Communists on one side, the nationalist, Gaullist right on the other – would be discredited and eroded, while Socialists and "respectable" right would draw together in a common theory and practice of democracy. Described briefly like that it sounds a pipe-dream, but propounded that night in his fast-spoken, elegant, precise French, Valéry succeeded in making it appear the only way forward.

Then something went wrong, not only with his Presidency but with our relationship. For no given reason, he would no longer agree to see me. Stories began to circulate, some of them well-based, about his monarchical illusions of grandeur. He seemed to lose whatever he had once possessed of the common touch. The country turned against this once attractive, youthful, new-style leader. Even the class from which he came – the *haute bourgeoisie*, with its spacious apartments in the 16th *arrondissement* and its pheasant shoots in the country – appeared to think that President Giscard d'Estaing had parted from reality. In the Presidential elections in 1981 he was beaten by that prototype of Fourth Republican Ministers, François Mitterrand. Like the overthrow of Mendès-France, Giscard's fall was in many ways a tragedy, his metamorphosis still inexplicable.

Compared with this new friendship, even if it did go sour, a renewal of old memories had a very different effect. The Duke and Duchess of Windsor, for years resident in Paris, asked us to dinner. The brief infatuation brought on by that week in Bermuda, years earlier, was totally dissipated by this later experience. In their big white house in the Bois de Boulogne, the Windsors, neither of them looking much older, had collected together a motley and not very attractive company: blue-rinsed widows of American millionaires, members of French café society, hangers-on of one sort or another. The Duchess, always the good hostess, provided an excellent dinner, at the end of which, after the *bombe surprise* had been removed, the servants trotted round the tables offering yet another course in little silver dishes. They contained angels-on-horseback, oysters wrapped up in a piece of bacon: the English savoury, in fact, unknown in France. Of the forty guests, none took any, save the host. "The Dook was brought up with savouries," explained the Duchess, in a voice which had lost its soft inflexions and grown raucous and cutting, "and always insists on them." "Isn't that just dahling," observed one of the blue rinses.

After dinner, the Duke took me off alone into a small inner drawing-room. He wanted to discuss world affairs with *The Times* correspondent. Eden had just become Prime Minister and he proceeded to blame the war on him. "There'd have been no war if Eden hadn't mishandled Mussolini," he said. "It was all his fault." He added, as an afterthought, "Together of course with Roosevelt and the Jews." Confronted with talk like that, what should one do? To make an excuse and leave was one possibility. But not only is it difficult to treat your former King like that, it is also the role of a journalist to listen to every sort of opinion, whether he agrees with it or not. A few weeks previously we had been to a private lunch-party where Sir Oswald Mosley was one of the guests. Discovering this before entering the room, we seriously considered sending in our apologies and leaving. Then realisation of the utter pomposity of such behaviour struck home. Similar thoughts presented themselves as the Duke continued to deliver himself of his bilious and distorted opinions. Besides, there was still about him some of that almost child-like charm which had carried him through his younger life and now made him as much an object of pity as of despisement. At one moment in our conversation, he opened his cigarette-case to find it empty. A touch on the bell brought his black valet, a legacy from the Bahamas, wearing royal livery. "Sidney," said the Duke with a beatific smile (though it is impossible on paper to reproduce the mid-Atlantic twang, strangely mixed with a Cockey vowel sound, with which he dwelt on the name), "Sidney, just fill this for me will you, there's a good man." A look of devotion crossed Sidney's face as he turned to do his master's bidding.

Though we did not go again to the house in the Bois de Boulogne, we were asked some time later to spend a day at the Windsors' country house, not far from Paris. It was an old mill which she had done up attractively inside while he had superintended the laying out of the garden. In this idyllic setting, with only a handful of guests, they both seemed more relaxed. At one point, the talk turning to eccentric signs of meanness, the Duke said the Duchess made him finish up the tablet of soap in his bathroom before issuing him with another. Evidently the passage of nearly twenty years had made no difference to the question of who wore the shorts. In the main sitting-room, part of the old mill itself, two large military drums, laid on their side, acted as low tables for drinks, ashtrays, magazines. Closer inspection revealed that they were formerly the drums of the King's Company of the First Battalion of the Grenadier Guards. In the same room, an enormous wall-map, equipped with flashing electric bulbs, traced the world travels of the then Prince of Wales. The Duke, operating the bulbs and explaining the map, seemed to regard it all as normal and unexceptional, like a man showing his holiday slides. He talked no more politics that day, although whenever we met in Paris, he would always embark on some issue of contemporary interest, on which his views would generally lie somewhere between the naive and the silly.

It would be tempting to write that, as the fifties wore on, and the toll and unendingness of the war in Algeria began to weigh more and more heavily, so life in France became increasingly doom-ridden and expectant. Certainly the war dominated most private conversations and underlay all politics. The difference between public and private utterance was remarkable. In the latter, even ministers and public men would avow that the present situation could not go on, that even if there were no rebellion, the prospect of a constantly increasing Muslim population dependent upon French financial support could not be considered acceptable. But very few said this in public. In general, hearts and heads were opposed, even within the same body.

It was not true, however, that this all-prevailing cloud made much if any difference to the content and quality of French life. Never before in her history had France worked so hard, had so many people in employment, produced so much. In that muddled and contradictory condition that seems the special gift and talent of economists to create, the prosperity thus engendered was accompanied by a series of austerity measures, designed to cut down imports. Scotch whisky suffered, to the pleasure of the Cognac industry. Even that had little effect on the delights, for example, of the autumn in Paris: a gentle season of marvellous, grey painter's lights and Sundays spent in the gold and russet woods of Senlis or Compiègne or strolling along Le Notre's noble terrace at St Germain, on a sunny afternoon one of the finest walks in Europe. Prescience is an enviable and useful quality, in journalists and politicians alike. It would be pleasing to show how I had foretold the impending break-up of the regime. But the Algerian abscess, though always there, did not, to change the metaphor, seem to have the proportions of a time-bomb. Even when outbreaks of Muslim violence in Algeria, in June 1957, evoked violent reactions from the *colons* (French settlers), including shouts of '*Massu au pouvoir*' (Massu was the tough parachute general in charge of security in Algeria) and '*L'Armée au pouvoir*', no alarm bells rang. The *colons* were always noisy and suspicious of Paris. As for the return to power of General de Gaulle, still brooding fitfully at Colombey, I had learnt, from my very first conversation with Gaston Palewski, ten years previously, to be wary of prophecies that this *deus ex machina* was about to manifest himself. Nonetheless, it is appropriate, if only in self-defence, to quote from a message I sent to Printing House Square, published on June 21, 1957. It spoke of the extent to which the General's name was now being mentioned. 'Though he has given no indication . . . of a wish to quit his present lofty isolation, the suggestion is being increasingly heard that the moment must inevitably come when this "man of the last resort" will have to be called upon.'

In February 1958 I paid a long visit to Algeria, returning with no good news about a situation so complex and difficult that a foreigner could only regard it with (in Burke's words) 'pious awe and trembling solicitude'. The views of the National Liberation Front, which I gleaned in Tunis, where they had an office, were obdurate: though they could never bring the French army to its knees, equally their men in the field could never be beaten, and national independence remained their unchanging target. For the French, the policy of 'pacification' – a mixture of military action against the rebels, combined with social and economic reforms – looked in theory to be workable. But the reforms, designed as part of an effort to capture the hearts and minds of the Muslim masses, had come very late in the day. Besides, in a cruel guerrilla war, in which the bomb and the knife often speak louder than a new bridge or a greater degree of local self-government, the measures to suppress such terrorism produce their own counter-effects. There had been many reports in Paris of torture and physical coercion being used by the army against Muslim suspects. I asked General Massu about this. His clipped moustache, close-cut hair, beak-like nose and six-foot presence made him, in his camouflage tunic, a formidable figure. It could not have been the first time he had been posed the question, and he had obviously decided to adopt the precept of never apologising and never explaining. After a long pause, he said defiantly, "*Je continue.*" This was more a confirmation than anything else of the methods his men were using. His argument, often echoed by those all over the world who are responsible, in a violent situation, for law and order, was in effect that ends, however unpleasant, justify means; the lives of those saved from the results of terrorism justify questionable interrogation methods. It is an old dilemma: in seeking to combat evil, you succumb to the temptation to resort to it.

There was no knowing what the Muslim masses thought and hoped. *Vox populi* techniques, inadequate enough in advanced European countries, become meaningless when practised in a totally different culture. Without any Frenchman being present in the room, I asked the members of a newly appointed all-Muslim village council what they thought of French plans for reform and development. Their handsome, burnous-crowned faces were inscrutable; one might as well have sought their opinion of the late Beethoven quartets. The *colons*, at least, did not suffer from such reticence. "You don't want to give the Muslim political power or equality of status," said a French vineyard foreman of Spanish origin, who spoke fluent Arabic and seemed on the best of terms with his Muslim workmen. "All he wants is to be administered justly by the French." How often in the future was I to hear nonsense like this from white apologists in Rhodesia. Baffled and depressed, I returned to Paris, to find yet another Government crisis, as a disparate majority, united by nothing save the desire to wreck, forced the resignation of the Prime Minister. The issue was the Government's proposal to resume negotiations with Tunisia for the evacuation of French troops from that country. For the time being, the question of supervision of the Algerian–Tunisian frontier was to be left in suspense. As many people in France believed that that frontier was used for gun-running to the Algerian liberation forces, the proposal was obviously going to encounter serious trouble, the more so because the Tunisian negotiation was based on suggestions made by a joint Anglo-American 'good offices' mission. In the eyes of the *Algérie Française* lobby, and indeed of many people of more moderate views, it was tantamount to surrendering vital French interests in North Africa to foreign pressures.

This was in fact the beginning of the death throes of the Fourth

Republic, although it was not apparent at the time where and by whom the murder weapon would be wielded. Very few people then knew – and I was certainly not among them – what somewhat later became general knowledge: namely that long before the events in Algiers on 13 May, which lit the fuse leading to the powder barrel, a large number of senior serving army officers and a certain number of Gaullist or self-styled Gaullist politicians in France were actively preparing *coups* against the Republic. General de Gaulle was, on the best evidence available, kept closely informed about these plans, both for a *coup* in Algeria and for one in France itself. He repeatedly told his informants that he was opposed to a *putsch* in France, and that he himself wished to return to power only by legal means. But this did little or nothing to deter the plotters, among whose aims was to provoke the army to seize power in Algiers, and then to 'invade' France, the capture of Paris being allotted to the parachute regiments.

'This looks like being more than just another Government crisis,' I reported, correctly as it turned out, in April. In fact, between April 16, when the Government fell, and mid-May, it looked exactly like other crises, with prospective Prime Ministers going down like ninepins, trooping back from Presidential consultations at the Elysée Palace in a bizarre and rapid succession, most of them unwilling even to try to form a Government. Though this only emerged much later, President René Coty, a well-meaning but undistinguished figure who had only been elected to the Presidency on the thirteenth ballot five years earlier, had through intermediaries appealed to General de Gaulle as early as May 5, when it appeared impossible to find a successor Government. But no suitable formula could be found, so M. Pierre Pflimlin, a familiar Fourth Republican figure, agreed to try his hand at the Premiership. Before he could succeed, indeed to stop him succeeding, Algiers erupted. On May 13, Rightist demonstrators there attacked and occupied the offices of the Government-General. To forestall further disorder, Massu, who had not been involved in the previous plotting, moved into the building and late that night a message went forth, signed by him, appealing to General de Gaulle to assume 'the leadership of a government of public safety'.

In Paris, extreme right-wing elements began to make a nuisance of themselves in the Champs Elysées. The long evening wore on, dark with consequence for the future of the Republican regime. Finally, in the small hours the National Assembly elected M. Pflimlin Prime Minister by a large majority. I remember feeling, as I left the Palais

Bourbon not long before dawn on May 14, that this looked like the reassertion, under threat, of constitutional authority. In fact, it was nothing of the sort. In the following twenty-four hours it became clear beyond all doubt that the *coup* in Algiers, far from being spontaneous, was something foreseen and planned, in Paris and Algiers, to prevent the establishment of a French Government which, according to the studiously disseminated propaganda of the *colons* and the military, was intent on an Algerian 'surrender'. Events were beginning to assume an uncontrollable momentum of their own.

Up to now de Gaulle had not shown his hand. He came to Paris, it is true, on May 14, but that was a Wednesday, a day on which he usually visited the capital. Then, the following day General Salan, the Commander-in-Chief in Algeria, whose position had been till then obscure, gave de Gaulle the opening he needed by shouting to the crowd in Algiers, "*Vive de Gaulle.*" Later in the day, a brief statement was issued in Paris on de Gaulle's behalf. It said that he was holding himself 'in readiness to assume the powers of the Republic'. The statement combined terseness with ambiguity. What did he mean? He had made it clear countless times that he was not interested in returning to power under the existing system of parliamentary government. But equally he had let it be known that he would not consider returning by any but constitutional means. Was he now asking Coty and the National Assembly voluntarily to yield up their powers into his hands, like spaniels rolling over on their backs?

In his memoirs de Gaulle has written that, from the moment he issued this statement about assuming the powers of the Republic, nobody doubted that the crisis would end with his restoration to power. This is simply not so. Despite – or perhaps because of – the rumours spread in Paris by the plotters and their agents – the chief rumour was that Massu's parachute troops were about to drop from the skies – there were plenty of people who resented strongly what appeared to be going on. If de Gaulle were to 'assume the powers' in such circumstances, he would be doing so as the nominee, as it were, of an insurrectionary clique of officers and *colon* extremists in Algeria. In Paris and the rest of France, there was no public outcry for de Gaulle's return, very little open expression of solidarity with the Algiers plotters. The streets were full of police, but people went about their business normally. Any sense of being on the edge of an abyss was almost totally lacking. The week ended on a welcome note of farce. The *Daily Mail*, in London, created a small sensation by reporting that thousands of civilian refugees were quitting Paris for the open country, 1940-style, their cars piled high with perambulators and mattresses. A London-based member of the paper's staff, visiting Paris, had driven to the airport on the Friday evening to take the plane to London and been misled by the long queues of weekenders' cars heading, as usual, for the countryside.

On May 19, the General returned to Paris and gave a press conference, his first public appearance for nearly three years. In my professional career, I have been to countless press conferences, but there was never anything like this. The setting was the ornate nineteenth-century ballroom of an old-fashioned hotel on the left bank of the Seine. Large forces of police surrounding the building made it difficult to get in, equally difficult to get out. Many of the huge audience, fighting for places near the front, were not journalists at all. The heat of the television lights became nearly unbearable. A few minutes after 3 o'clock the General stepped out on the platform. His hair was greyer than it had been on his last public occasion and he had put on some weight. But these were the only signs of increasing years. His step was springy, his long gaunt face as expressive as ever, especially when, to emphasise a point, his voice rose and fell from near falsetto to a gruff bass. He spoke, as usual, without a note and seemed fully aware, like everyone in the huge room, of the historic nature of the occasion.

Though there were certainly Gaullists, genuine or time-serving, present, there were also sceptics and outright critics. Memories came flooding back of the thugs at earlier Gaullist meetings, of the bombastic language used by some of the General's followers, of the scornful intolerance displayed on previous occasions by himself about those who were not of his opinions. Above all, the thought was inescapable that he would not be addressing this vast audience if plots and plotters had not prepared the way for him. So when the question was put: "Some people fear that if you return to power, you would attack public liberties", the tension, already considerable, rose higher. De Gaulle's reply, short though it was, was the most memorable moment of a memorable occasion. It did more than anything else he said that afternoon to assuage honest doubts and quieten dark suspicions. "Have I ever done so?" he asked, a note of indignation in the rising pitch of his voice. "On the contrary, I restored them [public liberties] when they had disappeared. Is it credible that at the age of sixty-seven I am going to begin a career as a dictator?"

When he answered a question about the army's conduct in Algeria, he was like a man threading his way through a minefield. As well as anyone, and better than most, he knew and understood the frustrations and mistrust of politicians felt by the army, all the way from 1940 through Indo-China, Suez and now Algeria. At the same time, he was aware of the meaning of the word sedition. So his reply was a skilful attempt to meet both points: "I understand very well the attitude and action of the military command in Algeria. And it is my wish in the national interests that the army should remain coherent and united and an exemplary element at a time when such things are rare." On the still unresolved problem of how he was going to "assume the powers of the Republic", he remained discreet. At the right time, he said, he would make known "to whom it might concern" the sort of procedure that seemed to him effective. "Now I shall return to my village [Colombey]," he concluded, "and remain there at the disposal of the country."

Although this dramatic episode had no immediate effect upon the situation in Paris, events now began to unfold at such a rate as to hasten a dénouement of one sort or another. On May 24, Corsica went over to the dissidents, a move planned from Algiers. In Paris, rumours circulated ever more strongly that the invasion of France was imminent. 'Operation Resurrection' was to seize Paris, using 4000 parachutists from Toulouse, who would work in conjunction with thousands of secretly mobilised paratroop reservists. De Gaulle knew about this and so of course did Pflimlin who, in a 2 a.m. broadcast to the nation, warned of imminent attack. The airfields around Paris were put under special guard – though it seemed dubious what sort of precaution that was, seeing that in Corsica gendarmes sent from the mainland had allowed themselves to be disarmed. News censorship was imposed, with the predictable result that rumours flowed faster and thicker. No sooner, late at night, had I completed and dictated long despatches to Printing House Square, reporting and analysing the latest situation, than I had to amend and add to them, often dictating, due to lack of time, straight into the telephone without a written text.

A midnight meeting between Pflimlin and de Gaulle prepared the way for the former's resignation, whereupon Coty, in a message to Parliament, warned of impending civil war and said he was calling on 'the most illustrious of Frenchmen to save the Republic'. Meanwhile de Gaulle, after his nocturnal meeting with Pflimlin, issued from Colombey another of those cryptic messages, in which he said he had embarked on 'the regular procedure necessary for the establishment of a Republican Government' and ordering the army in Algiers to remain obedient to their commanders. There were still Socialist objections to de Gaulle to be overcome, but finally, on June 1, more than twelve years after voluntarily stepping down from power because he believed the party system was unworkable, General de Gaulle had that power restored to him by a large majority of the National Assembly. Only a minority of the Socialists approved. The scene in the *Maison sans fenêtres* was hardly less dramatic than the famous press conference. The General himself, the scourge of the party system, sat, like any other Prime-Minister-designate, alone on the ministerial benches until the moment came for him to mount the rostrum. To a hushed chamber, he spoke, unemotionally and with a minimum of rhetoric, of the "unity, integrity and independence of France". He asked for special powers and outlined his plans for constitutional return. Then, without waiting to hear the ensuing debate, he returned, a tall and lonely figure, to his hotel to await the Assembly's verdict. For several nights that week, there were pro-Gaullist manifestations in the streets, consisting largely of young people waving tricolors, shouting *"Vive de Gaulle"* and blaring out the rhythm, on their car horns, of *Algérie Française*. Apart from that, and a general feeling of deliverance from danger and civil strife, there was surprisingly little public reaction to the stirring events of the last three weeks. Many intellectuals and men of the left, including Mendès-France, felt that de Gaulle had been planted on France by a seditious army and a bunch of *colon* extremists, and that Coty had given up too easily. I could see, and felt much sympathy with, their reasoning. The whole business smelt of a South-American-type *pronunciamento*, unworthy of a great nation. But it seemed equally arguable that however little was known about de Gaulle's intentions, however dubious the aims and reputations of those who had made his restoration possible, he had kept his pledge to return to power only by legal means. Almost the last act I can remember of the great drama was one of bathos: the expulsion of Mr Michael Foot from France, where he was providing special coverage for the *Daily Herald*, for what he had written about Coty.

This is not the place to repeat the oft-told story, fascinating though it is, of how de Gaulle patiently and with extraordinary sleight-of-hand tricked all those, soldiers and civilians alike, who thought that by making inevitable his return, so they had ensured that Algeria would remain forever French. De Gaulle, first as Prime Minister and then as President, turned out not to be the army's man or anyone's man. He was himself, a unique mixture of French pride, intelligence and low cunning, with a habit of thinking on the largest possible timescale and a well-developed sense of his own chosen destiny. It became easier to understand, as his grasp on power tightened, the strength and depth of the convictions of men like Palewski that de Gaulle and only de Gaulle could lead France out of her difficulties and into a brighter future.

When it was all over, Haley asked me to write three long analytical articles, with the general title of 'What went wrong'. They sought to explain how a faulty constitution and inappropriate electoral law had created a political and parliamentary system permanently incapable of responding to the challenges facing it. As under the system government had to be by coalition, and as coalitions were nearly always split internally, so the hammering out of policies was an almost impossible task. French party politics are never simple, but for simplicity's sake it could be said that the political map of those years was painted in three broad bands of colour: the Communists and their sympathisers on the left, implacably opposed to almost any measures put forward by a government of which they were not members; the Gaullists and their affiliates on the right, less completely negative but still a difficult and unpredictable mass of parliamentary opinion (though firmly pasting the label of right-wing on to the Gaullist package in an act of over-simplification); and in the middle an ill-assorted and shifting mixture, the only one on which a parliamentary majority could be built, of Socialists, some Radicals, some 'independants' (more right-wing than centrist), and the post-war Catholic party, now defunct, which went by the name of the Mouvement Républicain Populaire (MRP), to which Pflimlin belonged. The best tactic for a Fourth Republican Prime Minister from one or another part of this central grouping, indeed the only satisfactory, if far from permanent, safeguard against collapse, was to stand perfectly still. As one of these Prime Ministers put it, succinctly if unflatteringly, they were 'condemned to stick together'. The resulting immobility did not, with one great exception, matter very much. Events imposed policies in the same way that climate affects crops. But this comfortable determinism was inadequate for the troubles in North Africa. The task either of neutralising the nationalists and imposing a French settlement, or of admitting the principle of independence, was impossible. In the year before May 13, successive governments did little more than dither. When at last M. Pflimlin made – or was reported as making – a tentative suggestion for some form of disengagement in Algeria, the conspirators in Algiers and their friends in Paris moved quickly into action. What de Gaulle, in 1946, had described as the 'many and profound divisions among Frenchmen' had finally undermined the foundations of the State.

Yet until May 13 and the events that followed, the return of de Gaulle would have had no chance of approval by either parliamentary or public opinion. This is why I and so many others were unable to foretell the General's restoration until it was at hand. Only the really faithful, imbued with the sort of blind belief that insists upon the inevitability of the Second Coming, got it right, after having been wrong so many times before. For the despised and malfunctioning Fourth Republic had not served France all that badly. On the whole, as I was always learning from my travels in the provinces, people regarded the fall of governments and lack of policies with equanimity, content to share in the general prosperity which nothing had been able to stop. The end, when it came, was not by popular revolution, bloodless or otherwise. It was because action and authority had become so paralysed and sapped that a *coup d'état* could be painlessly organised and carried forward until the sovereign power, as vested in the Parliament and the President of the Republic, was glad to welcome and legalise it.

Covering the crisis was a considerable strain, involving a great shortage of sleep, long nights in the airless atmosphere of the Press gallery in the National Assembly and a constant need to distinguish fantasy from fact, rumour from report, personal persuasions from objective judgements. Luckily No. 7 Place de la Madeleine was close enough to the Chamber to make the use of a car unnecessary. Even so, it was sometimes difficult, on foot, to force a way through the ranks of police and Gardes Républicains (what were they thinking?) surrounding the building. All this had an inevitable effect on the nerves. One late night in the Press gallery, my seventh or eighth such evening running, I turned round to find Jo Alsop,* newly arrived from Washington and looking as fresh as paint, occupying one of the seats which resident Paris correspondents, given the smallness of the gallery, often had to struggle for. "This place", I said to Jo, "is reserved for working journalists." It was an unprovoked piece of rudeness only to be explained by fatigue. Jo, no mean hand at insults himself, repaid in kind, informing me in the bar later on that I knew nothing of French history and was writing the story all wrong. As I considered that my grasp of French affairs was far better than his, this was distinctly irritating. A terrible row ensued, but like most rows was blown away by

---

* Joseph Alsop, American journalist and for a time the second husband of Susan-Mary Patten

the winds of time. In later years, in Washington, Jo was often our generous host.

The remainder of my time in France until, at the end of 1960, I left *The Times* and joined *The Sunday Times* in London, was largely spent watching and describing the heroic efforts of the General to correct the mistakes of the past, above all to thread his way out of the Algerian maze. De Gaulle's towering presence was momentarily matched by one other personality of larger-than-life dimensions which crossed the French scene, like a comet on its celestial path. This was Nikita Khruschev. His reputation as a man of peasant wit and unpredictable temper was already well established, so that anticipations of his official visit to France in the spring of 1960 created large ripples of interest and (in the case of the Roman Catholic hierarchy) hostility. A colourful exception to the Church's attitude was the Chanoine Kir, the eighty-four-year-old mayor of Dijon, and member of the National Assembly. His place in social history is assured by his invention or patronage of the aperitif (white white and cassis) that bears his name. But at the time, he was better-known for his rather dotty ideas, Resistance record and devotion to the Soviet cause. As the doyen of the National Assembly it was his duty at the beginning of a new parliamentary term, before the President or Speaker was elected, to occupy the Speaker's chair and address the Chamber. This he did, clad in a fusty old soutane, with the utmost enthusiasm and marked eccentricity of views.

On arrival, Khruschev failed at first to live up to his fame as an ebullient performer. He had been ill and seemed subdued. But there was nothing half-hearted about de Gaulle's welcome. As a historian and a nationalist, he was deeply conscious of the significance of the Franco–Russian alliance of earlier years, a memory symbolised by his habit of always speaking of *La Russie*, never of the *Union Soviétique* (just as he always referred to Britain as *l'Angleterre*). In his speech at the inaugural banquet for Khruschev, he grandiloquently described France and the Soviet Union as "two daughters of the same mother, Europe". His habit of speaking without notes stung the still-torpid Khruschev, who had read his speech, into observing that he, too, could talk without notes; "that will be for later".

This indeed turned out to be the case. Two days afterwards he and his party set off on an extensive tour of France, pursued by a small army of journalists, among them myself. There were plenty of opportunities for seeing Khruschev at close range. The little piggy eyes, set in a large fleshy face, the extravagant gestures such as a double-handed boxer's salute to an applauding crowd, the sudden changes in mood, measured in bursts of uproarious laughter or the deepest of scowls: all this betokened a personality of intriguing and often uncomfortable dimensions. At one point, the programme called for a visit to a pumping-station near Arles. In the hot sunshine, Khruschev listened with growing signs of boredom to a lengthy explanation of the irrigation system which was already enriching the parched Provençal soil. Then one of the fruits of this process — a fine bunch of maize — was put into his hands. The effect was startling. In a second, he was off on one of his favourite subjects, boasting about Soviet agricultural achievements, throwing off real or possibly invented Russian proverbs, roaring with laughter. On another occasion, at the natural gas plant at Lacq, he rudely cut off the prolix explanations of the resident engineer with the words: "I know you engineers, you study for ten years and you want to explain it all in two hours." At Bordeaux, where the Mayor presented him with a fine sporting gun, he trained it with mock menace on the accompanying journalists. There was certainly a natural clown here, but unlike most clowns, one who could turn nasty with little or no warning or apparent cause.

The big disappointment of the tour came at Dijon, where the reception of Khruschev by the Chanoine Kir was guaranteed to make good copy. The party arrived to find no Mayor. He had been whisked away the previous night, in a kind of ecclesiastical kidnap, to the safe custody of a Roman Catholic agricultural college some fifty miles away. In a statement, the Cardinal of Lyons made it plain that, though he might be the agent, the wish was not his; the orders had come from Rome. I remember with admiration Khruschev's handling of this unexpected development. He could have been rude and mocking about the Vatican. Instead, he contented himself with lavish praise for the Chanoine and his work for France and peace. The waiting crowds, largely Communist, outside the Hotel de Ville gave him one of the loudest and most enthusiastic receptions of the whole tour. The next day, his mood had changed again. After a sombre tour of the battlefields of Verdun and Douamont, he spoke at the subsequent lunch at Reims angrily and obviously from the heart about German aggression, excusing his frankness on the grounds that he had not been trained as a diplomat. "Your speech was so diplomatic", he told the embarrassed accompanying French Minister, "that I could not tell whether the Germans had come to your country as aggressors or whether you had invited them." Two days later, in an impromptu press conference in the train taking him to Lille, Khruschev, whose remarks and general attitude marked him down as a true if exceedingly cunning child of nature, was holding forth about Christianity and Communism. "There is much in Christ that is common to us Communists," he said. "I only do not agree with Him when he says we should turn the other cheek; in my belief, if I am hit on the left cheek I hit the man who hit me on his right cheek so hard that his head falls off." Compared with the hackneyed and predictable statements which we in the West have over the years grown used to hearing from the grey *apparatchiks* of the Kremlin, this sort of language, for all its outrageousness, does strike a highly individual note. Khruschev's fall from power in 1964 was due to a number of reasons, but the historians have never, in my view, laid sufficient emphasis on one of the principal ones: the *enfant terrible* element in Khruschev's personality, which caused him to behave so mercurially. Soviet Communist party manners and *mores* are immensely conservative and formalistic and Khruschev's rodomontades must have been a constant source of embarrassment and irritation.

Within two months, Khruschev was back in Paris for the summit conference that never was. De Gaulle, Eisenhower, and Macmillan were due to discuss with the Soviet leader a whole range of topics involving peace and co-existence. Just before the conference was supposed to begin, a US reconnaissance U–2 plane was shot down over Soviet territory and the pilot captured. Soviet reactions were strong, but Khruschev, despite his claims to be no diplomat, was shrewd enough to express the belief that Eisenhower knew nothing of the flight. Instead of availing himself of the opportunity for some sensible if insincere face-saving, honest Ike not only claimed responsibility for ordering such flights but equally decided not to make public until later his decision to cancel them. In the unlikely event that he had ever heard of the Persian poet Sa'adi, he would have done well to recall the latter's maxim that 'a falsehood mixed with expediency is better than a truth which stirs up trouble'. Khruschev, by now in Paris, told de Gaulle that he would only attend the summit if Eisenhower were ready with a statement cancelling all future U–2 flights, apologising, and promising to punish those responsible. Eisenhower found this ultimatum unacceptable (de Gaulle agreed with him) and so the summit collapsed before it ever began. As an example of how not to handle delicate affairs of state, in which national pride and sensitivities are deeply involved, the story of the U–2 flights and their aftermath is probably unrivalled in the saga of modern East–West relations.

That is more properly for the history books. It touches personal reminiscence in the shape of the famous press conference given by Khruschev before leaving Paris. Press conferences seem to have played rather a large part in this chapter. Normally such occasions are unremarkable, fit only to be reported for next day's paper. But sometimes, as in the case of Dulles in 1953 or de Gaulle in 1958, they are so exceptional in nature and content as to leave at least a footnote, and sometimes more, on the pages of history. Khruschev's performance in Paris on May 18, 1960 clearly fell within this category. It was held in the largest hall of the Palais de Chaillot, the building at the Trocadero on the site of the 1937 international exhibition, and was attended by up to three thousand journalists from all over the world. As Khruschev took his place on the rostrum applause from Communist journalists was drowned by the booing of anti-Communists. This seemed to inspire him to excesses of eloquence. For over two hours – allowing for translation into French and English – he ranted and shouted and clowned, now exaggeratedly toasting the journalists in water, now tapping his head to indicate their folly, at one moment expressing affection for the American people, at the next working himself into a state of red-faced, stentorian-voiced anger as he repeatedly denounced the U–2 flights. On his right sat Gromyko, the Foreign Minister, stern-faced but occasionally betraying with a smile his membership of the human race. On the other side was the much-bemedalled Marshall Malinovsky, the Defence Minister, who allowed no such weakness to be seen in his square, expressionless face. When the whole extraordinary performance was over, it was still unclear just what lay behind Khruschev's tactics. Were he and his government genuinely outraged by the U–2 flights and Eisenhower's refusal to apologise? Or had a real and considered change in Soviet policy occurred? With hindsight, it is pretty clear that the first question supplied the right answer. Perhaps we should have paid more attention to what Khruschev actually said that afternoon, rather than have been side-tracked by his histrionics. "We came to Paris for the summit conference because we thought that the United States might be honest and apologise for the U–2 incident . . . it is a question of upbringing and manners. Someone tried to poke his nose into our affairs. We punched it and we shall do so again if necessary." It was not, as Khruschev himself would have been proud to admit, by any means the language of diplomacy, but should, for that reason, have been all the easier to understand.

At the end of the year, my career as foreign correspondent came voluntarily to an end. After thirteen years abroad I wanted to return to London, if only to avoid becoming, as time rolled on, a professional expatriate. *The Times* had nothing to offer in London. So with the idea of leaving journalism altogether, I consulted a merchant banking friend, Jack Hambro of Hambro's bank, about possible openings in the City or in industry. With total candour – the mark of a good friend – he strongly discouraged such a switch. It would be most unlikely to lead to happiness or job satisfaction, he said. Unless one was in on the ground floor, the only possible kind of job, even if it were available, was a consultative or advisory one, and it was, according to him, a known fact that institutions such as merchant banks or large industrial corporations, though they might be ready to pay someone to write informative or advisory reports, rarely or never imbibed the information or took the advice. Thus when Ian Fleming, who despite his growing absorption with James Bond was still connected with *The Sunday Times*, told me in confidence that that paper was looking for a new foreign editor, I followed up the hint. By the end of the summer, the die had been cast – not without some doubts, because *The Times* and I had come to suit one another very well. It was not because of discontent with my employers that I was taking this step. From Printing House Square came flattering letters of regret at my decision and appreciation for past services rendered.

Thirteen years of reporting from foreign capitals provided food for thought in two respects, one professional, the other personal. Firstly, they revealed the responsibilities of a foreign correspondent, responsibilities so great that they would have been frightening had one stopped to think about them. This may seem the language of a braggart, but in fact is no more than the truth. Millions of readers at home are partly, often largely, dependent for their views about a foreign country on the writings of the correspondents in that country. (This is equally true of course of the representatives abroad of the BBC and the independent television organisations.) If the reporting is trivial, inaccurate, biased, then the reading public's opinions of the particular country and its people will, in most cases, tend towards triviality, error and bias. All too often this is precisely what happens. Stereotypes are created – dirty and untrustworthy Arabs, wily Latin Americans given to intrigue, rapacious and inscrutable Japanese – and having been created, tend to be self-sustaining. Serious, 'quality' papers are less prone to this than the popular press, but for that very reason, and because they are addressing a more sophisticated and influential section of the population, correspondents of the 'qualities' bear a higher responsibility. Yet they will not necessarily discharge that by always allowing complete impartiality to rule their reports. 'One gets more real truth out of one avowed partisan than out of a dozen of your sham impartialists,' wrote Robert Louis Stevenson. Scarcely the advice to give to a reporter setting out for foreign parts, but there is something in it. To quote again from a very different source: 'The eye of the critic is often, like a microscope, made so very fine and nice that it discovers atoms, grains and the minutest particles, without ever comprehending the whole, comparing the parts or seeing all at once the harmony' (Alexander Pope). Comprehending the whole and seeing the harmony of a situation such as that which unfolded in France in May 1958 calls for very special efforts.

One of the most disturbing aspects of modern newspaper development is the gradual decline in the numbers of properly equipped foreign correspondents, living in the capital of the country to which they are accredited and establishing a close but healthily sceptical *rapport* with its policies and people. There are still, happily, a number of such journalists whose continued activity is made possible only by their enlightened newspapers' readiness to invest in them. But that is where the rub comes. The expense of maintaining a resident correspondent (plus perhaps his or her family) in a foreign capital becomes greater every year. So does the temptation to achieve foreign coverage by sending out, according to the flow and pressure of news, temporary task forces from London. Some of these may do good work, but the result can never be the same as that accomplished by constant contact and the knowledge and understanding that grows from it. I suppose the finest specimen of the kind of person whose gradual disappearance I am bemoaning was the Paris correspondent of the (then) *Manchester Guardian*. Darsie Gillie was large, scholarly, absent-minded, somewhat un-co-ordinated in his movements, given to passionate rages when gripped by some cause or injustice, often more interested in reporting the proceedings of a learned Paris institute concerned with the ancient world than in the contemporary scene. Yet over an unbroken period of more than twenty years he maintained a uniformly excellent service to his readers of accurate, well-balanced, well-written information and analysis about France. It was a tribute to the French authorities that despite his frequent castigations of what seemed to him their shortcomings in the theory and practice of democracy, they awarded him the Legion of Honour. No one could seriously have accused him – indeed, no one tried to do so – of having sung for his supper.

The second impression concerned the nature of French society. We had been warned, before arriving for the first time in Paris in 1947, of the inhospitable and impenetrable composition of the French social carapace. You will never, the lesson went, really be received within a French family, never make any real friends. The advice was nonsense then and is nonsense now. Most French people (like most British people) are reserved on first contact with foreigners, do not easily open their hearts or their homes. Moreover Paris and Parisians, unlike the people of the provinces, have a well-deserved reputation for gratuitous rudeness to one another. Diana Cooper, shopping one day in one of the big Paris stores, could not find what she wanted and asked the assistant in what other shop it could be found. *"Vous savez, Madame,"* replied the young lady, in tones which managed to be both aggrieved and surprised, *"je ne suis pas ici pour vous aider."* But this sort of bad humour apart, we soon found, above all as our capacity to speak French properly increased, that we began to make friends, to go to French houses as often as French friends came to ours, to enjoy the lively little dinner-parties at which either everyone tends to talk at once or all listen more or less respectfully to the 'lion' who has been specially invited for the purpose of roaring. French friendships, once well and truly made, endure for a lifetime; there is little of that casual drifting apart, of failing to keep in touch, which increasingly characterises English social life.

---

* (*page 149*) This episode could not have happened today, at least at Times Newspapers. There, and in an increasingly greater number of other newspaper offices, modern technology has at last overtaken the old, hot metal methods. The tyrannical power of the print unions and their restrictive practices has also, not without a struggle, been reduced.

7

'The Great Globe Itself'

One Saturday night in the composing room at *The Sunday Times*, where the pages of the paper used to be made up by fitting sections of lead type into large metal frames or formes, the paper's recently appointed foreign editor was leaning over one of these formes, inspecting its contents and preparing to shorten some of them in case the lead in which they were set would not fit its allotted space. At this stage in the process, the lines of this leaded type run backwards (right to left) and are therefore difficult, to those unpractised, to read. To make it less difficult, the foreign editor picked up a lump of metal which was awaiting its turn to be fitted in and held it up to eye level. The make-up man standing behind the forme, a member of the National Graphical Association, the union whose members consider themselves the princes of the print industry, emitted a low hiss in which a sense of outrage and a note of warning managed to combine. "Put that down at once," he said, in a voice muted enough to avoid attracting general attention, "or the Father of the chapel [shop-steward] will call everybody out." In the circumstances, it was nice of him to have treated the matter as something between him and me.

This was my dramatic introduction to the mysteries, unknown to me up to then, of newspaper production. Being a foreign correspondent, witnessing great moments of history, filing tens of thousands of words about them was certainly journalism of a sort. But the episode of the lead – I had transgressed the cardinal rule that in the composing room only members of the NGA can handle metal – showed up my total ignorance of the lore and laws of Fleet Street and of the demarcations and restrictions which in the early sixties made (and still make today) the production of a newspaper a nightly (or weekly, as the case may be) struggle between the opposing claims of efficiency and what are sometimes referred to as the old Spanish customs of the print unions.*

This was not the only new lesson to be learnt as the result of forsaking

Paris for London, *The Times* for *The Sunday Times*. The latter, in those days unconnected in any way with the former, was, or at least was shortly to become, a very different animal. It had recently been bought by the Canadian tycoon Roy Thomson from Lord Kemsley, the previous proprietor, for whom I do not think I could ever have worked. Contemporary accounts★ are full of phrases like 'outdated', 'impossibly autocratic', 'shut off from everything of significance in post-war Britain'. He seems – I never knew him – to have been at once pompous, self-satisfied, ignorant, snobbish and obstinate. Yet other witnesses speak of his essential kindness and integrity. Cyril Connolly, no respecter of persons, had written of Kemsley's *Sunday Times* as having 'a gentlemanly charm about it'. H.M. (Harry) Hodson, Editor when I joined the paper – a scholarly, gentle, harassed man who, with his silvery hair, Lock bowler hat and furled umbrella, projected the image of a successful merchant banker or perhaps a country gentleman up in London to see his wine-merchant – has described Kemsley as 'the bogey of our office lives', who insisted that on the Sunday after every Lord Mayor's Day the paper should carry a leader praising the retiring Lord Mayor and congratulating his successor. Yet Hodson adds that there was no senior member of the staff who did not regard Kemsley with admiration and affection – a statement that strains credulity.

Whatever Kemsley's limitations, there is no doubt that under Hodson's editorship, and helped by the far-sighted wisdom of C.D. (Denis) Hamilton, before long to succeed Hodson as Editor, *The Sunday Times* was forging ahead as a quality weekly paper strong on the arts and the literary scene and noted – once the Kemsley influence had gone – for the independence of its editorial views. After the Thomson takeover, there was inevitably a good deal of apprehension about what this bluff, philistine Canadian, reputed to be interested only in profits, was going to do with his new possession. No one need have worried. Roy Thomson was not only a great entrepreneur who liked laying out money to make more money (provided it was the bank's or somebody else's – never use your own if you can help it, was one of his maxims) but believed in and practised the theory of editorial independence. His creed was written on a card which he always carried in his pocket. (He also carried on his person typed collections of jokes for use in after-dinner speeches. They were divided into three categories: tellable in

★ Principally in *The Pearl of Days*, an intimate memoir of *The Sunday Times*, 1822–1972 (Hamish Hamilton, 1972)

11 Washington 1967:
President Johnson
and F.G.

12 Washington 1982:
President Reagan
and F.G.

13 Amman 1981: King Hussein and F.G. The portrait behind is of King Abdullah, Hussein's grandfather, who was murdered in Jerusalem in 1951

any company, slightly risqué and downright filthy.) According to this creed, 'I do not believe that a newspaper can be run properly unless its editorial columns are run freely and independently by a highly skilled and dedicated professional journalist.' Each paper in the growing Thomson empire would operate, the card went on, 'without advice, counsel or guidance from the central office of the Thomson Organisation'. Roy never broke or bent these rules. From the point of view of editorial independence, they were every bit as admirable and agreeable to work under as the Astor constitution of *The Times*.

Life in a big newspaper office bears more than a passing resemblance to the caricature of it in films and plays. True, the odds are against the news editor wearing a green eyeshade, no one ever shouts "Hold the front page", the medical correspondent is unlikely to be a dipsomaniac, disqualified Irish doctor. But typewriters are pounded furiously by shirt-sleeved reporters; telephones jangle incessantly; to the rage/despair of their creators, journalists' 'pieces' get 'spiked' – i.e. rejected by the responsible editor because they are unsuitable or inadequately done; picture editors are under constant pressure to produce a more striking/dramatic/eye-stopping contribution for page 1; the production editor, who is responsible for getting the paper out on time, becomes, as edition time approaches and the main lead to the paper is still in the author's typewriter rather than in the hands of the printer, increasingly irritable and foul-mouthed. In my first years at *The Sunday Times*, the holder of this office, an Irishman of normally genial disposition, was capable on a Saturday night of reducing strong men to nervous wrecks and girl reporters to tears.

The rhythms of a Sunday paper are very different to those of a daily. For the latter, the timescale is obviously of twenty-four hours. As the final edition comes off the presses at, say, 2.30 a.m. that is that; whatever has gone right or wrong in the selection, preparation and presentation of news and features, leading articles and pictures, whatever journalistic triumphs have been achieved or follies committed, tomorrow is another day which will in the same timespan spawn another paper. There is not much time for doubts or regrets. In a Sunday newspaper office, the working week usually begins on a Tuesday and runs on, for some, until the early hours of the following Sunday morning. The first part of the week is spent in planning the contents of the next issue and deploying the forces to supply it. By about Thursday, some of the plans will have to be abandoned, either because the subject has gone off the boil in terms of news interest, or because other topics have come up to push them away. As Saturday, press day, approaches, so anxiety mounts. Is the balance of the paper going to be right, are the stories and topical features which are going to figure prominently the appropriate ones for that particular issue, how is the new outbreak of fighting in the Middle East to be properly covered when the reporters despatched at great expense earlier in the week have been prevented getting anywhere near the scene of action? All this concerns news in one form or another. On both a daily and a Sunday, the Editor and the relevant members of his staff will have been busy with the arts pages, the book reviews, the women's pages, the business and finance section, the sports coverage. Those require planning on a longer timescale than a week, and a longer one still is needed for the choice of the book – diaries, letters, biographies, autobiographies – whose serialisation in carefully edited extracts has become the staple diet offered by posh Sunday papers.

In order to plan and monitor this wide range of material, much of the working week, above all the early part of it, is taken up with conferences: Editor's conferences, news editor's conferences, foreign editor's conferences, sports editor's conferences, conferences about long-term projects, conferences (these come later in the week) on what the leading articles are going to say. I sometimes wondered whether this unending and time-consuming process was always necessary. All too often, it gave rise to office politicking, as one departmental empire, ruled over by a rapacious executive, sought to extend its frontiers at the expense of another. But on the whole, the system worked well and justified itself, both in terms of ideas generated and cross-fertilised and in the avoidance of overlapping and duplication.

Journalists, as I soon discovered after returning to London and getting to know them and their ways *en masse*, are just as varied and unsuitable for generalising about as the members of any other profession. Probably the most legendary perceptions of them are as drinkers and submitters of inflated expense accounts. Many of them do like drinking, above all in a pub near to the office where, like the actors and actresses they often resemble, they can and do exchange endless gossip and rumours about the work, professional prospects and private lives of their colleagues. But, with some notable exceptions, they do not normally carry things to extremes. During my many years with *The Sunday Times*, only one or two people come to mind who could be called persistent over-consumers. In fact, many more people seemed to drift on to the marital rocks than were shipwrecked on the bottle; though

whether this would have happened anyway, because of their temperament and circumstances, or whether this sexual restlessness was the
result of the pressures of the job, there is no knowing.

The expense account legend is better based. Although the level of
Fleet Street salaries has been raised considerably since I went to work
for *The Times*, journalism is still not, and is unlikely ever to be, a career
into which people go to get rich. Most journalists regard a little padding
of their expense accounts – nothing too outrageous – as a legitimate perk
of the job. Sometimes even this is unnecessary. The sheer sumptuous-
ness (or over-consumption) of lunch with a contact at an expensive
London restaurant can be enough both to gratify the taste for good
living and genuinely to blow the chargeable bill up to a point beyond
which the financial scrutineer at the paper would begin to ask questions. The system is so well known that sometimes the recipient of this
form of subsidised hospitality joins the circus. A senior Labour politician, later to become Chancellor of the Exchequer, being lunched
one day by a *Sunday Times* man, himself chose the most expensive
claret on the wine-list because "we know who is paying the bill, don't
we?"

The colleagues with whom I was to work for the next twenty years
and more came in all sorts and sizes. At least until a later time, with the
introduction of a Young Turk element much given to office intrigue
and acrimony, it was a happy and generally harmonious team. Denis
Hamilton was an unusual Editor. He wrote little or nothing for the
paper and could be occasionally moody and difficult. His silences were
famous, creating – whether intentionally or not – feelings of profound
unease among his interlocutors. He also had a shortish temper, which
could suddenly and without warning flare into a white-hot rage. But
these moments were rare. For the most part, he was a far-seeing and
enthusiastic chief, with an undefinable quality of leadership which
found expression in his unerring ability to pick out able men and
women to work for him and in his power to delegate. During his time as
Editor, he created a sense of corporate pride among the journalistic staff
of *The Sunday Times*, akin to that to be found in a good regiment or
club. He also seemed to possess invisible antennae which told him with
enviable accuracy what the quality newspaper-reading public was
looking for in a Sunday paper. Above all, he knew and practised, both
then and later, after Thomson had bought *The Times* and he became
Editor-in-Chief and Chairman of the new company, the all-important
art of getting on with your proprietor. No doubt Thomson, with his creed-

on-a-card, his complete lack of status-consciousness, his easy-going and jovial ways, was not difficult to live with. Yet though he took little apparent interest in the editorial views and contents of *The Sunday Times*, he had very definite and progressive opinions about the future of newspaper publishing, views which included a healthy Canadian scorn for the stick-in-the-mud attitudes which characterise much of British life. He liked to tell the story of how, in Edinburgh after his purchase of *The Scotsman*, he felt the cold one winter's day and went into a shop in Princes' Street to buy a pair of gloves. It was just before 1 o'clock. Announcing his needs to the girl behind the counter, he was told: "We're just closing for lunch, we can't sell you anything now." His purpose as a newspaper proprietor in Britain was to combat and reverse this mentality by pushing forward the frontiers of knowledge and interest (not forgetting the profits which would ensue once the right formula was found). Hamilton knew exactly how to make use of and channel this purpose, taking endless trouble to keep Thomson informed of every step in the paper's development and working closely with him through what proved to be some very difficult moments. At no time was this truer than over the launch of the Colour Magazine in 1962. In origin Thomson's brain-child, it had an exceedingly sticky start. Even Thomson, the perpetual optimist, was dismayed. But Denis Hamilton, with a display of faith which would have done credit to a recusant priest on the run, weathered the storm. Within a year, the magazine was an outstanding success, to the point that the other quality Sunday papers were soon to pay the supreme compliment of ceasing to scoff and starting to copy, by producing their own colour magazines.

When I joined *The Sunday Times* at the end of 1960, William Rees-Mogg was its City editor. Later, under Hamilton's reign, he became political editor and then deputy editor, before transferring, once Thomson had bought *The Times*, to the editorship of that paper. He was thus a close colleague and became, with time, a good friend – kind, considerate, blessed with a lively sense of the ridiculous. Apart from his well-developed intellectual powers, there was no doubt that William was a character. In one of Simon Raven's novels,* about public school life, he is caricatured, under the not very subtle pseudonym of Somerset Lloyd-James, as a precocious and scheming prig. This may have been an accurate picture of him as a schoolboy. It was not true of

---

* *Fielding Gray*, one of the series with the general title of 'Alms for Oblivion'

him as a man. But he had certain traits which did lend themselves to parody. One was his voice, a rich, plummy, never varying sound with which, one imagines, he must have uttered his first, infantile syllables. Another was his readiness to form and express a view about absolutely anything. Ask William a question about apartheid in South Africa, bimetallism, Shakespearian metre, Mr Gladstone's first administration, the Congressional committee system in Washington: after a very short pause, during which a keen ear might pick up a faint whirring hum as he engaged the mechanism of his well-oiled brain, out would come the answer, perfectly formed in long cadences that gave a passable imitation of omniscience. Sometimes, listening to him, the vision of Anthony Powell's anti-hero, Widmerpool, flashed across the mind's screen. But there was a great deal more to William than his mannerisms might at first suggest. He had strong political convictions; on a good day he could write like an angel. His influence, both as an anonymous leader-writer and as the author of signed articles, became a national phenomenon. When Sir Alec Douglas-Home (as he then was) became Prime Minister in 1963, William, a strong R.A. Butler supporter, expressed his disillusionment in a signed article which pulled no punches: 'I know of no convincing argument which I could put to a young scientist or university teacher to persuade him that the Conservative Party was both the best way of fulfilling his political ideas and a party in which he would be at home . . . this is a new situation, a very sad situation, and I believe an extremely perilous one.' And on the Profumo affair, concerning which Haley at *The Times* had written a ringing denunciation with the title of 'It is a moral issue', William voiced a memorably dissenting opinion, arguing that 'in the end even a scandal has to be brought back into proportion: the life of Britain does not really pass through the loins of one red-headed girl.' It was his influence, backed strongly by Hamilton, which moved the paper's editorial stance away from the unthinking Toryism of Kemsley's day to a more radical and intelligent position. Over the years this developed into one of independence of any party label.

After I had been with *The Sunday Times* for about five years, Hamilton recruited to the staff a young, short, energetic north-country journalist, the very antithesis of the patrician Rees-Mogg. His name was Harold Evans, and when Rees-Mogg went off to edit *The Times* he became, and remained for the next fourteen years, Editor of *The Sunday Times*. To describe Harry's approach to life and work as 'energetic' is about as adequate as calling Goethe gifted, or Einstein numerate. John

Morley,* describing Theodore Roosevelt, said he was 'an interesting combination of St Vitus and St Paul', and this would not be a bad pen-portrait of Harry. The Pauline element was represented by his crusading zeal for the causes he believed in: open government, the showing up of secrecy and deceit in high places, the right and duty of the Press to report fully and accurately upon matters of public interest, a preference for evidence over propaganda, above all, perhaps, the importance of what has been called the citizen as victim – victim of misused power or business ruthlessness or racial prejudice or inferior services.† These beliefs found resonant expression in some of the campaigns and major efforts of reporting which Harry, as Editor, inspired and supervised. Like St Paul's, his enthusiasm could at times spill over into obsession. But much more usually, he continued to drive in successful harness his passions and his intellect, his heart and his head, avoiding altogether the earnestness and pre-Puritan streak which must have made the Apostle, at times, such a fatiguing companion. Whatever other traits people could, and did, associate with Harry, earnestness and Puritanism could not be numbered among them. His capacity to mock himself was a guarantee of that.

St Vitus, on the other hand, was represented by his working habits, which could be extremely disconcerting. He disliked doing anything for very long, above all sitting still. In the midst of an important conversation he would dart from the room, as he did so encouraging his visitor to keep talking because he would shortly be back. If, while that important, and perhaps confidential, conversation was taking place, somebody else stuck his head round the door, the newcomer would as likely as not be invited in to participate, even though he had nothing whatever to do with the matter under discussion. Never walking when he could run, Harry would streak along the passages en route to one or other of the editorial departments, there to discuss, advise upon, redirect or breathe new fire into whatever project was on foot. Sometimes his whereabouts, usually a mystery, could be traced by the roars of laughter coming from the office where he had temporarily hove to. At other times, his unexplained absences from his own office were marked by a growing queue of people waiting frustratedly to see him. It was a system (hardly the right word) just about as far removed as possible

---

* Viscount Morley, statesman and author 1838–1923
† See 'Rupert Murdoch and *The Sunday Times*: a lamp goes out' by Hugo Young (*The Political Quarterly*, Vol. 55, No. 4, October–December 1984)

from Haley's stately protocol at *The Times*.

But along with all this frenzy, occasionally approaching close to the point of exhibitionism, went the highest degree of professional skill and knowledge. There was almost nothing on the journalistic side of a newspaper office which Harry could not turn his hand to. Very often this is just what he did do, to the annoyance of the person whose job it was. His relations with his staff, despite the irritation he so often caused them, were characterised for the most part by warmth, veering towards affection. It was impossible to dislike him. Often, it was impossible not to admire him – for his ebullience, his humour, his devotion to his profession, his gamin-like charm which amply compensated for some of his more outrageous behaviour. I think the quality I found, over many years of working closely with him, the most uplifting was his readiness to praise where praise was due. Journalists, like actors, need constant encouragement and Harry was always ready to supply this. Sometimes indeed he could have been a little more sparing with it. Criticism and fault-finding, when they are deserved, are just as important a duty of leadership as commendation. But at the very least, Harry's career provided a living negation of the theory that to be a successful leader – in politics, business, journalism or any other branch of activity where human beings are required to work together towards a common goal – you have to be a bit of a shit.

All this, however, is running ahead of chronology. No one, least of all I, had any idea what Hamilton's ultimate plans were for Harold Evans when in 1966 he joined the staff as the former's Chief Assistant. Perhaps things should have become somewhat plainer when, after only seven months, he was appointed managing editor. Roy Thomson's purchase of *The Times* was by now more than a possibility. If and when it was achieved, and on the likely assumption that Haley were to step down, Rees-Mogg was obviously the most favoured candidate for the post. Who then would become Editor of *The Sunday Times*? I remember asking Ian Fleming, when I was negotiating to join the paper five years earlier, whether it was realistic to think of becoming its Editor one day. In his debonair way, he replied to the effect that such a prospect was indeed entirely likely. But I had not given much or any thought to the matter since then. Even a memorable night during the autumn of 1967 failed to alert me to what apparently other people claimed by now to discern clearly.

Harold Wilson, Prime Minister since 1964, had taken to entertaining at Chequers newspaper proprietors, their editors and one or two of their senior staff. The invitation was to dine and spend the night. When one Sunday evening it came to Thomson's round, he took with him Denis Hamilton who, in turn, brought along Rees-Mogg, myself and James Margach, the witty and experienced political correspondent of *The Sunday Times*. I do not recall much about the dinner, but remember vividly the rest of the evening. Wilson led us to the panelled long gallery where, gathered round a blazing log-fire, we talked far into the night. That is not in fact an accurate reminiscence. Firstly, Roy Thomson soon excused himself and was driven back to London. Secondly, it was not we who talked, except in short and ever shorter responses. From 9.30 until 3 a.m. the next day, Wilson held the floor, fortified by a bottle of brandy of which he himself consumed nine-tenths without betraying the least sign of having done so. Though his comments ranged over the whole political and economic spectrum, most of his talk was concerned with the inclinations and personalities of the members of the journalistic parliamentary lobby, the group of men whose duty is to report on the political and parliamentary scene. He appeared to know them all, or know of them, in the greatest detail. Anecdote after anecdote poured from him about what so-and-so had written years before, about how somebody else had fallen out with his editor about such-and-such. Assuming the stories were well-founded, it was an extraordinary feat of memory, though I recall wondering strongly whether the national interest was best served by the head of the Government spending hours of his time and depriving himself of his night's sleep with unimportant tittle-tattle of this kind. Eventually we all got to bed. When quite late the next morning – Monday is the Sunday journalists' day off – I awoke and was served by the efficient Chequers staff with a delicious breakfast in bed, the tireless Prime Minister had already left for London. Before driving away, I strolled about in the gardens for a while, reliving this extraordinary evening. Even then, I did not realise that Hamilton must have included Rees-Mogg and myself in the party in the guise of future editors of *The Times* and *Sunday Times*.

This was just as well, because when the moment came, he appointed not me but Harold Evans to run *The Sunday Times*. According to *The Pearl of Days*, I was his first choice, so much so that someone meeting Harry in the corridors at this time told him, "You'd be candidate for Editor, you know, but you're considered too left-wing," a remark which caused Harry, on his own admission, to 'go around looking as true blue as I could'. Hamilton is on record with the comment that he

wanted someone 'who would be innovative and who would take chances
. . . someone the young men around the office would be prepared to
follow'. In Harry, he certainly got what he was looking for. At the age of
forty-seven, I was appointed deputy-editor, a post to be held in
conjunction with that of foreign editor. The immediate effect was one of
shock and disappointment. But this very quickly wore off, partly
because I had never consciously worked towards the editorship, partly
because the fascinating life of travel and writing which had developed
soon after I joined the paper, and which formed such a contrast with the
relatively static jobs in Rome and Paris, was to continue unabated.

For twenty years from 1961 onwards, I travelled the world, summing
up situations, analysing, interviewing. The United States, East and
Southern Africa, the Middle East, the Indian subcontinent, Vietnam,
China, the Soviet Union: all figured on the itinerary, often several
times. Only Latin America and the Antipodes remained, for no particularly good reason, off the list. In the previous chapter there are some
critical remarks about the efficacy, or otherwise, of a journalistic task
force despatched from London, in the interests of economy, to report
on a foreign country. It could be objected that all this international
travel was an example of such a task force, even if it did consist of only
one man. But I did not see my function, as foreign editor, as that of a
reporter of news. It was more a question of looking, listening and
learning, so that when country X or Y came into the forefront of events,
I in London knew at least something of its problems and personalities.
On the whole these methods, which had the unstinted support first of
Hamilton and then of Evans, proved worth while.

Unless one is Hakluyt or Burton or Pierre Loti, the telling of a
succession of travellers' tales is a sure way to bore the reader. Travel,
while it widens the experience, also magnifies the details; there is a risk
of the canvas becoming clogged. But the memories of places visited and
revisited, or people talked to, combine to create a series of abiding
impressions, just as the recurrent study of certain paintings or works of
literature leave indelible marks upon the surface of the mind. Four such
places, or areas, were for me the United States, the Soviet Union, the
Middle East and China.

As any journalist with personal knowledge will attest, the USA is the
near-ideal place to get people in public positions to talk. I once tried to
explain to Senator Edward Kennedy, whom I was seeing in his Senate
Office in Washington, that our talk was not meant to be an interview
but was confidential, for my background information. He could not or

would not understand and became quite indignant at the thought of not being quoted directly. There are of course exceptions to this attitude. At the extreme other end of the scale was President Ronald Reagan, who received me in the Oval office in the White House in the autumn of 1982, when I had become Editor of *The Sunday Times*. The meeting was arranged with considerable difficulty. Before escorting me to the President, his public affairs man stressed the importance of asking no question of substance. The occasion was to be social and above all brief. I immediately resolved to disregard these absurd limitations. One does not often find oneself in the presence of the most powerful leader in the West. To waste the time in pleasantries would be a total disregard of duty. So after Reagan had stepped forward from behind his desk, hand out-stretched in genial welcome, I began, to the horror of the various members of the White House staff present, to ply him with questions. What were the prospects for a Middle East settlement, how did he assess the Soviet threat, what had he thought of the Falklands Affair? The public affairs man had been right after all. There was no point in asking these questions. Either through unwillingness to answer, or because he had no answers to give, Reagan turned them all aside with bland insouciance. Feeling more and more as though I had stumbled into a dream sequence, or become immersed in some strange sub-aqueous world where the ordinary laws of nature did not apply, I heard myself asking, in tones of near-desperation, under what sign of the Zodiac the President had been born. Reagan perked up. "That's the damndest thing," he said, smiling his crooked smile, "no one's ever asked me that before. The answer is Sagittarius." "And what do Sagittarians do?" I said, not through any curiosity but because it seemed impossible, having started it, to abandon this supremely un-likely dialogue. The smile widened still further. For Reagan it was equivalent to being presented with a one-foot putt to win the match. Expertly, he stroked the ball into the cup, "I guess you could say they go around doing good to people."★

It is nearly irresistible, after a visit to the USA, even if only to Washington and New York, to write a 'mood' piece, summing up what Americans appear to be thinking. It is a somewhat superficial practice. What do they know of America who only Washington know?

On my first visit to Washington, in 1962, the Kennedy legend was

---

★ In answer to my question, he must have said the first thing to come into his head. Born on February 6, 1911, his sign is Aquarius, the water carrier.

already in the making. 'One year of the Kennedy era', I wrote, 'has left the American people almost extravagantly hopeful that the new young team in Washington can somehow find a peaceful way out of international dangers . . . these people have a nearly unshakeable faith in their own future, a determination to take time by the forelock.' But then we went on to the University of Michigan and later to the city of Dayton, Ohio, to find the same optimism and confidence prevailing there. The mood was apparently indivisible. At Dayton, we put up at a scruffy hotel only to be whisked away from there by the President of National Cash Registers, the city's biggest industry. Someone had written to him about us, and we soon found ourselves installed in the lavish company guest house, a large and splendid mock-Colonial mansion which once was the home of the Wright brothers of aeronautical fame. The resident English butler there made a reflective remark: "Of course I miss the old country sometimes, but if I hadn't come to America, I could never have put my sons through college, could I?" One was a professor in nuclear physics, the other had a good engineering job. At this time a University education was available to only five per cent of British youth compared with thirty per cent in the USA.

This sense of a thrusting, ambitious, 'possibilist' society, with its simple, sometimes over-simple, belief that where a problem exists there must also be a solution, never changed in essence over the years. It is an integral part of the American dream. But the 'mood', depending upon the particular interplay of events and personalities, often differed. Lyndon Johnson's Washington was very distinct from Kennedy's, just as Nixon's Presidency was different from Johnson's. The latter was an extraordinary man to talk to. A rough-and-bluff Texan, very conscious that he lacked the graces and polish that the patrician Kennedys had laid claim to, he was secretive, autocratic, disdainful of criticism, evoking a sort of personal awe; so much so that even his own entourage tended to refer to him, behind his back, as "the Boss" or "Mr Big" or even "Old Slyboots". My meeting with him, in a tiny office leading out of the Oval office, where three television screens, tuned to different networks, flickered incessantly, ran well over its appointed time. He would not stop talking. It was one of the many moments during the sixties when the pound sterling was under pressure. Johnson was out to show that when it came to being pro-British there was no one to beat him. Even if it was only an act, he gave it all he had. "We depend upon you, we look towards you, we see you as our mother. And if my mother were in trouble [a reference to sterling's difficulties] why, I'd twitch open the bed-clothes and be in there between the sheets beside her." This weird analogy seemed to call for Freudian analysis, but without pausing Johnson swept on, jabbing at the air with his big fingers, sipping occasionally at the non-alcoholic beer his doctors had prescribed, while through the open door in the corridor beyond, unseen by him, frantic members of the staff signalled mutely to me to help restore the Presidential timetable by bringing the proceedings to an end.

Nixon was a different animal altogether, although he too suffered from a sense of inferiority vis-à-vis the sophisticated East Coast establishment which used to dominate Washington. Scotty Reston, of the *New York Times*, seeking to sum up the difference between the two men, put it to me thus: "Agreed, Johnson was a phoney, but a *real* phoney, Nixon is only a phoney phoney." How my meeting with Nixon in 1970 came about was a fine example of the bread-upon-the-waters principle. Some years earlier, at a London party, I had been introduced to a young visiting professor from Harvard. He was intelligent, witty, knowledgeable, even though his heavy German guttural accent made him sometimes difficult to understand. I liked him and asked him to lunch a few days later. At the lunch table, we had an agreeable and protracted discussion about international affairs. His name, at that time virtually unknown, at least in London, was Henry Kissinger. We remained in contact. By 1969, he had become Nixon's National Security Adviser. I wrote to him before going to Washington the following year, making an appointment to see him in his White House office. As we sat talking there, he kept glancing at his watch. I thought he was trying to get rid of me, but he explained that he was monitoring the time with a view to taking me "upstairs". This meant the Oval office, where a shy, unsmiling, swarthy President was waiting behind his desk to receive this foreign intruder. Like Reagan years later, he did not expect the meeting to be anything but brief and formal. But under pressure of my questioning and with promptings from Henry, he mellowed and began to talk, in a well-informed way, about international problems. At the end of a good half-hour, he brought the conversation to a close and walked with me to the door. As he did so, he asked, thoroughly relaxed by now, "What do you think I should do about bussing [the conveyance of children from one area to a school in another in order to create racially integrated classes]?" It was a burning issue in the USA at the time, but I did not feel in any way equipped to advise the President of the United States what to do about it, and respectfully told him so. We parted cheerfully and, as Henry and I walked through the White House passages back to his office, I thanked him profusely for the unexpected favour he had done me. "One good turn deserves another," he said; "I shall never forget what you did for me [i.e. one lunch] in London."

It was after this that I wrote a long article suggesting that, despite his unattractive ways and discreditable past, Nixon might one day deserve the world's gratitude for having abandoned the histrionics of the Johnson era and the high moral fervour of the Kennedy epoch, opting instead for a more limited and realistic American role upon the world's stage. The Watergate affair, and Nixon's part in it, makes this prophecy seem odd today. But despite the shame and shock of Watergate, I would still argue in favour of the original thesis. "We shall pay any price, bear any burden, meet any hardship . . . to assure the survival and success of liberty," proclaimed Kennedy. Such extravagant boasting, such a signature to a blank cheque, is no part of statesmanship. It induces a false sense of omnipotence on one side and raises false hopes on the other. Nixon's foreign policy, on the other hand, fashioned against the background of growing disenchantment with the Vietnam war, was based on the premise that the USA was *not* ready to pay any price and accept any burden. Admittedly, a US President cannot hope to please everyone. If he pitches the moral tone too high, he is criticised for lack of realism; if too low, for failing to provide the moral leadership which many Americans and many of America's allies consider should be constantly on tap in Washington. In my view, Nixon – or perhaps we should say Kissinger, for he was the principal formulator of these more modest policies – came much nearer to serving the true interests of his country and its allies than did the starry-eyed ardour of Kennedy or, in more recent times, the crusading rhetoric of Ronald Reagan. Henry Kissinger can be reproached for many things, intellectual arrogance and a crudely naked love of power among them. But there have been few if any men in recent American history who so effectively combined intelligence with action, theory with practice. Priding himself upon his pragmatic realism, he did generally manage to avoid the crude division, beloved by so many Americans, of countries and regimes into friends and enemies, goodies and baddies. At the more intimate level, his capacity to mock himself, added to his sophisticated internationalism, made him a consistently stimulating companion.*

* He was also the willing embodiment of the sexual lure of power. One day in New York, Kitty and I were invited by a friend to a cocktail party in her apartment. I asked if I could bring Henry. He was recognised the minute he entered the room and every woman under forty, and a good many over, pushed and shoved to get near and talk.

One visit, in the mid-seventies, took me right across the country on a lecture tour. A route from the East Coast to the deep South and the charms of New Orleans and thence to northern and southern California provided a constant reminder of how well-informed and interested in the outside world intelligent Americans can be. The audiences were mostly made up of academics, professional people, foreign affairs specialists. They evinced what appeared to be a touching interest in British affairs, wanting to know whether the country under its Labour Government was about to submerge beneath its weight of troubles: an outcome which they had apparently been led to expect by their earnest perusal of *The Economist*. I did what I could to reassure them. In the process, the nature of their apprehensions became clear. They were moved not by sentimentality or devotion to the British way of life in general but by the fear that if things went seriously wrong in Britain, the effect would rub off on the USA. While Britain may lag far behind the USA in technology or market techniques or the gadgetry of modern living, she remains, in many American eyes, the fountain-head of parliamentary democracy and political stability. If anything should happen to poison such a source, Americans would feel (or rather, Americans think that America would feel) far more direct and un-favourable effects than could come from some institutional upset in Paris, or Rome, or Bonn. This is the true and significant meaning of the 'special relationship' which so many pundits, on both sides of the Atlantic, have tried to kill off. (It was during this lecture tour that Mrs Thatcher was making her bid for the leadership of the Conservative Party. I was repeatedly asked whether it was likely that a woman could attain such a position, leading one day to the occupancy of No. 10 Downing Street. Without hesitation and with total conviction, I told audiences to dismiss such an idea from their minds. This was what I honestly thought at the time, and I was far from being alone. It is noticeable that I have not been asked back to lecture in the USA.)

Jimmy Carter from Georgia I never met personally, but the White House and Washington in his time exuded, as they usually do, the essence of the man at the top. Pomp and ceremony, the hallmarks of the 'imperial Presidency', were out, homespun qualities and Presidential prayer meetings were in. Jody Powell, the Press Secretary at the White House, displayed on his desk a sign which read "Draw nigh unto me and I will draw nigh unto you". Sometimes the Carter style proved too much for some to swallow. A normally well-balanced and reasonable Republican Senator, Mac Mathias, from Maryland, told me of an occasion when he and some of his Senate colleagues had been summoned to the White House for a briefing by Carter. He had been deeply shocked on arrival to find Coca-Cola being handed round *in cans*. Glasses or goblets would have been acceptable, but cans, in the opinion of my friend, lowered Presidential dignity to an unacceptable level. By contrast, the atmosphere of Reagan's White House was quieter, less tense and earnest. There was no more running in the corridors, and Reagan himself, even if his grasp of detail was so alarmingly uncertain, was infinitely more relaxed and comfortable with his job than his far abler predecessor.

Partly because most of these visits were to cities – Detroit, New York, Washington, Atlanta, Los Angeles – they failed to evoke the *genius loci* which everywhere is the greatest reward for the traveller. American cities are mostly soulless places. Even that is a questionable generalisation. New York has an ambience indefinably peculiar to itself, in which a sense of adventure and never-sleeping-ness is tempered by the sight of the East River glinting peacefully in the sunlight or by the unexpected, almost rural, tranquillity of Gracie Mansion, where the Mayor lives. San Francisco also can be a city of jewelled light, its steep inclines and hilltops contributing an almost Umbrian dimension to this twentieth-century, sea-girt, urban landscape. And Washington, provided it is not steaming with sticky summer heat or grey with fog and overcast, can be inspiring. One fine summer morning in the late sixties I went in search of the last resting place of the Kennedy legend. It can be found in Arlington Cemetery, just across the Potomac River in Virginia. There, side by side, are the graves of the two murdered brothers, Jack and Robert. The approach to the President's grave is flanked with granite slabs on which are inscribed some of the heady sentiments his speech-writers liked to put into his mouth. From the level of the graves, you look back across the river to the central buildings of the city, dominated by the great dome of the Capitol. In the bright sunshine of that morning they were sparkling white, their outlines slightly blurred in the heat haze that was beginning to form. It was a noble sight, recalling Prospero's cloud-capped towers and gorgeous palaces. But though the Kennedy legend had faded like an insubstantial pageant, here was no baseless fabric. On the contrary, the federal buildings of Washington are a living reaffirmation of the faith of the Founding Fathers: simple, dignified and possessed of an undeniable beauty.

Moscow is a different proposition altogether. The only previous time

I had been there was in 1946, when the Evgeni affair (see p. 48), occurred. Then it was a grim and forbidding place, ruled over by the grim and forbidding person of Stalin. The change, when I made my first journalistic visit in the early sixties, was amazing. Earlier, in the grey aftermath of war, the Kremlin was a nearly impenetrable fortress. Now it was the main attraction for innumerable groups of Soviet tourists come to look at the seat of their government. On a sunny Sunday morning, with the charabancs ranged in rows in Red Square, their passengers traipsing happily round the cathedrals and palaces of the Kremlin itself, the scene could have been Versailles or Windsor. Apart from this, Moscow as a city has its own peculiar charms. On a snowy winter's day, with the sunshine making the gilded onions of the Kremlin churches sparkle, or in early summer, when the pollen of the poplar trees covers the pavements and streets with a gossamer deposit that itself resembles snow (the Muscovites complain it gets up their noses), it has an atmosphere as distinctive as any European capital. But for a non-Russian-speaking visiting journalist, it is a famously difficult place to make inquiries. The most that can normally be hoped for in the way of contacts – and they usually only yield a stream of propaganda or special pleading – is a member of the Pravda or Izvestia editorial board or a middle-rank official in the Foreign Ministry. In the Khruschev era, there could sometimes be a special but unheralded bonus when that unpredictable man, attending some diplomatic function, would suddenly begin to sound off in the corner of the room, whither all the journalists present, and most of the guests, would soon gravitate, creating the effect of a mass meeting or the impromptu congregation of an itinerant preacher.

Otherwise you are dependent for information – or more likely informed speculation – upon the foreign embassies, some of whom are as knowledgeable as it is possible to be. In the years of my visits, there were a Yugoslav and a Canadian Ambassador who had been there for a long time and who knew a great deal more about the Kremlin and its personalities than most Soviet citizens. There was also Tom Brimelow,* the No. 2 at the British Embassy, a brilliant linguist and student of things Russian. For all his expertise a modest man, he liked to tell a story which could serve as a warning to all would-be Kremlino-logists. It concerned the early autumn of 1964, when there was no sound reason to believe that any question-mark hung over the future of

* Later Permanent Under-Secretary at the Foreign Office and Lord Brimelow

14 Mexico 1979: the self-exiled Shah of Iran at Cuernavaca

15 China 1972: Roy Thomson's party at the Great Wall: from the left: Ken Thomson, Denis Hamilton, Roy Thomson, F.G. on right in safari tunic

Khruschev, then First Secretary of the Party. Brimelow's opposite number in the Canadian Embassy telephoned to suggest a talk. The day being fine, he walked round to the British Embassy. On the way he saw – or thought he saw – a strange sight. It was that of Khruschev being driven in a Volga car towards the Kremlin. The Canadian mentioned his vision to Brimelow. The latter was inclined to disbelieve it. Its details conflicted with all the known evidence. Khruschev was not in Moscow at all, he was travelling in the Virgin Lands in the south. Moreover, it was unthinkable he could be in a Volga, a distinctly down-market product of the Soviet motor industry, almost a people's car, if only output and price were able to satisfy demand. Soviet leaders, like Chicago gangsters in the thirties, habitually move about in large black limousines, called Zils. In fact, it was Khruschev, already, as his humble conveyance suggested, in deep trouble. He was being driven to the meeting with his Kremlin colleagues which ended for him in disaster and disgrace. The moral of the story is that when a report or rumour conflicts with everything that is thought to be known about someone or something in the Soviet Union, that is the time to be on guard, to entertain every possibility, however remote or improbable.

The best method for a visiting journalist is to travel in the wake of a Very Important Person. In that way the Russians, whose system is geared to deal with groups, not individuals, consider you as an honorary member of the delegation (a key word in the vocabulary of official Soviet hospitality) and you can get into places and near to people with an ease that normally would be unthinkable. Three times I went to Moscow on such a footing: firstly with Harold Wilson's team in 1963, when he was leader of the Labour Opposition, secondly with Wilson again in 1966, when he was Prime Minister, and thirdly with David Owen in 1977, when he was Foreign Secretary. We journalists were allowed to follow Wilson and, later, Owen into the Kremlin, into the gilded splendours of St George's Hall, where official receptions are held, into the conference room where visiting grandees meet the Soviet leaders. These brief glimpses of the seat and personalities of super-power (we were unceremoniously bundled out once the serious talking began) were strangely unimpressive. Somehow the sight of Brezhnev, pudgy and bemedalled, or Kosygin, looking as though he had recently risen from the dead, or Gromyko, coldly impassive as ever, failed to evoke – in me at least – either awe or repulsion. They were men doing their job according to their lights and their creed. There was no reason to doubt Brezhnev's constant emphasis, in the public part of the ceremony, on *détente* and the unthinkability of another world war.

But as the splendid Russian vowel sounds rolled out (and were translated into the less evocative effects of Slav-accented English) so there was time to recall that the ornate interiors of the Kremlin had been the background for other tyrants, other tyrannies. Every student of the Soviet Union should read the Marquis de Custine's remarkable work *La Russie en 1839,*★ for as Mr George Kennan has pointed out, 'even if we admit that *La Russie en 1839* is not a very good book about Russia in 1839, we are confronted with the disturbing fact that it is an excellent book, probably in fact, the best of books, about the Russia of Joseph Stalin, and not a bad book about the Russia of Brezhnev and Kosygin.' This intelligent and observant Frenchman noted (as any objective visitor would be bound to note today) the exercise of sovereignty through fear, the widespread activities of the secret police, the operation of the bureaucracy, the secrecy and the deceit. Government in Russia, he observed, was 'the discipline of the camp substituted for the civic order; it is a state of siege made into the normal state of society.' Custine's words came back to me again in the course of a conversation in 1977 with Roy Medvedev, a distinguished Marxist historian who, while continuing to live, more or less unmolested, in Moscow, is an outspoken opponent of Soviet repression and a firm believer in free speech. "There has never been in our country a tradition for democracy or for freedom of speech or of the Press. The great mass of workers and peasants don't think of such things. It is left to the intelligentsia to feel and express discontent . . ."

Custine, in addition to his unfavourable view of the Tsarist system, found the Russian people 'naturally engaging', with many admirable qualities. That is the experience of most travellers. The chief, often insurmountable, difficulty is to climb over the barriers of language and suspicion and get invited into a Russian home. Once a friend took me to Peredelkino, the writers' colony in the countryside not far from Moscow, to have lunch in a dacha allotted to a celebrated author of children's stories. It was one of the happiest days imaginable. As well as the host and hostess, there were three very old black-clad ladies, aunts or perhaps cousins or even family hangers-on. Straight from the pages of a Chekhov play, they said almost nothing but looked continuously and humbly grateful. Despite, or perhaps because of, their mutism,

---

★ Published in Paris, in four volumes, in 1843; abridged and translated into English in one volume *Journey for our Time* (Arthur Barker, 1953)

they made a hearty meal of the good things set before us: huge quantities of blinis (thin pancakes), accompanied by baked salt fish, melted butter and sour cream, were followed by roast lamb cooked in herbs, after which came little sweet cakes and coffee. Vodka and fruit juice helped to wash down this feast. We talked, in French, about almost everything save politics. It was a day of classic Russian winter beauty, very cold and still, the pine woods suffused in pale but continuous sunlight, the trees casting long shadows on the virgin snow. Whatever the political convictions of our host, the Kenneth Grahame, as it were, of the Soviet world, he readily accompanied us when I said I would like to visit Pasternak's grave nearby. A Christianised Jew, the poet lies beneath three pines in the neighbouring churchyard. On a white headstone are sculptured his own features. The grave looks back across the valley at the substantial dacha where he had lived. In the dying light of that February afternoon, three fresh wreaths of chrysan-themums, laid upon the snow which covered the grave, stood out sharply. The sight was a striking expression not only of the esteem in which the officially disgraced Pasternak is held, but of the general regard which Russians have for great literature and those who help to create it.

As this book is concerned with reminiscence and not with punditry, it would be inappropriate to indulge in windy generalisation about the future of the Soviet Union and its relations with the rest of the world. Between the cold-warrior, Manichean view of Soviet acts and intentions and the naive adulation of the fellow traveller, there must be a middle way of looking at this huge and enigmatic country and trying to understand its peoples' hopes and fears. My experience has been that Soviet officials, while vigorously peddling their own line, do not mind if the capitalist hyena from the West disputes their arguments. Indeed, they tend to respect you the more for it. But that is not really the task of a journalist, however easily in Moscow he may find himself assuming it. His job, whatever the obstacles facing him, is to report as faithfully as he can what he sees and hears, trying always to explain the setting and conditions within which the situation lies. There have been some distinguished examples – British, French, American – of this sort of specialised journalism emanating from Moscow in the post-war years. Most, perhaps all, of these able men would, I think, admit to and welcome the special challenge and fascination which the Soviet Union presents to the journalist. Amidst all the suspicion and secrecy, it is a high responsibility to seek honestly to interpret the ethos of a country and regime which, however much some people wish it were otherwise, is not going to go away.

The same sense of challenge faces any one who concerns himself with Middle Eastern affairs. I paid my first visits to Arab countries and to Israel in the winter of 1963, and immediately fell under the varying spell of this enormous area and its intractable problems. Encountering in Damascus a Foreign Office friend who I knew had been for some years in New York but who had previously been a Middle East *habitué*, I asked him what brought him back there. He looked moodily out of the Embassy windows at the tawny rugged hillsides that surround the city, and replied, "I don't know really – when the chance came, I just couldn't resist getting back to the old dust-heap." As time went on, I understood his remark better and better. The combination of wide open spaces, ancient cities, iridescent light, talkative and hospitable people and the consciousness of the weight of history and pre-history can be overwhelmingly compelling. There were also startling contrasts. Some years later, I made an extensive tour of the Persian (Arabs, please read Arabian) Gulf. After meeting most of the rulers of the Emirates, drinking innumerable little cups of cardamom-flavoured coffee, talking far into the sticky nights with men (never women) of many persuasions, I acquired a general grasp of the situation, but lacked the vital bit of scene-setting which, at the beginning of a long article, is designed to capture the readers' interest. Quite unexpectedly, it came to hand. It was on a sultry morning at Bahrain airport. The sky was its usual shade of azure blue, disturbed only by the condensation trails of RAF Hunter jets as they dipped and wheeled in the still air. I took my seat in a Trident commercial airliner, bound for Qatar and Sharjah. With nose buried in a two-day-old London paper, I heard and felt the neighbouring seat being occupied by another passenger. Then, on lowering the newspaper, I got a sensational reminder that in the Gulf, as in much of the Middle East, the twelfth and twentieth centuries coexist. My fellow passenger was a patriarchal, bearded figure in flowing robes who supported, on his wrist, a large falcon. Its hooded eyes were within a foot of mine. The bird and its owner (or perhaps groom) were en route for a hawking engagement somewhere in the desert which lay to the east.

The high point of the 1963 tour came in Cairo. President Nasser agreed to see me at his modest bungalow at Heliopolis, a meeting which lasted for several hours, so incapable was he of bringing it to a close. This was a time when Nasser saw himself as the self-nominated leader of a new Arab revolution. He had good reason to do so. From millions of radios all over the area, his brand of anti-Western, anti-Israeli propaganda poured forth hour after hour. His picture adorned nearly every stall or shop in nearly every souk. On public platforms, his own oratorical flights of fancy and attempts at rabble-rousing knew no bounds. Yet to meet in private, he was a calm, rational person, with considerable charm of manner, fluent English, and an almost pathetic desire to be liked. Why, he wanted to know, were the British so hostile to him? Why had Anthony Eden always insisted on calling him Colonel (instead of President) Nasser? Why did King Hussein of Jordan adopt such consistently anti-Egyptian attitudes? Why did the West, particularly Britain, consider it necessary to maintain bases and deploy military forces in order to 'protect' the sources of Middle East oil? "We Arabs can't drink the oil," he said. On Israel, he was philosophic. "The Frankish Kingdom [the Crusader conquests] only survived for a century or so. We can afford to wait until this new Western attempt at domination [i.e. the State of Israel] similarly withers away." It was his children's half-holiday from school, and as he talked on and on their little faces repeatedly appeared round the door, full of silent beseechings to come to lunch and play with them. The afternoon was far gone – I had been there since 11 a.m. – before he rose to say goodbye. The overall impression was of a man of many different moods and natures, thrust by fate into a position where he was no longer the master either of himself or of events. In the months and years to come, as the level of his personal vituperation against Britain and her presence in the Middle East rose ever higher, so the memory of that day at the bungalow remained vivid. Were his assurances of goodwill, of wishing to be friends with Britain, only meaningless examples of Arab rhetoric and soft soap? Or had these hours of self-justification contained a real plea for mutual understanding? The answer is probably yes to both questions. What remains certain is that in his heyday, especially after the Suez affair, Nasser had a fair claim to have been the first Arab since Salah-el-Din (Saladin) worsted the Crusaders to establish a real measure of popular leadership over much of the divided Arab world.

Two other episodes, both affording insights into the Arab mind, stand out from that trip. On November 22, in Kuwait, I learnt of Kennedy's murder. Flying on the next day to Baghdad, still feeling sad and shocked, I was met at the airport by an Iraqi official from the Ministry of Information. As we drove into the city, where the flags on public buildings and embassies were flying at half-mast, he remarked with a broad grin, "You see, we are not the only people to shoot our rulers." Whatever the bad taste, it was an obvious attempt to put previous gruesome Iraqi blood-lettings into perspective, to show that Arabs do not have a monopoly of violence and disorder. A few days later, in Damascus, there was an example, at once touching and comic, of wounded Arab pride, involving denial of physical facts. I had asked for an interview with the Syrian Minister of Guidance, whose office was in the broadcasting and television building on the outskirts of the city. Like most broadcasting headquarters in *coup-d'état*-prone countries, this was surrounded with tanks, their guns in the ready position. As the car made its way through their ranks, I asked the young official accompanying me, with intentional naivety, what they were there for. Staring straight down the barrel of a gun whose muzzle was about one foot from the car window, he replied crossly, "What tanks?"

A few months later, I was in Israel, the first of many visits. It was only sixteen years since the founding of the state. Yet here was a country which, at tremendous odds, had fought off its Arab enemies, established its identity, realised the ancient Jewish dream of 'tomorrow in Jerusalem'. Whether it was the last bulwark of the West (as the Arabs asserted) or the first outpost of the new East, it certainly seemed worthy of sympathy and admiration. In many respects it has remained so. But I found my own attitude – and there were many who felt the same way – evolving after the Six-Day War in 1967. Israel had not sought this war, her armies had fought it brilliantly. They were surely entitled to the fruits of their victory. But by this time I had become more fully acquainted with the murky history of the Middle East settlements after the Great War, particularly the muddled thinking of the Balfour Declaration of 1917: 'His Majesty's Government view with favour the establishment in Palestine of a National Home for the Jewish people, and will use their best endeavours to facilitate the achievement of this object, it being clearly understood that nothing shall be done which may prejudice the civil and religious rights of existing non-Jewish communities in Palestine . . .' It may have sounded all right on paper. But even in 1917 the claims and intentions of Zionism were, or should have been, plain to anyone with ears to hear. Whatever might be said for or against those claims, they could never be compatible with the Balfour principles. Admittedly, Balfour could not have foreseen the holocaust (the dire work not of the Arabs but of a traditional Christian European nation) which did so much to strengthen the case for a sovereign Israeli state. But the foundation of that state, when it came, could not avoid being prejudicial to Arab rights. That great Zionist Chaim Weizman, pleading the Jewish case in the 1930s, had put it with brutal clarity: 'The Palestinians cannot stay where they are, yet have nowhere to go.' Six days of war in the summer of 1967 completed the process. With Israeli occupation of the conquered territories, the attractive if naive idea of a Jewish National Home had burgeoned into something approaching the likeness of Biblical Israel. The sound of the guns had hardly subsided when I was writing, in the leader columns of *The Sunday Times*, that prospects for a genuine long-term settlement had not necessarily been brought nearer by Israel's blitzkrieg. 'Badly though they have put it over,' the article went on, 'the Arabs do have a case, which has gone largely unheard in this country and the US. No settlement is conceivable which overlooks that case.'

This was the line that the paper consistently adhered to: Israel's right to exist as a nation must be recognised but so must the grievances of the displaced Palestinians. The trouble, as successive visits to the area confirmed, was that such sweet reasoning had little or no chance of appealing to the parties on the ground. Nasser proclaimed his wish for peace, so did King Hussein, so did the Israelis. But they all meant peace on their terms. It became increasingly difficult for an outsider to identify the rights and wrongs, to preserve an impartial position in the middle of the road. (Abba Eban, one of the most brilliant and original of thinkers ever to hold office in an Israeli government, used to maintain that the middle of the road is where the worst accidents occur.) Each time after the 1967 war that I went to Israel I was struck not so much by the justice of her cause as by the impossibility of getting any conceivable Israeli government seriously to modify their support of that cause. It was all very well to talk about magnanimity in victory, about handing back the spoils of war. But after three victories against the Arabs (1948, 1956, 1967), the Israelis did not see why they should give way to the demands – unreasonable and dangerous demands, according to them – of the vanquished. In the admonitory way that it is all too easy for pundits to adopt, I wrote that it was time the statesmen of the world realised that, like it or not, Israel was never going to yield sovereignty over any part of Jerusalem and was not going to relinquish any other part of her 1967 gains until she could be sure of a settlement with the Arabs that gave her real security. In Jerusalem, these arguments seemed unanswerable. But in Cairo and Amman they were stood on their head. We cannot, said the Arab protagonists, give Israel the recognition she demands until she withdraws from the conquered Arab lands she is now occupying. The situation was comparable to that of two card-players, each highly suspicious of the other and fearful of leading their top card lest it should be trumped by the other side, whereupon they would have no winner left. Meanwhile in the Palestinian refugee camps in Jordan the winter rains turned the red soil into a sea of mud and bitter winds blew under the flaps of the overcrowded tents. Small children ran about pointing imaginary guns at one another. "What is their game?" I asked. "They are playing at killing Jews," came the answer.

It was about this time – the winter of 1968 – that I had my first interview with King Hussein, an experience which was to be repeated many times. The survivor of several attempts on his life, this brave and diminutive Hashemite descendant of the Prophet was a most attractive personality, with the disconcerting habit of addressing all Englishmen as "Sir". (It apparently came from his days as a Sandhurst cadet. According to the highest authority, he calls the Queen "Sir" when he visits her at Buckingham Palace.) An alarming crisis of identity was thus created.

Me (entering the room and bowing): "It is good of you to receive me, Sir."
The King: "Not at all, Sir, I'm very glad to see you."

But once this awkwardness was over, Hussein's words flowed easily and were always worth noting. He never, despite the strength of his views, became excited, his voice remaining low, almost hesitant. Despite the sad little smile which lit up his face from time to time, he often seemed almost overwhelmed with cares. After the Six-Day War, he pointed out to me that until then, Israel had commanded wide sympathy because of her position as the underdog, "the little man fighting for survival. Now Israel has become an overdog, if there is such a word, and in doing so has lost a great deal of the world's sympathy." It was a point that the Israelis themselves came to admit. Despite his difficulties with the Palestinian militants, who later were to threaten the unity and stability of his Kingdom, the King always made it clear that it was the Palestinian people who were the main sufferers in the Arab–Israeli dispute; satisfaction for their grievances must lie at the heart of any settlement. Hussein also continued, whenever I saw him, to hope (rather unrealistically, in my view, though his hopes were shared by other Arab leaders) that the United States, Israel's main supporter, would adopt a more balanced attitude, would in fact 'lean' on Israel.

Naturally, a very different piece of music was played by the Israelis, and none played it more stridently than that remarkable instrumentalist Mrs Golda Meir. Chain-smoking and in her American-accented English, gesticulating with her enormous hands as she talked, she swept all counter-arguments aside. For her, there was only one version of history and of events. One interview I had with her made history, when she denied that the Palestinians existed. "There was no such thing as Palestinians . . . it was not as though there was a Palestinian people in Palestine considering itself as a Palestinian people and we came and threw them out and took their country away from them. They did not exist." She was right, of course, within strict definitions. Palestine, as an independent sovereign state, has never existed. But it was a long and imprudent step from there to assert that there were no Palestinians. Mrs Meir was also eloquent on a favourite Israeli theme, summed up in the words 'making the desert bloom'. One of the first sights that had shocked her when she arrived in Israel in 1921, she said, was of an Arab ploughing with a very primitive plough. "Pulling the plough was an ox and a woman. Now if that means that we have destroyed this romantic picture by bringing in tractors and combines and threshing machines, this is true, we have." Years later, when exploring the desert country round Riyadh, the Saudi Arabian capital, I had cause to remember these words. It was my second visit. On the first, a characteristic sight had been of a Bedouin family on the move, the patriarch on his camel, preceded by a line of women carrying the impedimenta and a mingled procession of sheep and goats. Now this glimpse of the picturesque, so scorned by Mrs Meir, had been replaced by a line of red Chevrolet trucks roaring across the desert, leaving behind them a cloud of dust. Making the desert bloom, if that is the appropriate description, is not an activity confined to the Israelis.

But it would be giving entirely the wrong impression to suggest that the people of Israel have been universally and consistently unrelenting. One of the many pleasures of visiting Israel is to find a wide and frequently expressed diversity of opinion. Soon after the 1967 war, an Israeli friend, contemplating the possible effects of a long-term Israeli occupation of Arab territories, said bitterly, "If we don't look out, we will become the Boers of the Middle East." The war after that, in 1973, when Egyptian and Syrian armies took Israel by surprise, was seen by many people, inside and outside Israel, as a case of Arab aggression. Nonetheless a left-wing Israeli paper came up with the following perceptive explanation: 'Despite the sins of Arab nationalism, much of the responsibility for the latest hostilities rests on the Israeli Government which seeks to annex territories and since the six-day war has opposed peace initiatives.' The following year, after another long tour of the area, I came to the conclusion that the outcome of the 1973 war had created, in the minds of each side, a mirror image: the Arabs, principally the Egyptians and Syrians, had convinced themselves that they had won a great victory, the Israelis that they had suffered a defeat. It was true that Israel had been caught napping, that in the early stages the Egyptians and Syrians had enjoyed considerable military successes. But it was also true that once they had pulled themselves together Israeli armies triumphantly drove the Syrians back to Damascus, and pushed their way across the Suez canal. This was conveniently forgotten by the Arabs. In the bars and coffee shops all the way from Cairo to the Gulf, the same remark could be heard again and again: 'the myth of Israeli invincibility has been broken . . . things can never be the same again.' It was all a striking example of how, in politics (and often in love) what counts is not the truth, even when that can be easily established, but what people want to believe.

As time went on, it became increasingly difficult for the persevering journalist to discover what 'the Palestinians' were saying and thinking at any given moment. I never succeeded in meeting Arafat, the leader of the Palestinian Liberation Organization, though it was not for the want of trying. Wherever one might seek him, he had always just left for somewhere else. As for the movement itself, it was perpetually divided into different and often opposing factions, whose leaders were usually holed up in small, dark, well-guarded rooms in the back streets of Beirut and Damascus. Whatever tendency they represented, they never ceased to be evasive when it came to the crucial question of recognising Israeli existence. Partly, no doubt, this was tactical, but also the fear of assassination was never far absent. Those poky meeting places had reason to be well-guarded. Constant exposure to this kind of equivocation can drive the non-Arab visitor nearly to distraction. Once in the seventies, forsaking the role of travelling foreign editor, I attended a seminar in the Lebanon, when representatives of the news-broadcasting and television media from the Western and Arab worlds spent several days discussing the communications gap between those worlds. Never was there such an out-pouring of self-pity and hyperbole from the Arab side. "The general picture of the Middle East", said one Arab editor, "is that it is a backward and a problem area." On my copy of his paper, I scribbled "Isn't it?" But such irritation, though understandable, should be no part of the journalist's equipment. Throughout these years of observing the Arab–Israeli dispute, I tried always to remember that the Palestinian cause was worthy of the understanding it seldom received, even if its proponents, by their words and actions, were so adept at shooting into their own goal. The British part in helping to create the mess, by promising different things to different people, should never be forgotten.

These travels could impose considerable physical strain. There was, during the long years before the Israeli–Egyptian settlement, no direct air route, for example, between Cairo and Tel Aviv. It was necessary to fly from one or the other city to Cyprus or Athens or even Istanbul, change airlines, and set out again. The journey would take all day and part of the night. Arab frontier formalities sometimes recalled the theatre of the absurd. Once, driving from Beirut to Damascus, I was turned back at the Syrian customs barrier because in my passport was the name of my eldest child. Sarah, decided the humourless sergeant, was a Jewish name. He was of course right, but arguments that Christian gentiles also gave it to their children were unavailing. There was nothing for it but to return to Beirut and get a temporary passport from the British Consulate, without the offending entry. To compensate for these and other ennuis, there was the joy of sights and places. The old city of Jerusalem, its honey-coloured stone eating up, as it were, the yellow light, remains for me the most desirable town in the world, just as the Dome of the Rock⋆ is the world's most beautiful building. Cairo, its overladen buses clanking across the Nile bridges to add to the vast traffic jams of ancient vehicles that block the city at morning and evening rush hours, has all the mysterious charm of total chaos. With its universities, its centres for Islamic studies, the intelligence of its educated classes, it is, and must always be, the true centre of the Arab world. Damascus, with its miles of souks and the huge Ommayed mosque, one of the noblest creations of all Islam, is somewhere to linger and stare. Travelling around the Gulf by air lends a new dimension to that normally boring form of transport. From your window seat you look down upon the translucent greens and blues of the shallow sea, upon the vast desert wastes of the mainland, dun and dull and uninhabited, until suddenly the capital – Doha, Dubai, Abu

---

⋆ Wrongly called the Mosque of Omar, this octagonal-based masterpiece was built between 687–691 by the Ommayed Caliph Abd el-Malik. In spite of many restorations, it still preserves its original majestic and harmonious design.

Dhabi – comes into view, a sprawling incongruous mixture of ancient and modern, where breathtakingly expensive hotels await your custom and where you wait, possibly for days, to be received by the Ruler or his advisers.

From the mid-sixties onwards, these Middle Eastern travels were extended to include a still older civilisation. The Shah's Iran was generally regarded at that time as (in Jimmy Carter's words some years later) an island of stability in one of the more troubled areas in the world. It was an autocracy, in which the word of the Emperor was absolute. Not surprisingly, the Shah himself, whom I interviewed for the first time in 1966, saw nothing wrong with this, indeed just the reverse. "Revolutionary socialism", he said (he was referring to Nasser's philosophy), "means, if it means anything at all, corruption and misery and concentration camps." Instead, he was creating "social justice". Greatly daring, I asked him why he had to flaunt the trappings of his imperial status so insistently. The newspapers carried daily accounts, expressed in the most sycophantic terms, of his doings and sayings. An English friend of mine, who had also been granted an audience, noticed on his way to the imperial presence a line of court officials in a corridor, being taught how to make a profound bow. In such a system, how is anyone ever going to tell the King what he does not want to hear? The Shah did not appear at all put out by the question. Westerners could not, he explained, be expected to understand the oriental mentality. In a country like Iran, the outward signs of monarchy were an appeal to the mind and the imagination. "The word of the King is all-important, the pomp is for the people to see and enjoy." It was not a bad answer, given the circumstances. Then this strange, shy, insecure man had to spoil it with a remark of utter bathos: "Anyway [the tone was defiant] even the Americans have a Dairy Queen."

Some of his claims – that under his rule, the battle against hunger and disease and illiteracy was gradually being won – were well founded. His motives and his methods as a social reformer were highly creditable, as I saw for myself in different parts of the country. His views about the Middle East, especially Israel's right to exist, were refreshingly realistic after all the bombast and striking of attitudes to be found in Arab capitals. But with the blessed gift of hindsight, it is now clear that the Shah's increasing tendency towards megalomania should have rung some alarm bells. When I saw him again in Teheran in 1974, he was talking in terms of Iran becoming the fifth most powerful nation in the world. He was also obsessed by what he saw as the permissiveness of

Western society and in particular by the iniquities of the Persian section of the overseas service of the BBC. I pointed out to him that his critics were claiming that the regime was becoming more repressive. He did not trouble to deny it, passing instead on to the offensive: "What do my critics know about this country, what have they done for this country?"

By 1978, with the economic boom slowing down, leaving a rising tide of unfulfilled expectations, Iran was faltering. Outbreaks of unrest and disorder were reported from many cities. Again I flew to Teheran and saw the Shah (he always seemed to be accessible, even though his own subjects could wait for years, often for ever, to be received). He did his 'it-can't-happen-here' act – except that with him, it was no act. The rioters were "a handful of poor, ignorant people", the trouble was due to an unholy alliance between Muslim fanatics and the Communists. He was ready to admit that for an absolute monarch to loosen the screws, as he had recently done by introducing a (relatively) liberal political programme, was to take a considerable risk. But as always, he was resentful of criticism, quick to point to real or imagined shortcomings on the part of the critics. On the question of human rights in Iran, "We have no lessons to learn from anybody."

It was impossible, after that, to doubt that the regime, for all the Shah's posturing, was in serious trouble. Just how serious was difficult to say. What few people, either inside or outside Iran, realised at the time was the degree to which the Shah's rule had managed over the years to alienate three large groups of Iranians: the students and the universities; the religious classes; and the bazaar. The first had been treated to the supposed advantages of Western-style education and technology, only to find that at the end of the process there were very few jobs available for Iranians. The second, the mullahs and their followers, were by definition the implacable enemies of the Shah's secular, modernising, Western-inspired ideas. The third, the bazaaris who provided the financial and commercial core of every Iranian city, and who might have been considered the natural allies of the Shah's monarchical system and its years of stability, found their power reduced and themselves humiliated by the introduction of modern, State-run credit organisations and price controls. These three groups, disparate though they might be in many ways, were broadly united in one respect: rightly or wrongly, they did not want Iran to be dragged, in the way the Shah was trying to do, into the twentieth century. In further-ance of their opposition to the Shah, they were ready to encompass his downfall.

Why did the Shah not sense this? "My advisers built a wall between myself and my people," he said in early 1979, shortly after leaving Teheran on the first stage of his exile. "I didn't realise what was happening. When I woke up, I had lost my people." This was a tragically belated recognition of the facts. I wish that, after that 1978 visit to Teheran, I had been able to forecast the future more precisely. Not that many people did much better in foretelling the collapse of the regime. But one prophecy I can claim to have got right. As the Iranian drama mounted towards its climax, I wrote, in the autumn of 1978, that Dr David Owen (then Foreign Secretary) was quite correct to say that it would not be in the interests of Britain or the West were the Shah to be toppled. 'If that embattled monarch succumbs to his enemies, it is more than likely that we shall quite quickly all be, literally, the poorer.'

The revolution that swept away the Shah was one of the most stupendous events of the twentieth century. Most revolutions are imposed by the top, or at least the middle, ranks of the society in which they occur. The Iranian upheaval of 1978/79 was, by contrast, a popular movement, revealing the sheer unbreakable power of the masses once they are aroused. The Shah himself, when I saw him for the last time in September 1979, readily recognised this: "I can recall nothing in the history of the world – not even the French Revolution – to compare with what happened," he said. This was in Mexico where, at the resort of Cuernavaca, about sixty miles from Mexico City, he had fetched up after extensive wanderings. Because of industrial troubles, *The Sunday Times* and *Times* had been out of circulation for nearly a year. With the promise of publication resuming in the autumn of 1979, Harold Evans asked me to try for an exclusive interview with the exiled ruler. One of the few people with knowledge of his exact whereabouts was Henry Kissinger, who had been instrumental in arranging for him to go to Mexico. From London, I telephoned Henry, who supplied a Cuernavaca number. When dialled, this brought the Shah himself directly on to the line. He agreed to see me. Two days later, I was sitting wishing I was not so jet-lagged, in the drawing-room of his luxurious Cuernavaca villa. In he came, informally dressed and accompanied by two Dobermann pinschers and a wolfhound the size of a small pony. The world, which included me, did not then know his secret: that he was, and had been for some time, suffering from cancer. He seemed calm and collected, even detached, as though he had not fully absorbed the impact of the tidal wave that had washed him up on this distant shore.

We will never know how far, in the closing months of his reign, his illness affected his judgement.

For three hours he talked, sipping coffee and stroking the great dogs at his feet. One of his main arguments was that he could have stopped the rot by using all-out force against the Iranian crowd. "But as a King and not a dictator [sic]," he had not thought it right to authorise massive repression, "though many people around me advised just this." He also maintained that had he not hearkened to advice to leave the country, the armed forces would have remained loyal. With bitterness in his voice, he recalled Carter's island-of-stability remarks. "Twelve months later . . ." the Shah's voice trailed away and he shrugged his shoulders and rolled his eyes upwards as a mark of incredulity that such bad faith could exist. He was just as harsh about the British, pulling a face when I mentioned the name of Anthony Parsons, the outstandingly talented British Ambassador in Teheran (though he too, by his own confession, failed to read the tea-leaves correctly), whom the Shah consulted frequently in the months before the end. But this rancour was a low-key affair. He only displayed some of the old fire once, when I asked him whether he knew, and if so did he approve, of the excesses committed by SAVAK (the Iranian intelligence service which was his special creation). "Tell me the name of one man who under my rule was murdered for alleged political offences." I began to interrupt, but he talked me down: "Terrorists are different, they must be dealt with firmly." The talk came to an end, and I made my way back to Mexico City, New York and London. It had been a remarkable experience, akin to interviewing King Lear or the deposed Richard II (though the Shah had stopped well short of the words put by Shakespeare into the latter's mouth: 'tell thou the lamentable tale of me'). According to his own lights he had, it can be argued, tried to do the best by his country. But he was ill-equipped, intellectually and emotionally, to meet the great challenge when it came. His corrupt and deplorable family, which he seemed incapable of controlling, gave his enemies a powerful weapon to use at the appropriate moment against him. Above all, he had no one round him really to play the part of candid friend. Despite his vast power, he was essentially a weak man, more interested in justifying his actions than in considering their wisdom.

For better or for worse, there are not many Emperors left in the world. My only other experience with one goes back to the early sixties, when in the course of a long African journey we spent a few days in Addis Ababa. The episode is a painful reminder of the dilemma which often faces a journalist: how much of what he learns at the social, intimate level can be regarded as legitimate grist to the mill? In the course of our African travels – Kitty was with me – we received a message from John Russell,* then Ambassador in Ethiopia, suggesting we spend a few days with him on our way back to London. It was an attractive invitation. On arrival, I told John that, with notebooks bursting with material about South Africa, Northern and Southern Rhodesia (as they were then) and Kenya, I did not want to report on yet another African country; I would sit in the Embassy garden and work up my notes; I would not write about Ethiopia. John was not only hospitable but also ambitious and a considerable showman. He was not going to let slip the opportunity afforded by having a reasonably well-known London journalist under his roof. He and his wife gave large lunch and dinner parties for us, at which a lot of local talk got talked. He organised a splendid mounted picnic of Raj-like proportions in the hills to the north of Addis: a spacious open tent, a long table laid for luncheon, a bar and buffet weighed down with food and drink, a quantity of servants with fly whisks and other comforts, grooms and ponies waiting in the rarefied mountain air for the descent back to the city. John liked to uphold and prolong the claim of a former British Ambassador that Addis was the last outpost where an English country gentleman could live as he was accustomed to do. He took me to see ministers. He talked a great deal and knowledgeably about Ethiopia: about the sheer inefficiency of the Emperor's government, about how all effective power lay in the hands of that melancholy but astute sovereign, about the dead weight of the triumphantly unreformed Coptic Church, about the double standards which enabled the Emperor, as would-be leader and representative of new nationalist Africa, to speak out against the continued existence of the Portuguese colonial regime in Angola and Mozambique, while in private assuring the Portuguese Ambassador that there was no need to take these words too much to heart. Above all, John Russell took me to see the Emperor.

Scanning the bookshelves in the Palace ante-chamber while awaiting audience, I found a small Victorian volume called *Rambles in Bath*, evidently a relic of the Emperor's exile in that city. But there was, not surprisingly, no sign of the most descriptive modern work of all on Ethiopia, Evelyn Waugh's *Black Mischief*. I was just thinking that much of the hilarious picture it had painted of the country thirty years

* See footnote p. 101

earlier evidently still held substantially true, when a chamberlain opened the doors of the Throne room and the Minister of Court made a beckoning gesture. I walked through to bow to the diminutive figure of the Lion of Judah, Haile Selassie the First, who began effectively to rule Ethiopia in 1916. The ensuing conversation, which went forward in French, his preferred foreign language, was memorably unmemorable. The little man, in sharp contrast with the Shah, was fearful of committing himself to any ideas at all. There were a good many grave, sweet, smiles, some hazy generalisations about the nature of African nationalism, a reference or two to his time in England. Then, after further bows and expressions of respect, we were being shown out and escorted through the ante-rooms, down the staircase and so to the entrance to the Palace, flanked on either side by two rather mangy chained lions.

Back in London, reliving these few days in Addis, I came to the conclusion that it would be a pity not to record some of the things seen and heard. Taking care not to reveal any sources or name any names, I gave in *The Sunday Times* what I felt to be a lively and accurate sketch, based upon what John and his friends had said, of modern Ethiopia. It contained a graphic description of the mounted picnic, including the interesting information that in Ethiopia you mount your horse on the off side. It was published with the headline 'Haile Selassie has the best of both worlds'. Ten days later came a letter from John, marked Personal and Confidential. Metaphorically speaking, it was smouldering even before being withdrawn from the envelope. Metaphorically speaking, it burst into flames on being exposed to the air. He accused me of bad faith, of going back on my word, of repeating things I had learnt in the privacy of his house, of ruining his career, of ruining Anglo–Ethiopian relations . . . Only the detail about mounting a horse seems not to have given offence. There never was such a letter. And the trouble was that some of his charges went home. I had succumbed to temptation and written after saying I would not write. Sick at heart, I went to see a senior man in the Foreign Office to find out whether the damage was as terrible as John had described. He was consoling. The affair would blow over, he said. John was given to exaggeration, especially when his own interests might be involved. The best course was to reply to him, adopting a low profile, and then wait for the wind to disperse the smoke. A letter of apologies was on its way to Addis that very evening. My friend was proved right. After a long period of refusing to have anything to do with me, John forgot and forgave, and we became friends once more. His reaction may have bordered on the hysterical, but I had not behaved well, and look back on the episode, even today, with no satisfaction.

Apart from the issue of the broken word, there was the fact of having given public notice to things heard in private. There is an argument that everything said in front of a journalist, unless the speaker explicitly asks for confidentiality, is for reporting. Any ensuing trouble is due to the indiscretion of the original source, who should have been more cautious and aware. But this harsh formula, if rigidly applied, would effectively rule out, or at least put an intolerable strain on, real friendships and shared intimacies. In such circumstances, the honourable method is to tell your informant that you are proposing to report what he said. If he objects to being quoted personally, his remark will have to be unattributed. If he objects to being quoted at all, you will have, if you set any value upon the friendship, to give way. That at least is one possible set of rules. Not everyone would agree. Certainly old Blowitz would not. 'A journalist is, first of all, the servant of his paper and the public . . . he ought to keep nothing hidden from them . . . all he knows, all he learns, all he sees, all he hears and all that he feels belongs to his paper,' he wrote robustly. As for people who specified confidentiality, he would tell them he did not want to listen: 'I am a journalist, not a confessor.' This is certainly a vigorous and honourable code. But under its influence genuine friendship could flourish only with difficulty. Doubtless Blowitz would contend that your friends must take you as they find you.

But of all experiences, the one that exerts the strongest power of recall is a visit to China in 1972. Today, there is almost no limit, save that of the purse, to foreign travel there. Then, in the wake of the Cultural Revolution, which had virtually closed the doors to the outside world, it was only just beginning. Our party was led by Roy Thomson. One of his harmless snobberies was to 'collect' Heads of State or of Government. He had already been the guest of the ebullient Khruschev in the Soviet Union, and had been angling for some time for a similar invitation from Mao Tse-tung. At last it came. Roy, and the Chinese authorities, agreed that the group should contain two or three journalists, of which I was one. The old man had by this time only four years to live and was not in good health, walking with difficulty. In China, age is an object of respect and the Chinese, who on every possible occasion rolled out the red carpet for him, detailed a minute woman interpreter to follow him everywhere, carrying an ordinary kitchen chair, which she deftly slid under his enormous bottom whenever the tour of the collective farm or textile factory came to a temporary halt. Although often showing signs of fatigue, he responded bravely to all the challenges. When we besought him to take a day off and rest at the hotel, his invariable reply was that he was the guest of the Chinese Republic and was in honour bound to look at everything they wanted to show him and go wherever they wished to take him.

His treatment of his son Ken, who was of the party, displayed a less admirable spirit. At each stopping place where a Chinese reception committee was on hand, Roy would introduce the members of the group – "Denis Hamilton, he's my right-hand man, Frank Giles is one of our senior editorial staff" etc. But when it came to Ken, then aged forty-nine, mild, courteous, likeable, even if he lacked the strong personality of his father, he would say: "and this is my son Ken, who doesn't do anything." Either the reception committee was too polite to absorb the remark or, more likely, they did not understand it when translated. But we were left chagrined by this boorish behaviour, so out of keeping with Roy's usually jovial style.

The Chinese, though still wary, seemed genuinely pleased to see us. At the innumerable discussions in factories, newspaper offices, universities – semi-ritual occasions, the Chinese on one side of a long table, the visitors facing them on the other, a white-jacketed girl distributing covered tureens of green tea at regular intervals – there appeared to be a sense of real relief, as they answered our questions about the nature of the Chinese Communist system, at being able to talk about such matters with some measure of openness. There was of course a great deal of stock Marxist dialectics; no one, at that stage, was ready to denounce the excesses of the Cultural Revolution. But the desire to open the windows and let in some outside air was already plain to see. Anti-Soviet sentiments were universally and vehemently expressed. (Pausing in Hong Kong on the way home, I went to see an old French friend* who was French Consul-General there. He was a distinguished China expert and Sinologue. When I described what we had seen and heard, he gave it as his opinion that Chinese Communism was only skin-deep, that it was indeed something alien to the national temperament and tradition, and that it could not be long before they began divesting themselves of it. He did not live long enough to see his prophecies begin to come true.)

---

* François Geoffroi de Chaume, later killed in a car accident when French Ambassador to Burma

By far the most important and memorable of our conversations was with the Prime Minister, Chou En-lai, by whom we were summoned without warning on our last day in Peking (to his disappointment, Roy never got to see Mao). Chou was without exception the most suave and seductive of the world's statesmen that I have ever met. This is not surprising. His personality was well summed up by a reviewer* writing in the *Times Literary Supplement* in 1984: '. . . cosmopolitan sophistication, charm, wit and style. He certainly was one of the greatest and most successful actors of our century . . . no interlocutors ever appeared too small, too dim or too irrelevant not to warrant a special effort on his part to charm them and win their sympathy and support . . . being pragmatic with the pragmatists, philosophical with philosophers, and Kissingerian with Kissinger.' A survivor by nature and design, Chou was a convinced and committed Communist who nonetheless developed to the highest degree the art of dissembling. Though he had shared in all the hardship and struggles involved in establishing the Communists in power, it had never been possible to pin him down to a definite political line or to know where he stood on any particular issue. Loyal and patriotic, he had become, by the time we saw him, the effective – far more effective than the ailing Mao – wielder of power in a regime which, in Leys's words, 'managed to kill more innocent Chinese citizens in twenty-five years of peace than the combined forces of all the foreign imperialists in over one hundred years of endemic aggression.' Most recently, he had once again demonstrated his power to survive by outliving the Cultural Revolution, whose chaos and violence he must have abhorred. Now this remarkable man sat, in an over-stuffed armchair, deftly and wittily answering the questions of these barbarians from across the sea. Time appeared to be of no account. Like Stalin, he was said to work for most of the night. We saw him in the early evening and were with him for nearly three hours. Though everything was interpreted, there were various signs that Chou understood English; sometimes he would not wait for the end of the interpretation of a question before answering it, a slow and infectious smile often spreading across his dignified features as he talked.

Roy, in his bluff way, tried to persuade him of the virtues of the capitalist system. Credit, he explained, was the way to success for a nation as well as a company. Borrow to expand; use the bank's money whenever possible. An economy founded upon cash settlements could

---

* Simon Leys on Dick Wilson's life of Chou, *TLS*, October 26, 1984

never thrive. Behind his glasses with their pebble-thick lenses Roy's eyes were twinkling, but there was no doubt that he meant what he was saying. It was, for practical purposes, his own religion he was pro-pounding. When he, and the interpreter, had finished, Chou replied. With exquisite courtesy, his graceful hands constantly gesturing, from time to time selecting a fresh cigarette from the box beside him, which a girl attendant proceeded to light, he explained that while the system propounded by Roy might work very well in capitalist countries, it was not suitable for China in her state of development. "We do not want to finish up like India, paying out a great part of our annual income to meet the interest on the debts we have contracted." The only way forward was the hard way – working hard, encouraging self-reliance, never again becoming, as China had come near to doing with the Soviet Union, dependent on outside support. At one point, he asked whether the new *Times* correspondent was present. This was David Bonavia, whom we had brought with us from London and who was to be left behind to open the *Times* office in Peking. His previous post had been Moscow, where his brilliant coverage had got up the noses of the Soviet authorities. "I want Mr Bonavia to know," said Chou, "that he is especially welcome here. If ever he meets with any difficulties in his work, he should get in touch with me personally." Perhaps this was Chou pouring on the 'charm and wit', but even allowing for that, I was surprised, for a man of his professional resources, at Bonavia's lack of reaction. He should there and then have asked for Chou's private telephone number – though whether in the end the Prime Minister's open-ended invitation would have proved to be what it appeared to be, is open to question.

Our final port of call was Canton, where we were taken to one of the main hospitals to witness two surgical operations involving the use of acupuncture as an anaesthetic. It was an extraordinary performance, comparable to some bewildering feat of legerdemain. We were installed in the students' gallery of the theatre, looking down on the operating table below. The first operation was on a middle-aged man with gallstones. The acupuncture needles were inserted – two either side of the abdomen, two in the lower part of each leg, one up the nostril and one between the eyes, just above the bridge of the nose. The needles in the abdomen and legs were connected to a low-voltage current which caused the muscles to twitch convulsively. A short pause ensued and the surgeon went to work. The man showed no signs of discomfort or indeed of any discernible feelings whatever. Presently a stone about the size of a peachstone was extracted and sent up to the gallery for us to admire. Down below, the stitching-up process completed. The unbelievable was happening. The man swung his legs off the operating table, stood up unaided and strode out of the theatre, not forgetting a cheery wave to us in the gallery.

The second operation was a much bigger affair: a birth by Caesarian section. The young woman was helped on to the table, the needles inserted in the same way as with the man, a little screen placed on her chest so that she could not see what was going on. After a long and bloody business, during which the mother remained expressionless (and I had temporarily and urgently to leave the theatre) the child was delivered and handed over to the maternity team to be cleaned and swaddled. This time there was no question of the patient striding out. She would, the doctors told us, be bound to suffer post-operative pain and be given Western-style analgesics to relieve her. But what pain, if any, had she suffered already? Was it all a trick, a case of hypnosis, a gruesome piece of play-acting? The Chinese doctors were unable to give any clear explanation of how and why the use of the needles induced anaesthesia, though they claimed a ninety per cent success rate; the remaining ten per cent were given conventional anaesthetics, which every patient had the right to choose.

Later, in the waiting-room, the gallstones man turned up, as cheerful as ever. Had he felt any pain? No, nor anxiety, "because I knew the acupuncture would work." He was followed by the young mother, wheeled in on a mobile stretcher, clutching her child, as inscrutable as ever. But she was capable of expression, as we had seen earlier, in a glimpse which was by far the most memorable event of that extraordinary day. In the theatre, after she had been sewn up, a nurse brought the baby back and, drawing aside the swaddling clothes to reveal its sex, showed it to its mother behind her screen. From our vantage point above, we could see her features at last register an emotion. A long, slow, contented smile crossed her face as she contemplated her boy, China's nine hundred millionth citizen, give or take a few millions. It was a moment of rare and profound beauty and meaning.

In these years as foreign editor and later deputy-editor of *The Sunday Times*, there was another series of journeys which, while the reverse of intercontinental, involved a lot of moving about and a constant espousal of and enthusiasm for a particular cause. This was the adherence of Britain to the European Community. During the Paris period, I had witnessed with growing dismay the efforts of the then Conservative

Government to delay and disrupt the labours of the Six – France, Germany, Italy and the Benelux countries – to create economic and eventually political unity between themselves. My old *bête noire* David Eccles and the far easier-going Reggie Maudling would, as Ministers responsible, descend upon Paris from time to time and irritate everyone, above all the French, with their openly displayed spoiling tactics. British ideas about Britain's place in the world still rested upon the hazy and ill-thought-out concept of concentric circles – Britain-and-the-Commonwealth, Britain-and-the-Anglo-American-relationship, Britain-and-Europe. There was no place here for the kind of European commitment which, especially after the Suez débâcle, seemed to many thoughtful people to be the true way forward. (A lot of other people, on the other hand, saw it as the descent into a morass.) The result was that the Six went ahead and formed their Community (a word which in French signifies a promising association of like-minded people but in English has an alien sound, suggesting an ethnic minority or a dissident sect. Still less attractive are exhortations to be *communautaire*, or community-minded), Britain was left at the bus-stop, while the bus, with its passenger load of jubilant Europeans, engaged gear and moved off.

By the early sixties, however, the Macmillan Government had had a change of heart. The policy was now to seek British entry into the EEC, to catch the moving bus. But it was not going to be an easy task. Previous emphasis upon the inalienability of Commonwealth trading links was going to be difficult to explain away, both in Brussels, where the negotiations took place, and to British and Commonwealth opinion and Parliament. I went constantly to Brussels, to Paris, to Bonn to assess and report on the chances. I also went, one August evening in 1962, to an anti-Common Market meeting at Evesham, in Worcestershire. This luscious vale, with its orchards and market gardens, is one of the centres of British horticulture, and not even the most optimistic marketeer was ready to deny that horticulture was going to be hard-hit if tariffs against continental produce were to be removed. But contrary to expectation, the arguments at the Evesham meeting were not primarily economic. Tomatoes and asparagus hardly got a mention. The main speaker, a failed Tory parliamentary candidate of right-wing views, preferred to dwell on the sacred nature of the Commonwealth link and the iniquity of any Government which was ready to place British citizens under the jurisdiction of a lot of faceless men in Brussels. In some of the things said there was an undertone not only of anti-Semitism but of old-fashioned xenophobia. At one point there was a reference, much appreciated by the audience, to the Duke of Edinburgh as "this German-born prince".

These Little Englanders need not have been so fearful. In January 1963 in Paris General de Gaulle slammed the door in Britain's face. His action should have been easily predictable. Had he not, with considerable slyness, said in 1960, in his address in Westminster Hall to a joint session of Parliament, "everybody knows that England, in her capacity of a great State and as a nation faithful to herself, will never agree to dissolve herself in some Utopian construction"? Despite this, I had, during the previous autumn, been optimistic about Britain's chances. My growing admiration for Edward Heath, the chief negotiator in Brussels, led me to think that, with him in command, we were bound to succeed (an assessment which in the end proved correct). His skill, knowledge and commitment won general admiration from the other negotiators. A reference to the files shows that I also wrote about his 'amiability'. This may sound surprising. As he himself is the first to admit, communication is not his strong point. Irritable, intolerant, an administrator more than a politician, capable of stony silences or massively squelching rejoinders, Ted Heath is not everyone's idea of either a first-rank statesman or a jolly companion. For me, he became from these early Brussels days onwards a friend who was always worthy of respect as well as being good company. His influence caused me to vote Tory for the first time in 1970. I was present in 1971 at the famous press conference in the ballroom of the Elysée where eight years earlier de Gaulle had announced his veto against Britain. Heath, as Prime Minister, and Pompidou, as President, proclaimed the Anglo–French agreement which subsequently opened the European gate to Britain. "Sate ung mowmong istoreek," said Heath in his execrably accented French. But it was the spirit, not the accent, that counted, the realism and persistence that had carried him through to its final goal. Later on, when he had become Prime Minister, at one of his formal dinners at No. 10 (followed by a concert of Tudor choral music which induced in most of the guests present a combination of sleep and bewilderment) he was kind enough to recall my writings about Britain-in-Europe. Being complimented in public by a Prime Minister is heady stuff, not in general to be recommended for journalistic health. But on this occasion, the sentiments were genuine; fortunately or unfortunately for him, the arts of flattery are unknown to Ted.

Despite the setback of de Gaulle's veto, I continued to preach, in articles in the paper, the eventual inevitability of Britain's entry into Europe. In this, I was encouraged by Jean Monnet, whom I saw from time to time in Paris. By now well into his seventies, this small, dapper, untiring Frenchman, chief among the fathers of Community Europe, refused to be dismayed. Because certain conditions and circumstances existed yesterday and today, there was no reason, he would argue, to assume they would exist tomorrow. In this pragmatic and optimistic approach, he was in fact untypical of his race. He once accused me of being an honorary Frenchman, in the sense of wanting to see every step ahead and every consequence of every action worked out. In these sessions with him in his flat overlooking the Avenue Foch, it was impossible to rattle him or catch him off guard. His quiet, precise voice flowed on and on, expressing in varying forms and cadences his central belief that 'nothing is possible without men, nothing is lasting without institutions.'* Such optimism, even if it sometimes recalled Voltaire's Dr Pangloss, was welcome at such a time. Even if there had been no de Gaulle, the return to office in 1964 of Labour, under Harold Wilson, boded ill for the European cause. His neo-Kiplingesque ideas about Britain's role in the world were little if any improvement on those ridiculous concentric circles. Moreover his tactics in general – described by William Rees-Mogg in a splendid phrase as his being 'so busy juggling with the plates that he forgets to lay the table' – were not of a kind to inspire confidence in Paris or anywhere else.

After Labour's second electoral victory in 1966, however, and with George Brown's appointment to the Foreign Office, things began to look up. George could be a horror. I was present at the famous dinner at the French Embassy in London when, drunk and not in control of his tongue, he publicly humiliated Rachel Reilly, the unoffending wife of the British Ambassador to Paris. It was on that occasion that he also propositioned Martine de Courcel, the beautiful wife of the host, who came back wittily with the riposte *"pas avant la soupe"*. But if at times he was a hairy-heeled sot, there was no doubt of his robust eloquence and sincerity as a European. I followed him and Wilson to Strasbourg and Paris early in 1967, when they went on a European reconnaissance to see whether a fresh attempt at entry should be made. By this time, Wilson had undergone a partial conversion. It was not enough, however, to convince the French. At de Gaulle's lunch for them at the Elysée, he singled out George Brown for special esteem, thus

---

* Jean Monnet: *Memoirs* (Collins, 1978)

recognising that Brown's Europeanism was a plant of mature and uninterrupted growth, by contrast with Wilson's dubious seedling, only recently bedded out. (This was the occasion when the British party, leaving the Elysée afterwards, were questioned by a crowd of French journalists in the courtyard as to the nature of the conversations. "*Pas de comment*," said George cheerfully, under the impression he was talking French.)

The reconnaissance came to nothing. Once again the colossus-like figure of de Gaulle barred the way. It was not until he had removed himself from the scene and been succeeded by Georges Pompidou that Britain finally caught the bus she ought to have boarded in 1957. Even then, the story was not over. Labour, returning to power in 1973, insisted on a renegotiation, followed by a national referendum. But the withdrawal of Wilson and his replacement by Jim Callaghan was no guarantee that Britain's European destiny was going to receive ringing affirmation. The new Prime Minister's reservations and half-heartedness were well-known. One night at a party in London, when he was still Foreign Secretary, he drew me aside and in the most porten-tous terms revealed the plans for despatching part of a British battalion to Belize (British Honduras) to deter Guatemalan claims. There was no questioning his enthusiasm and sincerity. He might have been describ-ing the preparations for the invasion of Normandy in 1944. But when I said that it would be an excellent thing if he could show the same spirit towards our membership of the Community, he became quite heated and accused me of lacking a proper sense of values. Combined with the world slump which followed the 1973 Middle East War and the consequent oil embargo, this attitude destroyed what little there was left of the lustre of Britain's entry. One eminent Labour leader who never wavered, however, in the strength of his European commitment was Roy Jenkins. He had become a firm friend back in the Paris days. His intelligence, his steadfastness, his good company recalled his mentor Hugh Gaitskell – though Roy, to his honour, had resigned from the latter's shadow cabinet because of Hugh's anti-European attitude. Despite a distinguished political career, culminating in the Presidency of the EEC Commission in Brussels, he was either too civilised or lacked the ambition and dexterity ever to have been a convincing candidate for the top of the greasy pole. Nonetheless, it was the likes of Roy who until 1970 kept me voting Labour. I could never see that the fact that he preferred a good glass of wine to a bad glass of wine disqualified him from sustaining liberal views and humane sentiments.

Another recurrent memory of these years has to do with conferences. Somewhere, at every moment of the day and often of the night, throughout the length and breadth of the globe, an international conference is going on between people and institutions of matching interests: historians, sociologists, friends of Marcel Proust, students of the Third World, enemies of apartheid, supporters of a united Europe . . . The fairly high boredom level of many of these meetings can be partly or wholly offset by the value of the friendships made, the places visited, the out-of-school activities, and the sheer relief of getting away from the office at home. For years I attended, and eventually became closely connected with the organisation of, an Anglo–German gathering called the Königswinter conference. This took place annually at the pretty Rhine-side village of Königswinter, on the opposite bank of the river to Bonn, or in Cambridge. It brought together MPs, bankers, industrialists, academics, journalists from both nations, who spent three days discussing, according to a prepared agenda, current problems affecting the two countries. Over the years, it built up an enviably high reputation for friendliness and plain speaking, so much so that when such bilateral encounters with other countries were under consideration, the best baptismal name that could be given to them was 'an Anglo–Königswinter'. The conference thereby acquired a considerable social cachet. Invitations were eagerly sought, and regular attendance induced the sort of pride and snobbishness associated with having been at an exclusive school. After a while, it amounted to a form of freemasonry, enabling regular clients to address the Chancellor of the Federal Republic as Helmut or the British Foreign Secretary as Jim or Geoffrey. The conference, usually confined to speech-making by day and much quaffing of green wine and singing in pubs by night, sometimes itself made history. On the hills above Königswinter stands a famous Rhineland landmark, the Drachenfels, a ruined tower of romantic appearance. One particular year, in the course of an important political exchange during an afternoon walk to this tower, David Steel and Shirley Williams are popularly supposed to have laid the foundations for that relationship between the Liberal Party and the newly founded Social Democrat Party known as the Alliance.

Another, rather different kind of conference setting where I was a frequent guest was Ditchley Park, near Woodstock in Oxfordshire. Here, in a magnificent early eighteenth-century mansion, the work of James Gibbs, men and women from Britain and the USA – and latterly from other countries – chosen specially to contribute to the subject of the conference (the Middle East, the Soviet threat) gather over a weekend to exchange views. Privately funded, Ditchley's standards of comfort and stateliness are such as to leave the *homme moyen sensuel* more than satisfied. It aims at being the model of a great private country house, which it once was. Dinner jackets are encouraged. There is a good deal to drink. At one conference, I recall talking to an eager young American academic from a distinctly non-Ivy-League university, who had never before been to England. It was a beautiful June evening and we were having pre-dinner drinks – large, strong, dark brown, well-iced glasses of Bourbon, not thimbles of hot sherry – in the White Drawing-Room. The rays of the dying sun were lighting up the formal parterre outside, the Lely portraits and carved panels within. A white-tied butler shimmered about, offering more Bourbons. My young American friend was transfixed with joy. "I always knew it would be like this, that this is how life in England is lived," he sighed in near-ecstasy. Here was a quandary. Should I enlighten him that there were few, very few, houses in England where such a scene was customary? Or should I leave him undisturbed in his happy illusions? Having elicited from him that he was going to stay on after the conference, visiting London and Cardiff and Manchester, I decided to leave him as he was, in uninformed bliss. He would learn the truth soon enough.

But if Ditchley is the Daimler or Cadillac of conferences, unquestionably the Rolls-Royce is Bilderberg. Founded many years ago by Prince Bernhard of the Netherlands, this high-level affair, which meets in a different country each year, brings together statesmen – Prime Ministers, Foreign Ministers, Leaders of Oppositions – very important business-men and bankers, parliamentarians and a sprinkling of senior journalists. Its proceedings are confidential, a provision which gives rise to intermittent speculation in the popular press that dark and dirty things are being planned by a group of men who either have done well or intend to do well out of a war. There is no evidence whatever that such suspicions are anything but pure fancy. I was invited to only one of these extravaganzas. The venue was an exceedingly luxurious mountain hotel near Geneva. Many of the participants arrived by private plane or helicopter, unthinkable conveyances at homely Königswinter. I do not remember much about the discussions, but the excellent food and the Château-Lafite which was served as house wine at most meals stays in the memory. So does one particular sight. For the debates, the company was grouped in a rough hemicycle and seated on benches according to alphabetical order. On one of the short benches was a trio consisting of Edmond de Rothschild (by far the richest of the French family) and the Rockefeller brothers, Nelson and David. On the scribble pad thoughtfully provided, I made a rough calculation of their worth, assuming that all their assets could be realised. The result, if anywhere near accurate, exceeded the sum of the national budgets of a sizeable proportion of the underdeveloped world.

All this time, the Giles family were living contentedly in the London home which we found and bought on our return from Paris. It was a white, stuccoed house, built in 1840 in the Nash style. Its setting was that district of canals and tree-lined streets near Paddington, called by Browning, who lived there, Little Venice. In almost no way or circumstances does it resemble Venice. On a good day, with the sun slanting through the leaves and making the surface of the canals sparkle, it looks a little bit like Amsterdam. But whatever it compares with, it is a pleasant neighbourhood. Swans nest on the island in the middle of Browning's pool, mallard duck swoop down upon the water, long boats move slowly to and fro, the gardens behind the tall houses impart a momentary illusion of country life. In good weather, the reflection of light on water creates a dappled, mobile effect on the ceilings of the well-proportioned rooms, thus introducing for once a truly Venetian element. We felt well pleased to have found such a spot, and when Pamela Berry* asked me where we had chosen to live, I proudly told her. Renowned for her malicious wit, she looked complacently round her pretty panelled drawing-room in Cowley Street, close to the Houses of Parliament and Westminster Abbey, and said, "It sounds very nice, but you'll have to have a flat in London, won't you?" Evelyn Waugh also had his word to say. Shortly after settling in, I received a postcard from him the message on which ran: 'Sorry to hear you have exchanged your fine Paris flat for the insalubrious surroundings of one of North London's slums.'

The other side of the pool lived another figure from the Paris past, Diana Cooper. Her lunch-parties, consisting mostly of men without their (uninvited) wives, were notable occasions. Among the regular attenders were Harold Macmillan (always referred to by Diana as 'my horse', because decades earlier, when no one could have foreseen his emergence as Prime Minister, she had pointed him out as 'a horse to back'), and the Queen Mother. As the years passed, Diana's power to

---

* The late Lady Hartwell, wife of the owner of the *Daily Telegraph*

amaze remained as great as ever. One day, soon after the Piccadilly traffic arrangements had been reorganised so as to allow for a one-way bus lane, Kitty, driving down the main thoroughfare, was startled to see a tiny vehicle proceeding at speed along the bus lane, in the opposite direction to the main flow. It was Diana, re-enacting, at the age of over eighty, the scene immortalised by Evelyn Waugh in *Scoop* when, caught in thick traffic, Mrs Stitch steers her baby car along the pavement and finally down the steps of a gentleman's lavatory. The day came when she had, or was persuaded, to give up driving. While this was a boon for other road users who might have to encounter her, there was a certain sadness in observing this end of a unique chapter in motorised and indeed every other sort of eccentricity.

At the house in Little Venice, something of the old routines of No. 7 Place de la Madeleine were resumed. Ministers, MPs, members of foreign embassies, academics, journalists came to lunch and dinner. Points of view were expressed, arguments conducted. It was a way, often an effective way, of keeping well-informed. On one occasion, such a dinner led to a valuable acquisition. Among the guests was Walter Annenberg, the rather larger-than-life US Ambassador in London, whose lack of professionalism was compensated for by his ardent love of Britain and things British (or anyway some things British – I doubt if it extended to the Labour Party or the trade unions). Over the pre-dinner drinks, which were handed round by the dressing-gowned figure of our youngest child Belinda, aged ten and a half, Walter said something about Sir Kenneth Clark, the art historian. "You mean Lord Clark," said the child. She was right; he had just been ennobled. Far from being annoyed at this piece of juvenile impertinence, Walter was overjoyed. A couple of days later, a large black car drew up before the house, and the chauffeur staggered up the path bearing a heavy crate. It turned out to contain a twenty-volume children's encyclopedia. A visiting card, inscribed by Walter, accompanied the gift. It read: 'To little Belinda, may she continue to grow in wisdom as well as in stature' (Walter was prone to rotund expressions like this). I do not remember Belinda making much use of the encyclopedia, but I found it invaluable, especially for explaining the rudiments of nuclear fission, a subject on which I was seriously in need of instruction.

8

Editor of *The Sunday Times*

On the morning of October 22, 1980, Harold Evans bounced into my office and revealed that the Thomson interests were going to put Times Newspapers on the market. The previous weekend *The Sunday Times* had had a shortfall in production, because of trouble with the print unions, of 328,000 copies, or more than twenty per cent of the whole. On another Saturday night a month previously, similar troubles had robbed us of nearly 800,000 copies, or more than half the number which should have been produced. All this on top of eleven months' suspension of publication of both papers (1978/79), which had cost the company close on £40 million, without gaining any substantial provisions from the print unions to secure unbroken production. Despite the huge sums of money that the Thomson family had seen disappear down the drain, what appeared above all to have stuck in Ken Thomson's* gullet was the decision by *The Times* journalists in the previous August to strike in support of a wage claim. For eleven months, the company had paid these journalists and those at *The Sunday Times* to do nothing. This was for the sake of keeping together a body of journalistic talent which, once scattered, would have been difficult to reassemble. Greed and ingratitude were the normal and predictable response from the print unions. That journalists should resort to the same tactics was too much for Ken Thomson. Who could blame him?

In the months that followed, Harold Evans was, if possible, even more than his usual frenetic self. He records in his book† how he had spent the suspension period 'trying to find a middle ground between management and unions'. Another, quite different, view was put to me

---

* He succeeded his father as the second Lord Thomson on the latter's death in 1976.
† *Good Times, Bad Times* (Weidenfeld & Nicolson, 1983). This was the book written by Evans after his dismissal as Editor of *The Times*, which, according to its paperback blurb, revealed 'the explosive inside story of Tycoon Rupert Murdoch and the battle for *The Times*'. There will be many references to the book in this chapter.·

long afterwards by a leading representative of the then Times Newspapers management: "Every time we felt we were nearing a point where
our pressure on the unions might bear fruit, Harry stepped in uninvited, and queered the pitch." Now, as the date for the sale of Times
Newspapers approached, Evans was here, there and everywhere, trying
to organise the support and finance for an independent consortium
which could buy *The Sunday Times* as a separate and going concern,
thus preserving its editorial independence.

There was of course nothing wrong in Evans's efforts. Indeed, quite
the contrary. Just as his activities, wise or unwise, during the suspension were motivated solely by a wish to see Times Newspapers back in
healthy production, so now his principal interest was to preserve the
prosperity and reputation of *The Sunday Times*. Personally, I did not
hold with his proposed solutions. I do not believe that large, important
newspapers, especially those as plagued with union troubles as Times
Newspapers had been, can be successfully financed and managed by a
consortium of owners. Naturally there would have to be guarantees that
a single proprietor would observe the principles of editorial independence practised under the Astor and Thomson regimes. But subject to
that, single and resolute ownership seemed, to me at least, infinitely
preferable to what appeared to be the other prospect: government by
committee.

I do not recall having expressed these views, at least at any length or
strength. There was no cause to do so. Early retirement, with as
favourable a pension and other leaving benefits as possible, was my
personal strategy. Whatever the future of *The Sunday Times*, it seemed
supremely unlikely that anyone would ask me, at the age of sixty-two,
to edit it. The struggles and passions over the sale, the emergence of
Rupert Murdoch as the sole purchaser of both titles, the efforts of some
of the *Sunday Times* journalists to file a suit challenging the sale to
Murdoch: all these left me obviously interested, but personally unin-
volved.

This dispassionate view of things continued unchanged after Murdoch had made good his bid. He had still to get the agreement of the
print unions to his proposed reductions in manpower, lacking which he
would not go through with the purchase. But in the interim period he
was thinking about senior appointments and one Saturday – February
7, 1981 – Murdoch, installed in a temporary office in the main *Times*
building, sent for me. As he intended to appoint Evans Editor of *The
Times*, he explained, he wanted me to take on *The Sunday Times*. "You

know it inside out, you'll be able to guarantee continuity and generally ensure a smooth transition . . . I see you doing it for two years or so." It was Murdoch in his most relaxed and charming of moods, leaning back in his chair, alternately putting his glasses on and taking them off again to twiddle them round and round by their side-pieces. I told him I had known his father. He did not seem particularly interested.

There is no knowing, or anyway I do not know, why Murdoch made this choice. His first instinct, so it was believed at the time, was to appoint either Hugo Young, the brilliant and much younger political editor, or Ron Hall, the editor of the Colour Magazine, a fine news-paperman with a good grasp of layout and the technical side but apparently lacking in political conviction or interest. The most likely explanation is that he found, or had pointed out to him, objections to both these names, whereas I represented an easy and, by virtue of my age, short-term compromise which would allow other contenders to emerge in the course of time. Another, more conspiratorial interpretation was that Murdoch intended the struggle for power to begin immediately, with Ron Hall being especially encouraged to undermine me and my authority. If this was the plan, it failed. Hall, appointed joint deputy-editor with Young, did little to help me, but also did nothing, so far as I was aware, in the way of sabotage.

At that first meeting, as so often in the future, I did not always catch every word Murdoch said in his light Australian drawl, particularly when he dropped his voice and threw away his words at the end of sentences. But there was no misunderstanding the main gist of his message. He was offering me, at the end of a long career which I had decided voluntarily to bring to a close, the eminence of the Editor's chair. It did not occur to me for one minute to do anything but accept. There had, of course, already been a great deal of unfavourable publicity about Murdoch and his methods, particularly his record for firing editors and breaking promises within his Australian newspapers and concerns. But these did not weigh heavily with me. Because Murdoch, an international operator, did one thing in one country did not mean that he would do the same thing in another. He was clearly a man of the world, he knew about newspapers (which was more than could be said about some of the would-be purchasers of Times News-papers), and I felt that the guarantees he had given on editorial independence were hard and fast enough to stick. Evans himself, than whom no one was more sensitive on such an issue, had given me forewarning of Murdoch's intended invitation, and spoken kind and encouraging words. Had not he also, a few days previously, sent a note to me and three other senior members of the *Sunday Times* staff which read: 'After all our agonies, I do feel we have been given the very best possible guarantees for an admittedly uncertain future . . . I had been worried that we wouldn't achieve anything as precise as we have . . .'

So I told Murdoch that I was ready and eager to become the first Editor of a Murdoch *Sunday Times*, assuming that his negotiations with the print unions were sufficiently successful to enable him to go through with the deal. I was due to leave the following week for a visit to Amman, to interview King Hussein; would he like me to cancel that visit and remain on hand in London? Yes, he said, he thought that would be best, a remark that led to some subsequent unpleasantness, when Evans chose to see it as an improper command from someone who was not yet formally the owner of the paper. Thus I did go to Amman, as planned, and it was there, listening in my room in the Inter-Continental Hotel to the BBC overseas service news bulletin, that I learnt that Murdoch and the unions had settled their accounts (though despite all the noise and bluster, in a way that resulted in only a very partial solution to the problem of overmanning).

Back in London, I tried unsuccessfully to discover what Evans's intentions were. Obviously I could not become Editor until he had left the chair vacant by accepting the editorship of *The Times*. He had gone to Amsterdam to judge a photographic contest. He seemed to be playing hard-to-get, though why is difficult to say; he had already signified, as his memorandum showed, that he was satisfied with the guarantees. Perhaps it was just one more example of his habitual tendency to cloak his doings in a mantle of theatricality. If so, the performance was sustained until the last moment, with Evans, in a near-incoherent conversation with me on his car telephone while being driven into London after arrival at Heathrow from Amsterdam, protesting that he had not had proper time to consult his lawyers about his contract. By the afternoon of that day, February 17, however, everything fell into place. Evans tearfully told a staff meeting of *Sunday Times* journalists that he was leaving them for *The Times*. To the same meeting I pledged myself to seek to maintain the standards of the paper and to safeguard its independence.

As in the farewell speech I made more than two and a half years later, so now I emphasised one particular and personal point. Because of those nine months with the Foreign Office, immediately after the war, I had been persistently described and regarded as some sort of superannuated Foreign Office hack, a smooth-tongued go-between who had somehow, and inappropriately, strayed into the steaming jungles of real journalism. In no way, I told the journalists, did I regret the nine months. They had been a fascinating and instructive period. But now, thirty-five years later, with literally millions of written words to my credit (or discredit), I considered myself, with good reason, to be a thoroughly professional journalist. To be appointed Editor was a great honour, which I had not expected. But it was no fluke. The speech seemed to go down well; though there was an almost tangible, and wholly justified, sense of dismay that Evans, whose editorship had been so consistently inspiring, was leaving.

In the interests of a good read, the story of the next two and a half years ought to portray the spectacle of a fearless Editor withstanding the nearly intolerable pressures of an overbearing and unprincipled proprietor or his representative. There were certainly elements of this, the choicest of which can be recounted. But there were other sides to the equation. Though many of the *Sunday Times* journalists, for example, were extremely talented and hard-working, a few were neither of these things. In the easy-going Thomson era, Evans had tended to take on staff with too much liberality and then failed adequately to monitor the performance of some of them. The result was that the paper was overstaffed. There were passengers and parasites, some of the feature writers, in particular, leading a life of almost leisured (though usefully subsidised) ease. There was as well, among the staff as a whole, a near-paranoic apprehension about Murdoch and his supposed intentions. An example of this occurred even before he had completed his purchase.

Evans in his book recounts an episode which, he says, has 'entered the lore of Fleet Street'. If it has, it has entered through the wrong door. He tells how one Saturday evening, before Murdoch had completed the deal and was not therefore the owner of the papers, he, Murdoch, was in the composing room of *The Sunday Times*, where the pages were being made up. Reading a proof of the leader page which contained a leader, written by Evans, about the impending change in ownership, Murdoch borrowed a pen, made an alteration, and gave it to Peter Roberts, the managing editor, to take to the printer for the type to be reset. Evans says that Roberts came to him for instructions and he, Evans, told him to forget it, though he did make the alteration in a later edition. I am sorry to have to contradict my old friend Harold Evans, but this is not exactly what happened. Murdoch did, it is true, write in a small factual amendment in the leader (it involved adding, correctly, the name of another newspaper belonging to Express Newspapers' empire) but he did not tell Roberts to have it put right. Nor did Roberts take it to Evans or anyone else for instructions. He was not in the least offended by what Murdoch had done. If a passing cleaning lady had spotted the omission, Roberts would still have done what he did do, namely take the corrected proof to the printers for resetting. Given the delicacy of Murdoch's position, it might have been better if he had not marked the proof, or at the most indicated verbally the mistake. But the idea that he was seeking prematurely to interfere with *Sunday Times* editorials and order senior staff about will not pass the historical test of accuracy. He might have been capable of doing so; in fact, he did not. What was true, however, was that other members of the staff present in the composing room noticed what had happened, jumped to the worst conclusions and complained to Evans, who later reprimanded his future proprietor. The latter, according to Evans's book, was penitent, though in fact he had little or nothing to be penitent about.

Thus the scene was set from the very beginning. On one side, an adventurous, thrusting, impulsive proprietor, prone to over-hasty decisions and with a proven record of ruthlessness; on the other, one hundred and seventy or so journalists quivering with nervous expectation, quick to identify or imagine the least sign of impropriety on the part of the new management. In the middle, in daily danger of being squeezed between these two opposing forces, stood the Editor. I had no immutable ideas about the job, but two things were very plain: first, that the loyalty and co-operation of the journalists must be won and retained if the achievements of the paper were to be sustained; secondly, that for an important national paper to function effectively, there must be constant and preferably friendly consultation between the Editor and the management. In the prevailing mood, how were these two requirements, not exactly incompatible but not easy to drive in tandem, to be achieved?

To begin with, it did not seem as though things were going to be too difficult. Murdoch came and went, in his peripatetic way, making a point, when he was in London on a Saturday, of dropping into my office in the evening, about the time the first copies of the paper came off the presses and were delivered to me. By no stretch of loyalty or imagination can it be said that these were all pleasant occasions. If I was alone, the situation was tolerable. Even when Murdoch, the paper spread out before him, would jab with his fingers at some article or contribution and snarl, "What do you want to print rubbish like that for?" or, pointing to the bye-line of a correspondent, assert that "That man's a Commie" (this happened most frequently when the man in question was reporting on Reaganite acts and policies in Central America), I tried silently to remind myself that just as any member of the public has the right (which he or she often exercises) to criticise the contents of a newspaper, so the paper's proprietor must be able to exercise the same right, however intemperate and disagreeable his language.

But it was when, as was frequently the case, other journalists were present in my office on a Saturday evening discussing the contents and appearance of the paper, that Murdoch's bitter animus, stridently voiced, became especially hard to bear. After a time, I evolved a simple technique of not attempting to answer his strictures. He may have had the right to make them, but I had no obligation to heed them. Here surely was the very essence of editorial independence. Besides, I became convinced that his performance – it was not invariable, he could on rather rare occasions find something good to say about the paper – was not wholly sincere. As time went on, he increased the pace and dimensions of his act, which consisted of regarding (or pretending to regard?) *The Sunday Times* as a nasty, left-wing radical organ, staffed for the most part by a bunch of left-wing layabouts. The insincerity would consist in deliberately seeking, through extravagance of language and extremity of views, to get a reaction or a rise. I schooled myself to avoid this trap, but sometimes some of my colleagues, when present at these scenes, were less able to contain themselves, and the ensuing slanging matches were not only undignified and embarrassing but encouraged, indeed tended to confirm, the worst fears of the journalists about their new chairman (and very probably the worst fears of the new chairman about them).

These Saturday night sessions had at least the advantage of being irregular. A cross that had to be permanently borne was Gerald Long, the man appointed by Murdoch to be Managing Director of Times Newspapers and his immediate deputy. Evans in his book has described so brilliantly what he calls 'this brooding and perplexing personality' that I can only add some touches – but fairly lurid touches – to the portrait. When I first heard of his appointment, I was pleased. I had known him slightly for some years, shared his interest in France and French affairs, was aware of his dazzling record as chief executive at Reuters, and looked forward to working with him and finding in him a friend and ally in our common endeavours. Quite early on, these hopes were somewhat blighted when I thought I spotted a tendency in him to egg on Murdoch in his impulsiveness and ape him in intolerance and rudeness. At the farewell dinner which the staff at *The Sunday Times* gave to Evans,★ I recall the pair of them hovering on the edge of the crowd, engaged in muttered conversation, their faces, as they surveyed the roystering company, framed in a scowl which seemed to stop not far short of malevolence.

In the early days, however, Long seemed, where I was concerned, quite affable and friendly. Knowing his interest in French linguistic usages, I told him of a conversation I had had recently at dinner at the French Embassy, when the proper use of the word *blet* (fem. *blette*) had come up. When applied to a pear, it means exactly the equivalent of the English word 'sleepy', a description so graphic, I maintained to my Embassy friends, that it should be possible to apply the word to people: did we not all know someone who was *blet* or *blette*? The French would have none of it; the word could be used only for fruit, they said. The next day came a home-typed, foolscap-sized letter from Long. Drawing on his large collection of French dictionaries and other sources, he pronounced my instinct about the use of *blet/blette* to be surer than that of the Embassy people, 'not unusual, since the French are so hidebound about their language'. There followed some learned disquisition, citing among other examples a fourteenth-century French poet and reaching back into Norman dialect and forward into Gide's journal, to illustrate the possible derivation and use of the disputed word. 'Faut pas se laisser faire,† Greetings' was the cheerful ending of this unusual and entirely amiable note.

Evans, in his book, writes that 'it was open season on Giles from the very first day: Long had conceived one of his instant dislikes.' The *blette* episode challenges this reading, but only in the matter of timing. Very soon, it did indeed become apparent that Long, for reasons best left to a psychiatrist to explain, had decided to harass and criticise me as often and as strongly as possible. I am sure I am right in deducing that he encouraged Murdoch to do the same. Indeed his publicly expressed contempt for newspaper journalists and their profession knew few bounds. The lines that Edmond Rostand puts into Cyrano de Bergerac's mouth can just as aptly be quoted to describe Long:

★ It is right to record that Murdoch and Long agreed that company funds should meet half the cost – £4000 – of this affair.
† You mustn't let yourself be taken for a ride

. . . Eh bien! oui, c'est mon vice,
Déplaire est mon plaisir. J'aime qu'on me haïse.*

The bombardment opened in earnest in early April, just a month after I had assumed the editorship. Memo from Rupert Murdoch:

Dear Frank,
   This is to confirm that both the Managing Director and I expect to be consulted about all senior appointments *prior* to their occurrence. We both recognise your ultimate authority in these matters (subject to budget limits). However, if we are to work together as a team we must all be involved.

There was nothing wrong, there was everything right, with the last sentence. But I smelt a rat. The famous guarantees, the bedrock, as it were, of the constitution, stated quite clearly that, 'subject only to annual budget factors the Editor retains control over the appointments, disposition and dismissal of his journalists.' What might be the outcome of the consultative process which Murdoch was now requiring? Was it not more than likely that the kind of people I might choose for senior positions on the paper would be just those to find themselves in Murdoch's and Long's bad books? It brought to mind the example of Guy Mollet, the French Prime Minister at the time of Suez. After it was all over, he was asked by journalists why he had not consulted the Americans before committing French troops to action against Egypt. "Because," he replied, with engaging frankness, "I knew that if I did, they'd object." So:

Dear Rupert,
   I have always found it very easy to tell you when I am not happy about something or disagree with it; and I would ask you to look on this letter in that light. I must say, I am not happy about your directive.
   You write that my ultimate authority in these matters (subject to budget considerations) is unquestioned. But your use of the word 'consult', especially when applied to both the Managing Director and yourself, does suggest to me the suspicion of a power of veto on your part. Discussion is one thing, prior consultation is another; I

* Well, yes it's my vice,/Displeasing people is my pleasure. I like to be hated.

interpret the latter to come close to meaning that there must be agreement before an appointment is made. This does seem to me to encroach upon my editorial independence . . . I feel there are the makings of misunderstandings here. What would happen if, in the consultation process, we disagreed over a nominee for a senior post and I went ahead and appointed him? That would leave us both (not to mention the nominee) in an awkward position.

I would prefer if we could leave it that I will continue to discuss with you and Gerry every subject under the sun affecting the paper and its future; but that there should be no quasi-constitutional requirement over these senior appointments.

The answer came back three days later: 'I do not understand the difference between you discussing something with me and consulting me about the same thing! I am sure that a little more experience and familiarity will solve this semantic problem.' There the matter rested. Murdoch had been perfectly courteous. It was of course a problem insoluble save in one overriding set of circumstances, namely that management and editor shared a broad measure of understanding about where the paper should be going, and who was best equipped to share in the task of taking it there. I did not, in those early days, appreciate just how far that essential degree of mutual trust was lacking. Evidence for that lack was not long in coming.

It is important here, for the sake of accuracy, not to exaggerate by suggesting a perpetual state of guerrilla, or sometimes open, warfare between me in my office, on one side of the street, and Murdoch and Long in their offices on the other side, each visible to the other. Evans tells the story of how Murdoch would amuse visitors to his office by firing imaginary pistol shots at my back, clearly discernible through the big plate-glass windows across the street. This may or may not have happened; I certainly never caught him at it, which I could have done easily, by turning the head. Again, life in a busy newspaper office simply does not provide time for uninterrupted strife with the management; there are too many people to be seen, editorial conferences to be held, articles to be discussed and written, plans to be laid. The life of a conscientious Editor is an immensely busy one, and even though I resolved from the start not to make any sweeping changes or startling innovations – why seek to turn a successful going concern upside down? – there were various delicate and urgent administrative tasks. These included persuading about fifteen members of the staff – the weaker element who had long since abandoned any sustained attempt to justify their salaries – to accept redundancy money and be gone. The success of this operation won Murdoch's warm approval, though it was perhaps typical that he never expressed it to me, so that I only learnt of it second-hand.

But Long began to vent his personal hostility with a persistence and mordancy that made nonsense of any earlier assumption that he would prove to be a friend and ally. He became famous – and risible – for issuing pompously worded memoranda, one of which forbade any director or head of department in Times Newspapers to authorise any increase in remuneration in any form, without the prior approval of Murdoch or himself. As a director, I knew – or rather had been informed, because detailed accounts which would have told their own story were never provided at executive board meetings – that the company was in low financial water. Clearly financial discipline was needed. Even so, Long's universal ukase was too sweeping. I wrote to him – the letter was marked strictly confidential – pointing out that though fully aware of the need for severe restraint and control, I must be enabled to exercise, on my own initiative, one of an Editor's rights, namely to make merit awards from time to time to individual journalists whose good work deserved recognition. 'I am not going to fling money around like a drunken sailor,' I wrote, 'but I do think I must retain the right to make these awards without a reference. This is an important point of principle.'

Long's reply was a studied – and undeniably successful – attempt at boorish rudeness. Without warning me, he copied it and my (confidential) letter to him to all directors. Its opening paragraph ran as follows: 'It seems faintly ridiculous to be writing back and forth, the more so since the matter raised in your letter is not an important point of principle, not a point at all, but an example of what seems to me your abnormal sensitivity about editorial prerogative.' It went on: 'Since you write, presumably for the record, I must record my reply, while wishing most heartily that you would not see points of principle everywhere and that you should not wear your editorial independence on your shoulder; I would have hoped you were sufficiently reassured by now that no one wants to knock it off.' The letter continued for two foolscap pages in similar vein, in the middle of which occurred the all-important sentence: 'I was not concerned in my note, nor in the preoccupations which prompted it (i.e. the financial difficulties of the company) with your ability to give rewards to journalists who have pleased you.' In other words, I had gained my point. All the rest was bluster and verbiage. I think it was at this stage that I told Joan Thomas, my personal assistant, to open a dossier called 'Long insult file'. Within the next few months, it became quite bulky.

These exchanges, whatever their underlying seriousness, happily had their comic aspects – at least they were comic to me – which were a great help towards remaining calm and preserving a sense of proportion. Nor were Long's interventions always unhelpful and officious. This is where any proper description of the period calls for special care. As I have already argued, he would be a fool (and there were plenty of those around) who sought to deny Murdoch the right to make comments about his own papers. The same should have been true about his deputy who, in his absence, acted in his stead. The difficulty was in deciding where comment, even if hostile, was justified and where interference began. Another exchange between Long and myself, dated August 1981, illustrates the point. It took the form of a written memorandum from him about the contents of the previous Sunday's paper, to which I replied verbally, after making careful and copious notes. (The amount of time consumed in conducting this traffic is another factor that needs to be weighed in the balance.)

Long took strong exception to a piece by a young-ish, radical-ish *Sunday Times* journalist which had appeared on one of the feature pages. It was a rather silly-clever analysis of the linguistic circumlocutions of Geoffrey Howe, then Chancellor of the Exchequer, about the economic situation. 'You have of course the complete responsibility for all this and I for one am very content to leave it with you. You will permit me however to say that in my personal opinion [the article in question] bordered on hysteria.' On reflection, I agreed with Long and wished, with hindsight, that I had killed the piece. The page on which it appeared was very late in going to press on the Saturday afternoon and in the last-minute rush had escaped my personal safety net.

Long's next point was far more contentious. The then Director-General of the BBC, Sir Ian Trethowan, had overruled some of his staff in deciding not to invite E.P. Thompson, the distinguished historian and notable campaigner for nuclear disarmament, to deliver that year's Dimbleby lecture. *The Sunday Times* had carried a leader critical of this decision. Long did not like this and contrasted it unfavourably with a piece that had appeared in the impeccably Tory *Sunday Telegraph*, upholding Trethowan's right to decide as he did, on the grounds that 'somebody's prejudices must prevail'. Long wrote: 'You have that authority here and in the end the decisions are yours but in preparation for what are often very difficult decisions it seems to me that discussions on the general lines of editorial policy would be useful . . . I hope that you will find it helpful to conduct in the autumn some discussions on the general question of responsibility and to give the rest of us some insight into your views on such matters as the political tendency of the newspaper.'

I told Long that I did not share his opinion about our leader on the Thompson affair, and went on to welcome his suggestion for discussions on general lines of editorial policy. It was only politic to go this far, especially in view of the scrupulously polite texture of his language, contrasting sharply with his earlier efforts. But the prospect was a daunting one. Though Murdoch had not up to then given me any explicit instructions about the political line of the paper – indeed he never did, throughout my editorship – I knew enough about his views, through hearing him express them, to recognise that he and I were a long way apart politically and could never agree on certain things, above all the duty and interest of *The Sunday Times* (as I saw it) to keep clear of any consistent political allegiance or dogma, in preference for a judgement of ideas and cases according to their merits. Not only was this my own profound conviction, but it was shared by the large majority of the senior staff who met in my office weekly to discuss the editorial attitudes of the paper. This need not and did not mean avoidance of any firm or consistent views. What it did mean was a maintenance of the paper's tradition, stretching back over the last twenty years and more, of true independence of mind and opinion.

Long's proposed forum on the political tendency of *The Sunday Times* was never convened. By the time I had been away on holiday and returned, Times Newspapers was faced with a crisis which made my skirmishings with the management – and theirs with me – look decidedly secondary. In September of 1981, the *Sunday Times* branch (chapel) of one of the main print unions, the National Graphical Association, threatened to withdraw co-operation, as a means of supporting the claim of some of their members to a wage increase which would have maintained their differential over the wage levels of another of the print unions. (Much of the industrial chaos in Fleet Street takes this form.) Such a threat, if carried out, must have affected, perhaps stopped, the production of *The Sunday Times*. When the NGA refused to give an assurance that its members would work normally, Murdoch (who was not in England) decreed what was in effect a lock-out, even if it was not called that. No one would receive any more pay until the NGA had promised normal production. There were to be no exceptions to this ruling. Unlike the period of the suspension of *The Times* and *Sunday Times* in 1978/79, when the journalists were paid for eleven months for standing by, this time they were to suffer, along with all the other innocent employees, for the NGA's militancy. The ostensible grounds for the lock-out were that with production under threat there would be diminished or even no revenue and without sufficient revenue there could be nothing to put into the pay packets. But it was not quite as simple as that. Murdoch was determined to break, or at least challenge in a way that had never been done before, the power of the NGA to call the tune. If this meant that unoffending people had to be penalised, so be it. As a director of the company, formally signifying approval at a board meeting for this policy, I had severe qualms. This was going to strain still further the already fragile relationship between the management and the journalistic work-force. But we had been through all this industrial mayhem before and nothing had changed. If Murdoch was now ready to stake all, who with any higher responsibility and understanding of the situation could demur? The attempted remedy was dire, but so was the illness.

What was much less easy, involving me in one of the most unpleasant experiences in my entire professional career, was when I exchanged my director's for my editor's hat. For it was my duty to tell the journalists of the decision. The legendary role of an Editor was to be reversed. In the idealised stereotype, the building is flooded, a partial power cut brings half the presses to a standstill, internal communications break down. Yet the Editor emerges from his office to exhort the staff to produce a paper by hook or by crook (the show-must-go-on tradition). On that September day I was going to have to tell them, with none of these conditions present, to go home and forget the paper. Admittedly, with the NGA threatening production, there was little or no likelihood that the journalists' stories would have appeared anyway. But that was a fact unlikely to weigh heavily with a group of professional people who were committed to the paper and tended to regard the production process as the management's business. By what right could anyone send them home without pay – thus breaching their contracts of employment, when they, as opposed to the NGA, had done nothing to warrant what was in effect instant dismissal?

A staff meeting was called and was fully attended. It was a Friday afternoon, normally a time of great activity in a Sunday newspaper office. The journalists in the news room were pounding away at their typewriters as though they had never heard of the NGA. This is not as foolish as it must sound. We had lived, in the last years, through so many industrial disputes, had seen so many last-minute settlements, that the only responsible course was to assume, whatever the portents, that there would be a paper for which copy would be required, quite possibly very urgently once a settlement was reached and production resumed. So when I stood up and told everyone to put the covers on their typewriters, go home and not return until further notice, adding that they would in the meantime receive no pay, the effect was traumatic. No Editor had ever issued such an order before. From amidst the ground-swell of shock, protest and indignation, there rang out one plainly audible and none-too-affectionate voice. "What happens to your salary?" it said.

As Editor, I was paid by News International, Murdoch's main London company, the owner of the *News of the World* and the *Sun*. My salary, which I received both as Editor of *The Sunday Times* and as a director of Times Newspapers, was, like my duties, in another category from those of the journalists. But in the two or three seconds available before an answer had to be given to the question, something stopping a good deal short of inspiration told me that it would be a disastrous step publicly to separate myself, or rather my salary, from the fate of the journalists. I would never win back whatever of their confidence and respect I enjoyed. I therefore replied that, whatever the circumstances, I would wish to undergo the same sacrifices now being imposed upon them. (After the affair was over and life had returned to normal, Roy Ekburg, the financial director of News International, told me that my words at the meeting had been reported back to him and that he had made a note accordingly on my salary sheet. He was only doing his duty.)

It was a very sad and disturbed body of men and women who left their editorial desks that Friday evening. Many of them had young families to provide for. There was no knowing for how long the stoppage would continue. Above all, as I had foreseen, the already considerable degree of mistrust for Murdoch and his methods had been increased a hundred-fold. By what right, moral and legal, was he imposing decisions which could endanger the careers and prospects of a whole section of professional people who had done no wrong? Even if this cloud passed, the same thing might happen again. There could be no confidence, no security, and not much pleasure working for such an employer. 'I regard this as one of the most disgraceful episodes in the history of British journalism,' wrote one of the more excitable members of the staff to me that night.

Similar fears and woes were voiced when a deputation from the committee of the journalists' chapel came to my house on the following afternoon, where I was failing by a large margin to enjoy the enforced and unusual experience of a Saturday at home. I received them as sympathetically as I could. Their worries were real and easily comprehensible. But it was no good side-stepping the realities. I reminded them of the appalling record of industrial disorder at the paper, of the financial difficulties of the company, and of the need for an end to precipitate and crippling action by one or another section of the print unions. I even mentioned the possibility, if the dispute were not settled, of liquidation. Dejectedly, the deputation left, its female member in tears, a fact duly recorded by the television camera team waiting in the street outside.

The dispute was settled, reasonably quickly, largely through the efforts of Len Murray, the General Secretary of the TUC. The NGA men returned to work without any increases in wages. Murdoch's tough tactics had paid off. Only one issue of the paper went unpublished. No one lost any pay, except the offending NGA men, though inevitably the company lost revenue. Once work resumed, my principal concern was to heal, or anyway seek to narrow, the alarming breach in confidence which had been created between the journalists and the management. I persuaded Long, and Murdoch, now back in London, that it might be helpful if the latter could see a representative group or groups of journalists for a free and frank, as the saying goes, discussion of the situation. There were two such meetings, the second of which I attended. It was not a successful experiment. Sensing that feelings of discrimination or unfairness might arise if I picked only a handful of people to see him, I built up each group to the number of about eighteen. It was a mistake. Murdoch is at his best in a small company; in larger gatherings he tends to be ill-at-ease and either non-communicative or abrasive. Nor were the journalists exactly tactful. "You can't think what we've suffered," one of them told him. They had certainly been given major cause for worry. But in fact they had not suffered materially at all, whereas the company had lost about £1 million – one entire, profitable issue of *The Sunday Times*, and three issues of *The Times*, after the NGA had picketed the building. Murdoch's response, as reported back to me, was predictably tart. The breach was not healed; if anything, it was made deeper and wider.

Two further exchanges of fire with Long, neither of them of my own choosing, occurred that autumn. One day he sent for me and told me, in ostensibly friendly tones, that unless I could learn to communicate more freely with Murdoch, to cease to hold him, as he put it, at arm's length, my position as Editor might have to be reviewed. There is no knowing whether Long said this on his own initiative or whether Murdoch encouraged him to do so. Had I been the worrying sort, the advice – or was it a threat? – would have meant some sleepless nights. But if I had been a worrier, I should by now have been in hospital undergoing treatment for acute ulcers. As it was, I resolved, after reflection, to continue on the same course as hitherto, listening to Murdoch whenever he wanted to talk, telling him of future plans for the paper, not feeling unreasoningly obliged to disregard his wishes because they were his wishes but equally not feeling professionally bound to follow up every one or possibly any of his ideas. Apart from the fact, admittedly an important one, that we were obviously not the same sort of animal and unlikely to see eye to eye on everything or indeed on much, I do not recall such sessions as I had with him in his office (in contrast to the embarrassing Saturday night performances in mine) being particularly unpleasant or doom-laden. Despite his frequently earthy way of expressing himself, he certainly never treated me as he did, at one board meeting when he was in especially savage mood, the director responsible for advertising. He asked this man whether he granted his staff special financial bonuses for bringing in extra advertising. It was a perfect example of Morton's fork, which the poor wretch had no means of avoiding. If he said he did, then he could be publicly admonished for extravagance in paying extra for services which ought to be rendered in the ordinary course of business. If he said (as he did) that there was no such bonus system, then he could be (and was) roasted for not sufficiently encouraging his staff.

The second brush with Long concerned a *Sunday Times* journalist whose alleged shortcomings over his expense account constituted grounds, according to Long, for considering dismissing him. The case was indeed a potentially alarming one. The journalist, who had done excellent and sometimes dangerous work in Northern Ireland, had furnished inadequate accounts, and sometimes no accounts at all, for expenditure of more than £40,000 over a period of three to four years. More serious, there was a suspicion that, as well as being lax, he was claiming more than he was entitled to as 'expenses'. Long's concern was justified, but he was unable to leave the affair alone, repeatedly speaking or writing to me in his most bureaucratic manner. One of his memoranda contained the sentence: 'The burden was now on you to show why a man who had failed as [the journalist in question] has failed in his administrative duty to the Company should continue to be employed by Times Newspapers . . . I find it difficult to believe that [his] behaviour does not offer proof of disabling irresponsibility.'

I needed no prompting from Long. Together with some of my senior executives, I examined the case at length and in detail. I saw the man myself, warning him of his serious position. The management accounts staff also examined the figures. The upshot of all this was that it was established to my satisfaction that although the man had been careless and made serious errors, he was not guilty of malpractice. I wrote him a letter of stern reproof which included a warning that any repetition of such conduct would result in instant dismissal.

Long remained completely unappeased. I had failed to pass his bureaucratic test of providing proof of why, after what had happened, the man should continue to be employed. We were back at the point I had earlier tried to clarify with Murdoch: that the Editor 'retains control over the appointment, disposition and dismissal of his journalists'. The case had been thoroughly investigated, the man's innocence of dishonesty proved to my satisfaction, and I had no intention of sacking this valued, if administratively scatter-brained, member of the staff.

The affair culminated in a ludicrous parody of a court-martial (except that the accused was not present). On one side of the table in one of the board room suites sat Long, exuding bad temper and frustration, flanked by a representative of the company's solicitors and a member of the management staff. On the other side were myself and two of my senior men most closely involved in examining the case. Long led the prosecution attack with such ferocity that, after a while, I heard myself asking, like the prisoner at some Communist secret trial, for the right to speak. I had previously taken some private legal advice and felt perfectly confident about where my rights and duties started and stopped. When it came however to analysing the letter I had written to the miscreant, warning him of dismissal in the event of repetition, the solicitor said that in his view the letter did not properly establish the necessary grounds for future dismissal. "I knew it," exclaimed Long, "this case has been mishandled from start to finish," and he swept up his papers and stumped out of the room. No more was ever heard of the

16 London 1983: Someone at *The Sunday Times* was able to get a laugh out of the Hitler diaries fiasco: montage by Michael Cranmer, of the S.T. picture desk

17 London 1981: Kitty

matter. The rest of the staff got to know (not from me) about the affair and reacted accordingly. The story spread even further. A friend in Washington reported to me that my refusal to yield up to Long his intended victim was the talk of the town there. While this needed to be taken with plenty of salt, it was satisfying to know that my efforts, most of them behind the scenes, to defend the legitimate interests of the staff and resist attempted trespassing on editorial ground had not gone unnoticed and unappreciated. Being pig in the middle can be dispiriting and above all lonely work.

There was to be one more, and the worst, storm before calmer waters were reached. One day early in January 1982 Murdoch sent for me and told me he wanted to get rid of Hall, the editor of the Colour Magazine, and to bring in as senior deputy-editor Brian MacArthur, a former *Sunday Times* man whom Evans had taken with him to *The Times*. This would make Hugo Young, the political editor whose judgement and experience were for me a constant and unfailing source of strength, junior to MacArthur. Murdoch also said that he intended to replace Hall at the Colour Magazine with Peter Jackson, the unknown-to-me editor of the *News of the World* magazine, which he was to continue simultaneously to edit despite its wide difference in taste and readership from the *Sunday Times* magazine. There was no pretence, in this sudden and totally unexpected expression of his wishes and intentions, of consulting me, of asking for my opinions about, still less consent to, these changes. There was no pretence they would be of my doing, though I would have to announce them in my name.* It was an instruction, an order as imperative as that issued by a commanding officer to a subordinate. There was not even more than a perfunctory attempt at justifying the changes, except to claim that Hall was not pulling his weight and to allege, without any detail or documentation, that the paper had become 'flat' and needed fresh ideas. Such a judgement must always be unscientific and subjective. What was proveable, on the other hand, was that the circulation, though it had fallen sharply, had fallen proportionately less than that of the other Sunday 'quality' papers, the *Observer* and the *Sunday Telegraph*. *The Sunday Times* still led the field by its habitually huge, commanding margin.

---

* Though Evans, in his book, quotes Murdoch as having told him, "I'll tell the national directors [the four outside directors who were supposed to be the guardians, as it were, of the constitution] at lunch Frank Giles asked for it all."

For once, I really did have a troubled night. Some of what Murdoch was demanding was not, in itself, objectionable. Hall, with his specialised flair for presentation and layout of the printed page, had not made the contribution which, as joint deputy-editor of the paper, was expected of him. I liked him well enough – we shared a passion for music and an enthusiasm for things Greek – but could not honestly say that his departure would be a loss to the paper. Indeed, rather the reverse: the arrival of MacArthur* – a pleasant personality, industrious, and well-endowed with a sense for news – would be likely to strengthen the team at the top. But the negative indications were seriously worrying. On the personal level, it went completely against the grain to demote Young, whom I looked upon as my natural successor. He had done no wrong, unless it was wrong for him to continue to pour out, in his weekly political column, a stream of independent minded, elegantly expressed and original opinions which evoked appreciative, if sometimes critical, reactions from readers. I knew that Murdoch tended to regard him as an undesirably left-wing influence. But then he saw many of the *Sunday Times* staff in that light. Anyone who deviated from Ronald Reagan was left-wing. That thought led on to a further objection, this time one of principle.

This was the point I had raised with Murdoch nine months previously, involving the formal declaration, enshrined in the guarantees in return for which the Secretary of State for Industry had given his consent to Murdoch acquiring the papers, that the Editors should be solely responsible, subject only to budget factors, for the 'appointment, disposition and dismissal' of their journalists. What he was now demanding was in complete breach of that undertaking. Surely not even by chicanery could it be claimed that 'budget factors' were the reason for the changes; Murdoch had not even bothered to make the claim. So what should be done? Was this at last the ground on which to offer serious battle, to refuse to carry out the Chairman's orders, to appeal to the national directors to ensure that the guarantees were upheld?

Thomas Gainsborough had in his studio a sand-table on which he built up scenic effects designed to help him, before painting a landscape, to assess the interplay of form and perspective. I tried, in thinking of the next moves, to create a sand-table of the mind on which to work out the consequences of a number of options once applied. The

---

* Later he became Editor-in-Chief of the new daily paper, *Today*.

first, based upon the premise that Murdoch, given his character, was going to get his way, national directors notwithstanding, was that my resistance would mean my removal. Personally, this would be at once manageable but regrettable. Pension arrangements were satisfactory, compensation for dismissal could almost certainly be arranged. In return for losing a job which, despite all the tribulations, I loved, I might become, if only for a fleeting moment, a minor hero, a splendid casualty in the fight against bad men and bad faith.

But was this not too histrionic? What would be the advantage to the independence of the paper, and the interests of the journalists, of my departure and replacement by a Murdoch nominee who would obviously not be Young and might well come from outside the stable altogether? Besides, I agreed with some of the changes, even if I had not thought of them myself. Would it not be wiser to seek to remove the disagreeable parts of the package and then accept the rest? The sand-table, however often rearranged, failed to provide any answer to the problem of how, in announcing the changes, they could be presented as my free choice, made within the terms of my editorial responsibility, and not just the (illegal) order of an authoritarian management. But that would have to be worked out later. The first task was to amend the order.

The next morning I arrived unusually early at the office to find Murdoch already there and engaged. I was going to say to him first that Young should not be demoted; MacArthur could be made joint deputy-editor, but Young would continue to be, as before, my No. 2. Secondly, I must see Jackson; it was ridiculous to expect me to appoint to an important post a man I had never met. Murdoch's personal assistant, always pleasant and helpful, bade me wait. He would not be long, she said. At that point, some unseen and ill-inspired influence guided my steps down the passage and into Long's office next door. I revealed my intentions to him. What could have prompted this act of folly is impossible to say. I think – though it is difficult when recollecting fraught moments such as these, to distinguish between hindsight and the actual mental process at the time – that I must have hoped that Long would for once abandon his remorseless hostility and be a little understanding and even helpful. It was just about as sensible as to appeal to a crocodile for help in fording a swollen river. Long left the room and was closeted with Murdoch for ten minutes or so. When he returned, it was to say that unless I carried out Murdoch's bidding forthwith, my editorship would come to an early end. The only concession was that I should see Jackson before announcing his appointment. I could also tell Young that he could still consider himself a candidate for the editorship – a patently empty assurance, but one that might do something to save some of Young's innocent face.

Had I waited to see Murdoch, I believe – though naturally there can be no proof – that I would have won my point about Young's position. Murdoch alone and uninfluenced could be reasonable and willing to meet one half-way. But Long's attitude could be calculated to stiffen Murdoch's already considerable resolve. There was nothing for it but to submit or be sacked. Mindful of the model that the sand-table had outlined, I opted, with a heavy heart, for submission. Naturally enough, Hall and Young when informed, were distressed, the former especially so, for he was being told to leave the paper. As Prime Ministers and heads of great concerns know very well, asking people to leave, even with golden handshakes, is no fun. I had never dismissed anyone of Hall's standing. "I need your job," I said to him, for want of anything better to say. (It is good to record that not only did he collect a handsome sum in compensation, but within a few weeks was appointed to another highly paid post in Fleet Street.) To Young I explained, as best I might, that the introduction of MacArthur would bring (as indeed it did) a fresh and more news-oriented element to our team. I also assured him, and later confirmed this in writing, that whatever his official place in the hierarchy, I would continue to regard and use him as my principal political counsellor.

There remained the almost insuperable – as it turned out, entirely insuperable – difficulty of how to present these changes. Everyone in the place sensed they were not of my doing. Yet to admit this, thus freeing me from any responsibility for them, was also to admit that I had become simply the instrument of Murdoch's whims and wishes. It was hard, after the struggles about which most of the staff knew little or nothing, to have arrived at this point. But there was no alternative to pretending – for form's sake – that my independence was not in question, even if few if any were going to believe in the pretence. What made the whole situation so depressing was the thought that with a civilised management, working in an atmosphere of friendly give-and-take, discussions with the Editor about senior appointments, about the performance of those holding them, about the thrust and direction of the paper, could and should have been a continuous process. As it was, there was nothing but a bleak ultimatum and a demand for instant action; no sand-table formed part of Murdoch's working equipment.

In answer to queries from the journalists about my share of responsibility in the changes, I issued an intentionally Jesuitical statement that, as Editor, 'I was involved in the discussion with higher management that led to these decisions.' After lunching with Peter Jackson, whom I liked and found highly professional even if his knowledge of quality newspaper readership was limited, I announced to a meeting of the Colour Magazine staff that I was appointing him in Hall's place. They wanted to know whether this was my personal choice. I could only reply that had I not taken to Jackson I would not have made the announcement. What would have happened had I conceived a violent dislike for him and thought him disastrously unsuitable for *The Sunday Times*? Then there would have occurred, I think, the battle which I had deemed it better, up to then, not to fight. As it was, the changes were completed, whatever the journalists may have thought about my part in them, and I received a call from Murdoch – was it a sudden onset of sympathy, a sign of jubilation, or merely a metaphorical patting of the head of the dog that had carried out its master's orders? – thanking me for being so helpful over a difficult time.

I have said that after this, intensely distressing, drama was over, the going became easier. This was true at the personal level. But other sorts of troubles now built up in a sky that was already far from serene. Early in February 1982, Murdoch announced that both *The Times* and *The Sunday Times* would be closed down unless the print unions agreed to yield up another six hundred jobs within 'days rather than weeks'. The papers, he said, were bleeding to death. The objective was to seek agreement on voluntary redundancies; 'the alternative is no work for anyone and only the minimum pay-offs.' This was the background to the affair of the titles, described at length in Evans's book. Murdoch wanted the titles of both papers transferred to News International, the owner of the *News of the World* and the *Sun*, because this would give him a far greater field for manoeuvre in his battle with the print unions. In particular, by thus stripping Times Newspapers of its principal assets, the transfer would mean that, in a liquidation, minimum or possibly no payments to creditors could be made, because there would be no assets from which to pay them. Among those creditors would be members of the work-force made redundant. Such a transfer would also mean that, in the event of a close-down, nobody else could buy the papers; Murdoch could keep them in cold storage for as long as he liked. The strategy may have been cleverly conceived, but the methods of carrying it out were, as Evans explains most lucidly, improper. The *Sunday*

Times journalists, more wide awake than their colleagues at *The Times* to this sort of thing, addressed a powerful letter of protest to me; and both I and Evans made known our objections to the management. In the end, the plan to transfer the titles was abandoned.

Whatever the wisdom or lack of wisdom of his tactics, Murdoch's analysis could scarcely be faulted. He had failed, on acquiring the papers, to achieve the measure of de-manning that was economically necessary. As a result, Times Newspapers' finances were in such a state that they now constituted a threat to the prosperity of the *News of the World* and the *Sun*, Murdoch's other London properties, which had been playing the role of milch cow to the two quality papers. (Though whether *The Sunday Times*, an habitually profitable concern, was really in the red was a proposition constantly and angrily challenged by my journalists. The weirdly uninformative way in which the accounts were presented made it impossible to answer the question. What was known was that the Murdoch management, in contrast to its Thomson prede-cessors, loaded *The Sunday Times*, a weekly paper, with a disprop-ortionately large burden of charges for facilities shared in common with *The* (daily) *Times* – presumably to diminish, on paper, the losses of the latter.)

Another painful period of doubt and uncertainty ensued. Coming so soon after the lock-out of the previous September, it had a profoundly demoralising effect upon the journalists. To try to offset this, Kitty and I held a series of supper parties at our London home for members of the staff and their spouses. The gesture was appreciated, as the subsequent thank-you letters revealed, beyond all expectation. I had feared that the formula might lend itself to a charge of paternalism, something akin to the way in which a nineteenth-century factory-owner, at the same time as paying miserable wages, also organised and underwrote the annual works outing. Happily, our little entertainments were not seen like this. Like most people, journalists, despite their reputation for being hard-boiled, need some tender loving care from time to time. The wives were especially grateful. Extraordinary though it may seem, many of them had never met the men and women with whom their husbands worked day in and day out. Murdoch got to hear of our efforts and, far from scoffing, expressed his gratitude.

The trouble finally resolved itself by Murdoch getting most of the de-manning he was asking for. I then left for a much needed holiday in Florida. This meant I was absent throughout the period of the Harold

Evans defenestration.* The news of it was painful. Harry, in spite of his sometimes capricious ways, had been a splendidly inspiring colleague and a good friend. He was certainly undeserving of the treatment he got from Murdoch. On the other hand, it was equally certain that, in one way and another, his brief tenure at *The Times* had marked its transformation into an unhappy ship, its journalists into a divided crew. The wretched episode imparted at least two lessons: firstly that, whatever the rule book may say, no situation where the editor of a newspaper is consistently at odds with his proprietor can have any permanence; secondly, that there are horses for courses. Evans's outstanding success as Editor of *The Sunday Times* was no guarantee that he was equally destined for the same success at *The Times*.

For me that spring, the piece of unexpected good news on arrival back from Florida was that Gerald Long had ceased to be Managing Director. Murdoch extracted him from Times Newspapers altogether and gave him a senior post at News International. Never again would I have to deal with, and be harassed by, this Iago-like character, whose ill-feelings towards me had succeeded, inevitably, in evoking similar sentiments in reverse. To describe his nature as complex is about as observant as pointing out that Schubert's Eighth Symphony is unfinished. There was certainly great intelligence, there must have been some good in him; but he took extreme precautions to conceal the latter, at least from me. Why Murdoch translated him to another sphere can only be guessed at. Perhaps he, too, applied the horses-for-courses rule. Despite his superb performance at Reuters, few people can have been less suited than Long to the style and rhythms of a great newspaper office. His place as Murdoch's immediate deputy was taken by Sir Edward Pickering, who knew newspapers as an instrumentalist turned conductor knows his orchestra. Pickering had been Editor of the *Daily Express* under Beaverbrook, and then had spent the rest of his career on the management side of the Mirror Group. Bald-pated, usually expressionless behind his large spectacles, always imperturbable, he was at least in one important respect the antithesis of Long: he was there to help rather than to hinder. For the rest of my editorship I invariably found him approachable, understanding, wise in judgement, scrupulously fair and endowed with a good measure of dry humour.

* In March 1982, Murdoch asked Evans for his immediate resignation. After a fiery rearguard action, vividly described in *Good Times, Bad Times*, Evans resigned on March 15.

Well past retirement age, he had nothing to fear about his future. His comportment in public towards Murdoch was one of total acquiescence, but behind the scenes he had, I suspect, a calming influence upon that restless temperament.

Life now became, if not exactly easy – no editor has the right to expect that – at least less marked by unpleasant surprises and disagreeable encounters. This was just as well, because in the next eighteen months, two national and international events occurred which called for a maximum amount of uninterrupted concentration. The first was the Falklands war, the second the general election of 1983. I was away in Cambridge, attending the annual session of the Königswinter conference, when the news came through on April 2, 1982 that Argentina had seized the Falkland islands. It was a Friday. I walked round and round the courtyard of St Catherine's College with Peter Shore,* another attendant at the conference, wondering aloud what the Government should do and what *The Sunday Times* should say about it. Shore, who combines a passionate belief in democratic socialism with a no less passionate sense of national pride, was in his most Churchillian of moods, contemptuous of all doubt, adamant for action: "It's perfectly simple, we must go and chase the Argentinians away." I was not so sure. The sheer dimensions and difficulties of such an enterprise were formidable, even to think about. Surely there must be diplomatic means for righting the undoubted wrong that had been done to us? One of the Germans at the conference gave it as his opinion that if we deliberately drew back from confronting the aggressor, who would ever again believe in Western, including British, guarantees towards Berlin?

Early the next, Saturday, morning I left the conference and returned to London, together with a number of MPs en route for the debate in the House of Commons, the first Saturday sitting since the war. I listened to it on the radio in my office. Never was there such an outpouring of patriotic fervour, such a concern for the rights of the Falklanders to remain British, such a contempt for the Foreign Office for having (so the critics argued) brought about national humiliation, such excoriations of the fascist regime in Buenos Aires. When a Tory back-bencher (Mr Ray Whitney), a former member of the Diplomatic Service who had served in Argentina and knew at first hand something of the problems, drew attention to the difficulties of a military operation and dared to hope that the interests of the islanders could be protected by negotiation rather than by naval and military action, he found

---

* Leading member of the Labour Front Bench

himself the object of general contempt, another Tory specifically accusing him of defeatism.

In the leader that I wrote against the clock, while still listening to the debate, I sought first to establish that the much maligned Foreign Office had done its best, over the years, to dispose of this awkward remnant of empire in as honourable a fashion as could be managed. These efforts had foundered, either because of Argentine intransigence or on the insistence of some British politicians and pressure groups that the Falklands and their people are and should remain British. Nothing wrong with that, of course, if that was what the islanders wanted. What was wrong was the refusal of successive governments and their majorities to provide the means – in terms of defence and social expenditure – which would cloak these fine feelings with reality.

The leader went on to pose two broad choices. The first was to recognise the inevitable, to admit that the Falklands chapter was closed and to arrange for the islanders' resettlement in this country. While there was something to be said for this argument, there was still more to be said against it. The Commons debate had shown no disposition whatever to write off the Falklands. So the other choice remained, which Mrs Thatcher had already taken: to despatch a large task force to free the islands from occupation in a manner and at a time as yet unspecified. While the force was steaming along to the South Atlantic, there would still be time for diplomatic efforts to resolve the crisis. If at the end of that period, nothing had changed, the Government would be faced with some hard decisions. But whatever happened, we were on sound moral grounds and should stay there. The leader avoided fence-sitting but also avoided jingoism, of which there was plenty to be found in some of the other papers. Harold Lever* telephoned the next morning to say he was thankful for "a breath of sanity at last".

In the next few weeks, as the task force neared its target and Alexander Haig, the US Secretary of State, shuttled back and forth across the Atlantic in a vain quest for peace, the paper maintained its line: if in the last resort we had to use force, so be it, but we needed to be clear about how much force was necessary and clear that we would be using it to punish and deter aggression and protect the islanders' rights, not simply to restore the colonial *status quo ante*. Once the peace-seeking process had, because of Argentinian intransigence, broken down, and British Forces were fully committed to the recapture of the islands, I

* Lord Lever of Manchester, former Labour Cabinet Minister

wrote a leader headed 'The war that had to be', whose closing thought was that, whatever the outcome, in the end the Falklands and Argentina would have to live together. The same idea was hammered home in the leader column on succeeding Sundays; 'the simple restoration of British sovereignty cannot be the final outcome of the war in the South Atlantic.' This line differed considerably from the more strident tone of much of the rest of the press. *The Times'* leaders brayed and neighed like an old war horse, but the prize for repulsiveness went to Murdoch's *Sun*, with its notoriously exultant headline, after the sinking of the Belgrano: 'Gotcha'.

Yet Murdoch himself never questioned or criticised these *Sunday Times* editorials, directly or indirectly. I cannot recall his making any comment whatever at the time, though his own sentiments and nature must have placed him squarely in the 'Gotcha' camp. It was only some time after the Falklands campaign was over that he disparagingly referred, in one of the Saturday night sessions in my office, to our Falklands arguments. Despite my resolve not to cross swords with him on these occasions, I protested. "But Rupert, our line – that force should only be used as a last resort but when it was used we supported its use – was entirely consistent and unchallengeably patriotic." "Yeah," he replied, grinning sardonically, "but ya didn't mean it, did ya?" There was no point in further argument. Murdoch was wrong. I did mean every word I had written or had caused to be written. But what *The Sunday Times* was not going to do, so long as I was around, was to glory in war as a sign of national virility, or endorse any policy which would result in a heavy, open-ended commitment in the South Atlantic.

There was an encouraging, indeed inspiring, sequel to this line of thinking. John Shirley, one of our reporters, a fairly typical Fleet Street type – bright, veering between cynicism and idealism, left-wing – was sent with the task force to cover the operation for the paper. Despite the frustrations and difficulties encountered by all the journalists with the task force, he did good work and returned, unscathed, in mid-July. A normally cheerful and out-going person, he seemed subdued, almost disoriented, by his experiences. With some difficulty and a good deal of prompting, I persuaded and helped him to write for the paper an account of his feelings, especially towards the armed forces. The result was highly successful and very moving.

'I did not do national service,' he wrote (he was far too young). 'Before this fierce campaign (the Falklands war) my experience of the British army was limited to a few encounters (generally hostile) in

Northern Ireland. I took to the Falklands what I suspect is a fairly standard stereotype for my generation: the officers, I anticipated, would be effete and upper class and stupid; the men would be stupid too and would have joined up only to escape the misery of unemployment and/or boredom in civilian life. It was not like that at all. There were exceptions but in the main I found the officers perceptive men. Below them, the marines I came to know were just as bright . . . they were not automatons, they were human beings too. And their ability to show grief helped me to cope with mine. In our anguish and our doubts about the whole damned thing, we shared something very special . . . these men, paraded in the press as some sort of macho supermen, turned out to be thoughtful, reflective human beings, not only capable of feeling grief, remorse and pain but also of saying so.' Ten days after this article was published, Dr Runcie, the Archbishop of Canterbury, preached at the service in St Paul's held to give thanks for the courage and endurance of the forces involved in the battle for the Falklands. The Archbishop (who with other Church leaders had withstood all attempts to turn the occasion into a victory parade) quoted from Shirley's article which had, he said, particularly impressed him.

The other event which demanded special treatment was the general election in the summer of 1983. *The Sunday Times* had been out of circulation and thus unable to express a view four years earlier, when the Conservatives had turned Labour out of office. Since then, under both Harold Evans and myself, the paper had often criticised Mrs Thatcher and her ministers – for unimaginative and constricting economic policies, for a shrill and over-simplified approach to East–West relations, for lukewarm where not actually hostile attitudes towards the European Community. At the same time, we had given credit where credit seemed to be due – the Rhodesian settlement, for example, achieved principally thanks to the patience and resolve of my old friend Peter Carrington, the person in the Government to whom I felt the closest ties, derived from a mutual distrust of ideology. He had now been swept away in the Falklands flood. Another significant development since the previous election was the emergence of the Liberal/SDP Alliance. Yet another was the increasingly incredible posture of the Labour Party, under Michael Foot.

My own feelings about Mrs Thatcher (and I think those of many of my senior colleagues) were somewhat ambivalent. When she spoke in the House of Commons or appeared on television, her nagging, schoolmistressy voice and unquestioning assumption of a monopoly of wisdom were enough to jar every nerve in the body (although she obviously commanded a wide measure of popular support and admiration, and not just among Conservatives). When however we entertained her to lunch at *The Sunday Times*, which we did both before and after she was Prime Minister, there was not one, I think, among the senior writers who were present on such occasions who was not impressed by her articulateness, her grasp of detail, and the strength and reality of her convictions. In these respects, as well as in her bluntness and freedom from any discernible sense of humour, she was comparable to Heath. Indeed, a senior Tory had early on expressed in private his view of Mrs Thatcher's conduct and manner as party leader in the inelegant words: "It's Ted with tits on." (Another, even more senior Tory, not given to exaggeration or embellishment, once described to me a scene in the Cabinet room at No. 10 during Heath's tenure. The story adds a new dimension to the feelings of the two leaders about one another. According to this man, a leading member of that Cabinet, Mrs Thatcher, who was Secretary of State for Education, made a practice of speaking, and speaking at length, on subjects which had nothing to do with her departmental brief. One day when she was, with more than usual volubility, thus engaged, Heath's patience, never very elastic, snapped. Leaning forward from his centrally placed Prime Minister's chair, he shouted down the table to where the Education Secretary was sitting: "Shut up, shut *up*.")

My first proper meeting with her was on a social occasion when she was still Leader of the Opposition. In a friend's country house one winter weekend, we stood in front of a log-fire and talked politics. At that time, the most likely outcome of a general election was widely considered to be a hung Parliament. In that case, would Mrs Thatcher consider a coalition with the Liberals, which was what Heath had sought to construct in 1974? There is a phrase, usually associated with love stories, about 'her eyes burning with passion'. Mrs Thatcher now gave a practical demonstration of this feat. Her deepest emotions had obviously been stirred. Never, but never, she said, would she consider a coalition, from which could only come irresolute and debilitating government. The Conservatives would win with a working majority and would then supply the country with the leadership it needed. As to the philosophy underpinning that Government or at least underpinning her, she said that the book whose influence upon her had been paramount was F.A. Hayek's *The Road to Serfdom*.

Soon after I became Editor, a message came from No. 10 that the

Prime Minister would like to see me on a certain day. This was somewhat unusual. It is quite normal for Prime Ministers to talk tête-à-tête with a national editor, but the request usually comes from the editor himself. Had Murdoch engineered this meeting, in the hope that I might be converted to the one and only true faith and henceforth lead *The Sunday Times* along the paths of righteousness? This is guesswork. What is certain is that no serious journalist would refuse such a chance. At the appointed time, I was therefore ushered into Mrs Thatcher's sitting-room on the first floor of No. 10 and given a smiling welcome. (By a stroke of chance, the appointment became public knowledge. A confidential list of the Prime Minister's private and public engagements for that period of May 1981 was left lying about in the House of Commons, whence it found its way into the hands of the *Daily Mirror*. That paper devoted a whole page to the matter, beginning with the words 'in the hands of a terrorist group planning an attack on her it would become a highly dangerous document', and going on to publish three-days'-worth of Mrs Thatcher's engagements. According to the paper, any item on the programme involving a risk had been omitted. Evidently I was not considered a risk. On my day, Friday May 15, I was allotted one hour, between '11.00 the Prime Minister of Papua New Guinea' and '13.00 Lunch in flat'.)

The exchange was largely a monologue from the Prime Minister, occasionally prompted or redirected by my questions. The state of the economy, particularly the rising level of unemployment, took up much of the time, with Mrs Thatcher insisting that as the old, "sunset" industries and their work-forces declined, so the new technology would open up fresh fields for British skills to conquer, the resulting excess of work-hands being mopped up by service industries. She was especially eloquent on this prospect, arguing that it could be no fluke that Japan, the country which had invested in high technology more than almost any other, also had such a low rate of unemployment. Reminders that the Japanese worker has, for better or for worse, a very different set of habits and values from his British counterpart, were brushed aside. This sounds discourteous, but it was not really like that. Mrs Thatcher is never rude unless she means to be, as when she engages the Opposition front bench in a name-calling contest. In private, she is low-voiced, smiling, patient, as though she were an instructor trying to impart a simple lesson to a rather slow-witted or less gifted pupil. The possibility that she might be mistaken, or even that an interpretation of events different from her own might be allowed to exist, does not seem to arise. For a fleeting moment, as we sat facing one another at No. 10 that May morning, the image of Mrs Jellyby, from *Bleak House*, flashed incongruously across the mind. Between the dishevelled and *distrait* appearance and style of that lady and the immaculately turned-out and self-disciplined Mrs Thatcher there was not indeed the smallest resemblance. But, in the words of her creator, Mrs Jellyby was 'a lady of very remarkable strength of character, who devotes herself entirely to the public'.

There were other opportunities to sample Mrs Thatcher's courtesy and her hospitality.* Kitty and I were invited to No. 10 functions from time to time – dinner for the Italian Prime Minister or an evening reception for the Secretary General of the United Nations, for example – and always the Thatchers – the Prime Minister and Denis – were excellent and attentive hosts, Mrs Thatcher usually accompanying her parting guests to the door of No. 10. The last time we were there was after I had ceased to be Editor, in the autumn of 1983. Mr Andreas Papandreou, the Greek Prime Minister, was being entertained to lunch and we were asked, I suppose, because of my interest in Greek affairs. It was very soon after the American intervention in Grenada, which had evoked some rather surprising condemnatory remarks from Mrs Thatcher. She felt that Western countries ought not to walk into other people's countries unless they were certain there was no other choice. My own feelings were even stronger. Reagan had, it seemed to me and plenty of other people at the time, decided to mount the Grenada operation (which could not, given the disparity of the forces involved, fail to result in a 'victory' for the USA) not because the situation called for such drastic action but principally in order to offset the effect on American public opinion of the disaster in Beirut, where nearly 250 US Marines had earlier died in bomb attacks on their camp. Seeing that Mrs Thatcher was momentarily not talking to anyone as the assembled company waited for lunch to be announced, I went up to her and said that, though I did not agree with all she said and did, I must congratu-

---

* The courtesy did not stop at the lunch or dinner table. One day in January 1982, I received an appeal from No. 10 not to disclose, as we were in a position to do, the address of Mark Thatcher's business premises. This seemed reasonable, on security grounds, and the address was kept out of the paper. Shortly after came a handwritten letter from Bernard Ingham, the Prime Minister's Press Secretary: 'As you may imagine, I do not like making requests to Editors and I seek to do so as little as possible. But I am sure there was a serious point in this request and the Prime Minister is very grateful to you for your help.'

late her on her courageous stand over Grenada. This was not a tease. It must have required a considerable moral effort for her, the friend and admirer of Ronald Reagan, to speak out as she had. The Prime Minister, standing in her own drawing-room, actually blushed. "It's been so difficult," she said in a care-laden voice, "you've no idea how difficult it's been." (Just to show how things strike different people differently, Rupert Murdoch, in an interview with an Australian paper about this time, declared that Mrs Thatcher, his former idol, had 'gone out of her mind', had 'run out of puff', was not 'listening to friends'.)

That No. 10 occasion was, of course, after the General Election, in the run-up to which *The Sunday Times* had week by week in the previous May and June put the manifestos of the Alliance, the Labour Party and the Conservatives under the microscope. Although Mrs Thatcher, through her dominant personality and her tendency to use the royal 'we' in talking about herself, had managed to introduce a quasi-Presidential note into the electoral process, the importance of issues and programmes remained primordial; at least, if it did not it should do so, and we had a duty, as a serious newspaper, to examine those issues. A series of protracted discussions with senior staff in my office determined our line. It was not difficult to reach general agreement that Labour's manifesto, reflecting all the incoherence and contradictions which existed within the Labour Party, failed utterly to provide a realistic basis on which a real-life government could attempt to operate. With the SDP/Liberal Alliance, on the other hand, we were on more challenging ground. Many, probably a majority, of the senior editorial group, felt drawn, even strongly drawn, towards the ideas of the Alliance. I certainly did. But it was fantasy to suppose that an Alliance Government would emerge from the election. Its manifesto, we wrote, had enough appeal in it for any voter 'who wishes to put him or herself behind a non-doctrinaire third force in politics'. But in an age of ideology, the time could well not be ripe for such a prospect. The best that could be hoped for was for the Alliance to do well enough at the polls to 'maintain a heavyweight political presence' and to reinforce its case for proportional representation.

The leader on the Tory manifesto was headed 'Manifesto or blank cheque?' It conceded that the Conservative Government of Mrs Thatcher had broken the old political concensus, thereby doing quite a lot of good. But the fault with the manifesto was not that, like Labour's, it lacked coherence or a sense of reality, but that it left too many questions unanswered. What sort of a Government would a new

Thatcher administration provide? 'Having changed the national mood once for the better, Mrs Thatcher might set about exploiting it further, for the worse. That would be moral re-education gone wrong.' Despite these misgivings, I decided when I came to write the final, pre-election leader, to come down for the Tories, though with certain reservations. The Alliance had no chance of winning a majority, so the choice was between Conservatives and Labour. There could be few doubts about the wisdom of wishing for a Conservative victory. Point by point, both in domestic and foreign policy, the Tory record, blemished though it was in some respects, had shown a capacity to govern. But two other outcomes to the election would, the leader said, be desirable: that there should be no Tory landslide and that the Alliance should get a sizeable share of the popular vote and a respectable holding of parliamentary seats.

In the event, these hopes were not to be fulfilled. In terms of seats, the Conservatives did have a near-landslide, and though Alliance candidates clocked up 25.4% of the popular vote, they secured only 23 seats (17 Liberals, 6 SDP). This was disappointing. But the paper's reputation for independence of mind, for judging things on their merits, for refusing any fixed affiliation to any party, had been steadfastly upheld and I felt well satisfied with the performance. Whatever he may have tried to glean from other members of the staff, at no period had Murdoch raised with me the question of our political line. Nor had Pickering. For this, most important moment in a paper's discharge of its political responsibilities, the proprietor and management appear to have behaved with as much regard for editorial independence as the earlier Thomson regime, and with a great deal more regard than the interventionist, high Tory Lord Kemsley.

18 London 1983: Rupert Murdoch and F.G.

19 London 1981: F.G. in the Editor's office, *Sunday Times*. The windows across the street were those of Murdoch's office, whence he is alleged to have fired imaginary pistol shots

9

The Affair of the Hitler Diaries

The episode of the forged Hitler Diaries, in April and May 1983, created a sensation, in many ways a very unfortunate one for Times Newspapers, especially *The Sunday Times* and me personally. The bare bones of the story consisted of the successful efforts of the Hamburg-based magazine *Stern* to sell to News Corporation, Murdoch's parent company, the English-language rights to sixty handwritten volumes said to be Hitler's missing diaries; the last-minute decision to begin publishing excerpts from these diaries in *The Sunday Times*, and not in *The Times*, as originally planned; and the discovery, after *The Sunday Times* had trumpeted the acquisition of this alleged historical miracle but before it began publishing the extracts, that the whole thing was a massive forgery.

The story began, so far as I was concerned, when, towards the end of February 1983, Peter Wickman, the *Stern* correspondent in London, telephoned to say his magazine had a highly important and highly confidential matter to put before me. He refused to be explicit and his conspiratorial manner could not fail to awaken my natural scepticism. I would, I told him, have to know the nature of his wares. In fact this was not the first time that the diaries had cast their shadow over Gray's Inn Road.

Unknown to me, the highly contentious David Irving, who was later to be among those claiming that the diaries were forged, had approached some members of the staff, towards the end of 1982, about twenty-seven alleged volumes of Hitler diaries. The journalists in question made some provisional inquiries, on the basis of which they decided not to follow up Irving's lead. One of them, however, a German speaker, did, in January 1983, go to Hamburg to see Gerd Heidemann, the journalist who 'found' the diaries. Nothing of this was reported to me. This may seem to the outside reader, and with good reason, a pretty weird way to run a newspaper or any other sort of office. Whether my being kept in ignorance of this earlier approach made any difference to the final outcome is doubtful. But it would have been tidier, to say the least, and would specifically have prepared me for Wickman's telephone call, had the right hand, at this important juncture, known what the left was doing or had done. One of the more questionable practices to have grown up over the years in *The Sunday Times* was for important departments to have become quasi-autonomous empires of their own. This was especially true of the Features Department with whom Irving made contact.

Soon after my conversation with Wickman, I went on a short visit to the United States. In my absence Brian MacArthur, as Acting Editor, met Wickman, who asked for a formal oath of secrecy before he would reveal anything. Having obtained it, he then explained that *Stern* had got the Hitler Diaries and had come to see if *The Sunday Times* was interested in purchasing the serial rights to them. MacArthur's first thought was that as *Stern* magazine is published on Thursdays, and since the publication of the diaries in Stern would be a major news event, other London daily papers would obviously follow up and milk the *Stern* extracts on Thursdays and Fridays. What was in it, therefore, for *The Sunday Times*? We would be left repeating, admittedly with rather more detail, what other newspapers had already printed. MacArthur therefore suggested, with the idea of some sort of dual sale of the diaries to both newspapers, that *Stern* should approach *The Times*.

On my return to London, I spoke to Wickman and said that, if *The Sunday Times* was going to be in any way involved, then we must see the material we were being offered. It was eventually arranged for Wickman to meet Sir Edward Pickering. At that meeting there was mutual agreement that the serialisation of the diaries was probably more appropriate (because of *Stern*'s Thursday publication) for *The Times* than for *The Sunday Times*. Once this important decision was made, I lost most of the interest I ever had. This was not true, however, of Rupert Murdoch. He seems to have regarded the possible acquisition of the diaries as a potential boost to his publishing interests, not only in England, but in the USA and Australia. Assuming they were genuine, no one could blame him for wishing to secure them.

But precisely on the point of genuineness, one of the difficulties, and one that persisted throughout the whole saga, was *Stern*'s near-paranoic fear of leaks and premature publicity. They had, they believed, the scoop of the century, and they were going to do everything in their power to keep it to themselves. This passion for secrecy accounts for

Stern's reluctance to allow independent examination, particularly by historians, of the diaries. News Corporation and *The Times* very properly insisted that these conditions were not acceptable and in the end *Stern* agreed to Professor Hugh Trevor-Roper (Lord Dacre) examining them. Trevor-Roper was not only an expert on the Hitler period – his book, *The Last Days of Hitler*, had been both a scholarly and commercial success soon after the war – but also a long-standing Director of Times Newspapers, going back to the Astor days. While this fact later invited criticism, it served at the time to satisfy *Stern*'s insistence on secrecy. Trevor-Roper was asked to go to Zurich where the diaries were lodged at a bank. His brief was to assess their authenticity and judge whether they would provide suitable material for newspaper serialisation.

As he was later to write in an article for *The Times*, he approached his task with a large degree of scepticism. No historian had ever hinted at the existence of these private diaries. The market was flooded with Hitlerian forgeries of one kind or another. 'However, when I entered the back room in the Swiss Bank,' he wrote, 'and turned the pages of those volumes, and learnt the extraordinary story of their discovery, my doubts gradually dissolved. I am now satisfied that the documents are authentic, that the history of their wanderings since 1945 is true; and that the standard accounts of Hitler's writing habits, of his personality, and even, perhaps, some public events may, in consequence, have to be revised.'

He had been promised, on his return to London, a sight of the typed transcript which, according to *Stern*, existed 'up to the end of 1941'. As he prepared to leave for Zurich, however, he was telephoned by Charles Douglas Home, Evans's successor as Editor of *The Times*, and asked to give his immediate reactions after a first sight of the diaries. Today, he admits he should have refused. At the time, he was taken by surprise and agreed. In the Zurich bank vault, surrounded by five members of *Stern* (and a Spanish journalist) he simply handled the volumes and listened to the *Stern* men's (false) assurances that the paper had been scientifically tested and that they knew and could vouch for the identity of the 'Wehrmacht officer' who was supposed to have had the diaries in his possession all those years. On the basis of this, he telephoned Douglas Home in London and said that on external evidence, which seemed to him conclusive, he was convinced of authenticity. He never did see a typed transcript, as promised.

Nonetheless, Trevor-Roper's words caused the machine to slip into top gear. Douglas-Home, Pickering and Murdoch himself went to Zurich, accompanied by Gerald Long, no longer with Times Newspapers but still in Murdoch's employ, and with considerable knowledge of German. They all examined the volumes. Douglas-Home, according to what he subsequently said on television, smelt them and liked what he smelt (though what sort of a scientific test that was supposed to be was far from clear). A little later, Murdoch visited Hamburg in pursuit of his quarry.

The decision was taken to buy. Very high-level negotiations ensued between News Corporation in New York and *Stern* in Hamburg. The American weekly magazine *Newsweek*, which had already accepted the authenticity of the diaries on the assurance of Gerhard Weinburg, a distinguished historian, was also party to the incipient deal. An agreed sale price of $3.75 million was arrived at, but then *Stern* raised the figure to $4.25 million, at which point News Corporation and *Newsweek* walked out. Despite this setback, Murdoch did not abandon his plans. At a lunch held in London on April 13, presided over by Murdoch, and attended by Douglas-Home, a number of senior *Times* journalists, Pickering, and Bruce Rothwell, a senior News Corporation employee, plans were discussed for *The Times*' serialisation of the diaries on two or three days a week throughout *Stern*'s publication of the first set of extracts. I could not attend this lunch, but MacArthur represented me. Not wishing to be excluded altogether from what at that time appeared to be a great publishing feat, I told him to mark out a stake for *The Sunday Times*' serialisation of the second instalment of *Stern*'s series, due to begin in January 1984.

Despite the fact that negotiations with *Stern* had broken down, Times Newspapers continued with its efforts to authenticate the diaries. On April 19 Trevor-Roper went to Hamburg to see Gerd Heidemann whose 'remarkable collection of Nazi documents and mementoes' he had been shown in Zurich. Trevor-Roper was a few days later to write, in his long article for *The Times* which appeared on the morning of April 23, about these documents – 'letters, notes, notices of meetings, minutes, mementoes, and, above all, signed paintings and drawings by Hitler, all covering several decades – which convinced me of the authenticity of the diaries'. Meanwhile, the plans for publication of the material, whose existence *Stern* was proposing to announce to an astonished world on May 11, accelerated sharply. Fearful that its scoop was in process of escaping – *Stern*'s principal rival, *Der Spiegel*, had got wind of it – *Stern* brought forward the date of the announcement of the discovery of the diaries by almost three weeks. On the same day that it took this decision, April 21, British and Commonwealth rights to the diaries were sold to News Corporation for $400,000.

That Thursday evening, April 21, I was on the point of leaving my house to dine with friends, when a trans-Atlantic telephone call came in. It was Murdoch in New York. He explained that the deal was done, and that *Stern* would be making an announcement on the following Monday, the 25th. *The Sunday Times* of the 24th would carry the news of the diaries' discovery, and thereafter would be publishing *Stern*'s first extracts. This change in plan, substituting *The Sunday Times* for *The Times* as the paper in which the diaries were to be serialised, seems to have been prompted by the realisation that *Stern*'s material – three instalments on the Hess flight to Britain in 1941, amounting to 20,000 words – would not be suitable for *The Times*. At this point I had not seen any part of this material.

I therefore questioned Murdoch about authenticity, and he replied that Trevor-Roper was satisfied. This was no more than the truth. It is easy, with hindsight, to wonder why I did not immediately insist on a far greater degree of authentication, above all by modern German scholars. The reason why I did not revert to my earlier scepticism is two-fold. First, the material had hitherto been handled exclusively on the basis that, provided News Corporation and *Stern* completed their deal, *The Times* would win the prize: at no stage in the authentication process, such as it was, was I involved or required to be involved. It would have been very difficult, to say the least, to demand a new authentication process. Secondly, like Murdoch himself, I was genuinely impressed with the weight of Trevor-Roper's opinion. I had known him well for thirty-five years, respected his scholarship, appreciated his values in general and his unemotional approach to facts in particular. Was it conceivable that the former Regius Professor of History at Oxford, now the Master of Peterhouse at Cambridge, could have declared himself so positively had there been even a small risk of his being proved wrong? Who was I, who had never seen or handled the diaries, who was not, by a wide margin, an expert on the Hitlerian period, to challenge the opinion of such a man? It never occurred to me to do so. Indeed, talking to Murdoch that evening, I felt, rather than reluctance, a sense of elation that *The Sunday Times* was to be the medium through which this amazing discovery was to be made known to the world.

Late that Thursday night, I despatched MacArthur to Hamburg, and also sent there the able and energetic European correspondent of *The Sunday Times*, Antony Terry, a man with bilingual German who had himself, at the end of the war and the beginning of the peace, while still in the army, been an interrogator of German prisoners-of-war. In Hamburg, MacArthur and Terry found Bruce Rothwell, representing Murdoch's American interests, and another Murdoch employee representing *The Australian*. This was the first time that anyone from *The Sunday Times* saw what *Stern* was intending to publish; and that first sight was only achieved with great difficulty. All that the men in Hamburg were shown were the articles and pictures *Stern* was planning to publish the following week, which Murdoch had now decided should be carried by *The Sunday Times*. This material consisted of the story of the find, with some of the juicier diary extracts. Our Hamburg team had their work cut out, given the short space of time available, to get this material translated and transmitted to London, together with accompanying pictures.

In London, I received on that Friday, April 22, several memoranda from members of the *Sunday Times* staff, emphasising the incomplete nature, to put it mildly, of the authentication process. These warning memoranda were, as events were to prove, extremely perceptive and fully justified. They came from the same people who had dealt with the earlier Irving approach. Without wishing in any way to detract from their assiduity, it occurred to me later that these memoranda might have been made more significant for me had their authors also told me of the Irving episode, and of the reasons which led them to the decision not to follow up that approach.

On Saturday morning, April 23, Trevor-Roper's impressive article, already referred to, appeared in *The Times* under the headline 'Secrets that survived the Bunker'. He had to write it in a hurry once the news of *Stern*'s change of timetable became known. But that did not affect the outspoken nature of his positive judgement. He admitted that there would be critics who would certainly assail the discovery. His short answer to them was that the whole archive 'coheres as a whole and the diaries are an integral part of it.' In addition to this imposing piece, *The Times* on that Saturday morning also gave full rein on its news pages to the discovery. It was as though, baulked of its prize, it was resolved nonetheless to squeeze as much juice as possible from the fruit which chance had prevented from falling into its own basket.

When the first copies of *The Sunday Times* arrived in my office from the presses on that Saturday evening, there was an understandable sense of excitement. 'World exclusive: how the diaries of the Führer were found in an East German hayloft' ran the line immediately under the paper's title on page 1. Also on page 1 was a piece from MacArthur, consisting of a series of 'nuggets' from the diaries as supplied by *Stern*, while in the centre of the paper was a three-page treatment, telling the story of the find and including the statement: 'Hitler's diaries, which *The Sunday Times* is to serialise, have been submitted to the most rigorous tests to establish their authenticity. One of the world's leading experts on Hitler and the Nazi period, Hugh Trevor-Roper, Lord Dacre of Glanton, has staked his academic reputation on his conclusion' (the words were the journalist's, not Trevor-Roper's). There was also a description of the handwriting tests arranged by *Stern*.

Trevor-Roper was due to return to Hamburg the following day to be present on the Monday when *Stern* formally announced their treasure at a press conference. After repeated but vain attempts throughout the Saturday to reach him, we finally got from *The Times* the codeword which would have the effect, when transmitted to the Porter's Lodge at Peterhouse, of opening up the line to Trevor-Roper. What I wanted to do was to describe to him what we had run in *The Sunday Times* and to see if he had anything to add verbally to his article in that morning's *Times*. It was about 8 p.m. My room was full of excited journalists who, though they could obviously not hear what Trevor-Roper was saying, could not fail to follow my words. Thus it came about that this terrifying conversation, as retailed later by the journalists to their friends and contacts on other papers, received wide publicity. Trevor-Roper told me, rather in the manner of a nineteenth-century divine assailed by thoughts of Darwin and the rationalists, that he was having doubts. "I hope you are not going to make a hundred and eighty degree turn, are you?" I asked. His reply caused me to say, to the fascination and horror of the assembled journalists, "Oh, you are, are you." It was indeed a dreadful moment. Given the difficulties of *The Sunday Times* production run, and given also the massive treatment that we had accorded to the affair in the paper, it would have been impossible at that stage to go into reverse, even if I had wanted to. Besides, my distress and bewilderment were compounded by the fact that Trevor-Roper, though he had certainly talked of making 180-degree turns, was clearly in a state of stress and confusion, most unusual in a man of his meticulous mode of thought. He had apparently changed his mind once; might he not change it again?

I did two things that night. The first was to ask MacArthur, together with another able journalist, Paul Eddy, to return to Hamburg on the following day to look after Trevor-Roper, ascertain the true nature of his doubts and generally be my ears and eyes in a situation which was becoming hourly more and more gruesome. The second thing was to despatch a telex – via Murdoch's private office, so that the text would not become generally known – to Peter Koch, the Editor of *Stern*. This read as follows:

> Trevor-Roper as you know will be in Hamburg on Sunday for a meeting with you and Heidemann. I cannot emphasise too strongly that unless *Stern* is ready to release to us in confidence and not for publication more data about the provenance and bona fides of the diaries, there is a grave danger that the authenticity of the whole affair will be threatened to the point that everyone – *Stern* and *The Sunday Times* – will be disastrously compromised. It is imperative, repeat imperative, that you provide evidence which will withstand the attacks now being made upon us.

The reference to attacks was all too well founded. It is natural enough, in Fleet Street, for an important scoop on the part of one newspaper to invite the envy of the others. It is also natural, though usually rather childish, to try to devalue the scoop by seeking to cast doubts upon its validity. Throughout the week that followed, these procedures were followed by other papers with the utmost vigour, the general attitude being a mixture of glee and derision. The hardest part to bear was that the scoffers this time had something genuine to scoff about. Trevor-Roper duly went to Hamburg on Sunday, April 24, where he had an extremely unsatisfactory conversation with Heidemann. The latter refused to reveal anything about the Wehrmacht officer who, he claimed, had salvaged Hitler's diaries from the wreckage of a plane in April 1945, and kept them hidden for almost thirty-eight years. Trevor-Roper's efforts to persuade Peter Koch to reveal the name were equally unavailing. At the press conference the next morning, arranged by *Stern*, Trevor-Roper, under pressure from Douglas-Home in London, said that he was suspending judgement until the full text of the diaries had been examined. Two days later, unable to contain himself any longer, he appeared on West German television to denounce them as prima facie forgeries.

Throughout that week, in Hamburg, MacArthur and the others did their best to pin down and make public the evidence which would refute the critics. It was an intensely frustrating period, not helped by difficulties in time between Hamburg and New York. *Stern* resisted unyieldingly any attempt to provide additional authentication (Koch did not even trouble to acknowledge my late night telex to him). Murdoch, in New York, would talk to Schulte-Hillen, *Stern*'s Chairman, and they would agree that progress could be made. MacArthur and Rothwell would then go around to *Stern*'s offices only to discover that the contract was not quite as it had seemed to be the last time they had been told of it. It became clear that the diaries themselves were not going to be made available for examination. In the middle of the week, Terry managed to persuade Professor Jacobsen, the only distinguished German Hitlerian historian who had not called into question the genuineness of the diaries, to examine them on behalf of *The Sunday Times*. But this was dependent on their being available. When Mac-Arthur telephoned the *Stern* offices at 1 a.m. on Friday, April 29 to report this arrangement, he was told that it was not in the contract. All that could be done that Sunday, May 1, was to publish in *The Sunday Times* a long account of our efforts to secure proper authentication. That account included the words: 'For all the fuss they [the diaries] have caused they seem rather insignificant.'

This assessment erred on the side of understatement. By this time I had read the material from the diaries, prepared by *Stern*, about the Hess flight to Scotland in 1941, which is what we were due to publish as the first complete extract. I was horrified by it. It contained a minimum of Hitler's actual words quoted from the diaries and such 'diary extracts' as there were had been swamped by *Stern* in a great morass of their own historical explanation and setting. I sent a memorandum to Murdoch, pointing out these shortcomings, and advising against any attempt at a rush publication of the Hess material. 'Once the contract with *Stern* is signed,' I wrote, 'I hope it will not be impossible to go back to them and persuade them to allow at least one reputable German historian to look at the diaries and report privately to us.' I therefore suggested that we should consider May 22 as the earliest possible publication date, 'always assuming that the balance of probability remains on the side of authenticity.' I further proposed that we should get hold of an English historian to write the surrounding material.

The pressures on me were increasing. It was only after a good deal of argument with Murdoch that it was possible to agree the wording in the paper of May 1 about our future intentions. That formula read: '*The Sunday Times* itself, which is carrying out its own investigations, is planning to publish extracts from the diaries later this month, unless, on the balance of probability, they are shown not to be authentic.' At that moment, my own feeling was that, while it might be impossible to prove that the diaries *were* authentic, it was likely to be equally difficult to prove that they were *not*, a view which explains the words 'balance of probability'. Trouble also loomed in another quarter. The day before I addressed my note to Murdoch, I received one from the Father (shop steward) of the *Sunday Times* branch of the National Union of Journalists. It expressed 'wide concern about what happened last weekend and how it happened', and invited me to address the branch, or chapel, and to answer questions.

With one part of my mind I sympathised with this request and the anxiety it revealed. Even though nothing had at that stage been proved or disproved, it was not pleasant for *Sunday Times* journalists to be asked by their colleagues and contacts in Fleet Street or the other media difficult questions to which they lacked the answers. But though a strong believer in discussions and consultation with the journalists, I was still more opposed, as a matter of principle, to allowing them, whatever their worries, to share responsibility for the contents of the paper. Once this principle had been breached, an Editor's authority would be undermined forever. I therefore replied that, apart from my intention of being absent on a week's holiday and therefore unable to address the chapel the following week, I did not think the matter appropriate for the chapel. 'I value your concern and that of staff members', I wrote, 'about the implications of the Hitler diaries for *The Sunday Times*. But I am the appointed guardian of the interests of the paper and I shall continue to do my best to protect those interests.'

The bit about a week's holiday was not a diplomatic ploy. Every spring towards the end of April or beginning of May, Kitty and I spent a week in our holiday home in Corfu, opening up the house after its long winter slumber. There seemed to me no good reason to allow Hitler to distort this pattern. I had arranged that no portion of the diaries would be published before May 22. This left three weeks, of which I was to be away only the first one, during which the investigating process could continue. The dispositions for that were all in place. While MacArthur was back in London, deputising for me in my absence, Terry and Paul Eddy were in Germany, testing the strength of Heidemann's story. There was little or nothing, so it seemed to me, that I could do until these procedures had advanced a good deal further.

In fact, things went quicker than this timetable might have suggested. By the middle of that week, while I was still in Corfu, *Stern* at last agreed to release two of the original volumes of the diary to *The Sunday Times* for independent examination. On Friday morning, May 6, these two volumes were flown to London from Hamburg and handed over to *The Sunday Times*. Dr Julius Grant, of Hehner and Cox, the leading chemical analysts, agreed to begin his tests on the following Monday. Meanwhile in Hamburg, the resourceful Terry had managed to get his hands on a facsimile of the volume of the diaries devoted to the Hess affair. He reported that read as a whole this was far less fragmentary than the *Stern* extracts which had so resoundingly failed to impress me.

Then, at about noon on that Friday, came the final blow. *Stern* telephoned to Gray's Inn Road to announce that the German Federal Archives at Koblenz, who had earlier been given seven volumes to examine, had denounced them all as forgeries. Chemical analysis had shown that the paper, the binding, the glue and the thread were all of post-war manufacture. MacArthur and his men then took two steps. Dr Grant was asked to begin immediate tests on the two volumes in London, in order to determine the age of the paper. Like the Federal authorities in Germany, he found that the paper was manufactured after the war. 'Hitler could not possibly have written on it.' Secondly, Mr Norman Stone, then lecturer in German and Russian history at Trinity College, Cambridge, was asked to read the two volumes of handwritten diaries, supposedly Hitler's inner thoughts for the years 1933 and 1935. Stone, after consulting contemporary history, reported that the diaries were simply a digest of this historical record. The game was up. *Stern* had been tricked into buying a forgery, and News Corporation and Times Newspapers were also victims.

I received this news by telephone in Corfu, and began to wish most fervently that I was in London, that I had never set out on this brief holiday. There was nothing that I or anyone could have done to repair the damage. But at least I could have been there, unhappy though the atmosphere would have been, to put the best possible face on what was, by any standards, a regrettable episode in the paper's history. As it was, senior members of the staff hammered out a formula for page 1 of the issue of May 8 in which we offered the readers a sincere apology for what had happened. We had not acted irresponsibly, they wrote. But 'our mistake was to rely on other people's evidence and to be governed by their demands for urgency. *Stern* magazine . . . previously enjoying a reputable standing in world journalism, insisted it had established the

diaries' authenticity. This was confirmed by Hugh Trevor-Roper . . .'
The piece went on to explain that we had given ourselves three weeks to
determine, by our own investigations, whether or not the diaries were
authentic. 'In a sense we are relieved that the matter had been so
conclusively settled . . . We are unreservedly delighted that the proof
was made before we had published any portion of the serialisation.'

Back at my desk on the following Tuesday, I did my best in talking to
the chagrined journalists – I shared their chagrin – to put things in
perspective. Yes, it had been a fiasco. Yes, the paper's good name and
credibility had been damaged. But, as had been emphasised in the
apology, serious journalism is a high-risk enterprise. We had taken a
high risk, and it had failed to come off. The effects of this failure would
not last. The reputation of *The Sunday Times* was too well established to
have suffered more than a passing blow. It was now, I said, up to us to
demonstrate that, by its skills and enterprise and its sense of balance,
the paper had lost nothing of its old and proven touch.

I did not make anything of the fact that the Hitler episode had
increased the circulation of the paper by 60,000. Such an achievement
would normally be a subject for rejoicing, but to accomplish it by
promising to peddle what turned out to be a forgery was not a reason for
any pride or satisfaction whatever. Neither did I underline the point to
which our innocent readers' attention had been drawn in the issue of
May 8, that we never actually began serialisation of the diaries. After all
the publicity, the razzmatazz, the references to world exclusives, the
assurances that the great Trevor-Roper had stuck his neck out, the fact
that the fraud had been discovered before we began formally to publish
it could not be, at the time, of much consolation. Nonetheless, it is, I
believe, a fact important for the record. We said that we would not
publish if 'on balance of probability the diaries were shown not to be
authentic'. They had now been shown, not as probable but as indisput-
able forgeries. Our pledge could be redeemed without hesitation,
argument or pressure from anywhere.

On May 14, Trevor-Roper published in *The Times* an article of
recantation. It began: 'Last month I rashly declared the "Hitler
diaries" to be genuine. I then compounded this grave error by admitting it . . . I therefore feel that I owe some explanation of my unique
double-fault.' He went on to explain that in examining the so-called
diaries he had sought to apply three criteria: form, provenance, content. On form, he was reassured, because 'who would forge 60 volumes
when 6 would have served his purpose?' On provenance he thought he

could accept the assurances of Heidemann and of the Editor of *Stern* that they knew the identity of the Wehrmacht officer who was supposed to have salvaged the diaries from the crashed plane in 1945. On content, Trevor-Roper wrote, he was at a disadvantage. He had seen the documents for a few hours only. 'The proper course, I believed, would have been to refer the texts to a qualified German historian.' But *Stern* with its fears of leakage had confined such a check to its own, domestic historians. 'I did not like this answer, but since I took the bona fides of the Editor [of *Stern*] as a datum, I accepted it as an unfortunate necessity. This is what I meant when I afterwards regretted that normal historical methods had been sacrificed to the necessities of a journalistic scoop.'

He went on to explain how the seeds of doubt were planted and grew in his mind, and how he told *The Times* of his doubts. Professor Weinberg, *Newsweek*'s expert, who had first been convinced of the diaries' authenticity, underwent a similar conversion. He later discovered that the so-called handwriting test mounted by *Stern* was not a test at all. None of the samples of Hitler's handwriting sent to the experts, and authenticated by them, had come from the diaries themselves.

The article concluded:'Looking back on the affair I recognise that I made a grave error in my first judgement . . . I blame no one except myself for giving wrong advice to *The Times* and *The Sunday Times*, whose Editors have behaved throughout with more understanding than I deserve. I apologise to them, and to the public, for my error.' The publication of this article would seem to have brought the long, sad story to a final, sad ending. But for me personally there was more to it than that.

In the final draft of Trevor-Roper's article, which I saw before publication, he had written that once his doubts began to assail him, he at once informed *The Times* and *The Sunday Times*. I knew this to be untrue, and therefore arranged with *The Times* people that the reference to *The Sunday Times* should be omitted. But I also discovered that Trevor-Roper was entirely accurate in saying that he informed *The Times*. In the course of the fateful Saturday of April 23, when I and my staff, in total ignorance of Trevor-Roper's doubts, were preparing to give the discovery of the diaries the maximum treatment, Trevor-Roper did indeed speak more than once to the Editor of *The Times*, Douglas-Home, and to his deputy, Webb. Neither of them passed on this information to me. It was not, as I have already described, until 8 o'clock in the evening when I telephoned Trevor-Roper in Cambridge, that I first learnt of his change of mind. The more I thought about this timetable the more bitterly I felt. Had I known in the course of that Saturday of Trevor-Roper's new thoughts, we at *The Sunday Times* would have presented the affair very differently. It would have been impossible, at that short notice, to have killed off all the Hitler pages and replaced them with something else. But we could and would have used more guarded language, would have toned down the headlines, would have allowed specifically for the possibility that the diaries were not authentic: we would, in short, have avoided the major pitfalls which our critics were so quick, not without reason, to gloat over.

I felt I could not leave the matter there, and went and discussed it with Pickering, expressing to him my distress and indeed indignation that I had been left in ignorance of something that it was vitally necessary for me to know. Pickering was sympathetic, and agreed – how could he do otherwise? – that I had a grievance. He said he would speak to Douglas-Home. Later that evening, May 13, the latter telephoned me at home. In the course of a long conversation, he apologised for not having passed on the information reaching him from Trevor-Roper on April 23. His excuse – though he admitted that his error stood – was that Trevor-Roper was in such a condition of doubt and perturbation that it was very difficult at any moment during the day to gauge his exact state of mind. In the circumstances, Douglas-Home thought it better to say nothing to me, though he realised that this was a mistake. Like Murdoch, he too seems to have become so immersed in the business of wanting the diaries to be genuine that he was unable to face the possibility that they were not. The rub for me that fateful Saturday was that it was I and *The Sunday Times*, not Douglas-Home and *The Times*, who had to pay the price for his clouded judgement. I nonetheless thanked him for, and accepted his apology. Nothing could now undo the errors that had been made. It was not even practicable, at that stage, with so much blood on the walls and mocking laughter in the streets, to make public the true course of events, especially Douglas-Home's apology. Today, when the affair of the Hitler diaries has entered into the archives of Fleet Street and been largely forgotten by the public, it is only right that the full story should be known.*

Even that was not, for me, the end. Later that summer, on a hot day

---

* After a courageous struggle against cancer, Charles Douglas-Home died in October 1985, at the tragically young age of forty-eight.

in July, Kitty and I went to a party in London where Trevor-Roper was among those present. I did not see or talk to him but Kitty did. She tore into him for the way in which he had put me on the spot. A few days later I received a long, personal, handwritten letter from this old friend. The relevant parts read as follows:

I have genuinely forgotten some of the details and order of events in the hectic period 22–25 April; but let me begin, without *ambages* or qualifications of any kind, by expressing to you (since my public apology was evidently insufficient) my great regret that, through an initial error of mine, which I have admitted, you were, most improperly (as I believe) put in an embarrassing and indeed impossible position. I think you were treated very badly and you certainly deserved an apology from those who put you in that position. I *thought* that I had sufficiently apologised to you; but if not, let me do so now. I apologise very sincerely *ex animo*.

That said, let me explain the reasons which have governed my action or inaction hitherto. I was asked to look at those diaries by *The Times*, not *The Sunday Times*. I reported to *The Times*; and on the basis of my first report (which I had never expected to have to give by telephone within a few hours of seeing the stuff) the management of *The Times* took over and thereafter forced the pace. At the request of *The Times* I wrote (under great pressure) my first article. In none of this history was *The Sunday Times* involved. What I understand is that Rupert Murdoch, having acquired the rights from *Stern* on – I think – 21 April, imposed (if that is not too strong a word) the stuff suddenly on *The Sunday Times*, which had had no opportunity of examining, considering, or criticising it. If this is true (for I speak from hearsay), then it is my own opinion that you were badly treated, though not by me, and were owed an apology, though not directly by me. In fact I believe that I too was badly treated both by *Stern*, which misled me with false evidence of fact (which I could not doubt unless I were to accuse them of bad faith), and, to some extent, by *The Times*, which did not allow me the conditions which I had at first been promised in order to check the material (i.e. a typed transcript of the German text on which I was to make a written report). However, I have refused to make any complaint or excuse on these grounds for I recognise that I should have been firm and refused to commit myself in the circumstances which actually obtained. So, when I first doubted the authenticity of the material, I decided to take the whole blame myself – and I must admit that *The Times* and *The Sunday Times* were very happy to place it there. I apologised in writing to Rupert Murdoch (who wrote very civilly in reply, accepting part of the responsibility), and in print to the Editors of *The Times* and *The Sunday Times*.

Trevor-Roper then turned to the question of why he had not been in touch with me during the course of Saturday, April 23. He explained how, having written his article for *The Times*, his doubts began to gather to the point that, by the morning of that day:

> I had to face the fact that the documents might be forged. But this entailed such large consequences – grossly unprofessional standards, even bad faith by *Stern* – that I could not, at that stage, call them more than doubts. I telephoned Charlie Douglas-Home early on Saturday morning and told him the position. I *understood* that my doubts would be passed on to you. Charlie's attitude was that so long as there was any chance that the diaries were genuine, we should keep to our course . . . If I had thought that I could have stopped – or postponed – the publication in *The Sunday Times* on the Saturday [i.e. Sunday morning's paper] I would certainly have done so; but matters were out of my hands.

This long and highly relevant letter ended: 'It was a horrible experience for me . . . it was a horrible experience for you too – and less deservedly, for I at least must admit to an error, which you need not. If my understanding of events is correct, *The Sunday Times* alone comes out of the affair quite blameless.' While telling me little that I did not know before, this letter, with its unqualified apology, was a great consolation. I thanked Trevor-Roper warmly for the additional, personal apology. Indeed, apologies to me, either solicited or freely given, seem to have been the order of the day.

There is no side-stepping the conclusion of Trevor-Roper, whatever his part in contributing to the fiasco: the imperatives of a journalistic scoop had been allowed to take precedence over the need for proper tests to establish historical truth. The main culprit was *Stern*, to whose cocksureness and passion for secrecy can be attributed most of the ensuing folly.* But if they were the fools, Murdoch, the supposedly shrewd publisher with a reputation for seeing off most of his rivals and opponents, was the dupe, comparable to a man who buys a horse upon the recommendation of its vendor's vet. Yet though hindsight renders his action blameworthy, his initial enthusiam is understandable, and it was perhaps inevitable that some of this spirit should have inspired his henchmen. MacArthur reported to me from Hamburg that, during the week he spent there with Bruce Rothwell (a Murdoch man unconnected directly with the interests of Times Newspapers), the latter began to show increasing impatience with the case for further authentication; publication became the goal, the nature of what was to be published seemed of lesser importance. As he had done with Trevor-Roper, so Murdoch later admitted to me his responsibility in the affair, though as I noted at the time, his remorse did not appear to be excessive. He even had the satisfaction of seeing his money refunded to him by *Stern*.

The reverberations of this affair had scarcely died away when the Fleet Street rumour factory, one of the most prolific and hardworking plants in the business, began to hum with stories that Rupert Murdoch was planning a change in the editorship of *The Sunday Times*. Though the episode of the diaries had nothing to do with it, Murdoch's mind was indeed moving in this direction. Not long after the general election, he sent for me and said, in essence, that he wanted me to retire early, so as to make room for another, younger man whom he wished to appoint in my place. I had already been Editor for more than two and a half years, so the proposition (if such it can be called) should not have come as a complete surprise. It was unaccompanied by any criticism or reflection upon my record; the temperature of the conversation was low; 'time for a change' was the burden of the message; the diaries had nothing to do with his decision. Later, stories circulated (I cannot personally vouch for their accuracy) that Murdoch made his move because of *The Sunday Times'* less than one hundred per cent support for the Conservative cause. If this is true, then he observed the niceties over editorial independence at the time of the election, but exercised his

---

* On July 8, 1985, a Hamburg court, after a case lasting for eleven months, sentenced Heidemann and Kujau (the actual forger of the diaries) to more than four years' imprisonment for their part in the fraud. The judge said that he considered *Stern*'s publishers bore at least some responsibility for the fraud, by their failure to examine the fake volumes before buying them. He also had some harsh words for the small group of *Stern*'s senior editors who were involved in the project.

power to dismiss the Editor immediately afterwards.

It was a shock, in the sense of something immediately unexpected. My contract was due to expire on my sixty-fifth birthday, so that what Murdoch was asking was that I should forgo just about one year's editorship. For a moment, visions of lawyers, law-suits and compensation payments loomed before the eyes. My only response, however, was to ask him what exactly he had in mind for me. He said I could either stay on for two more years on full salary as "Editor Emeritus" (a title devoid of meaning, which I am nearly sure he invented on the spur of the moment) and Director of Times Newspapers, or take an equivalent sum of money and sever connections altogether. It was an extremely generous offer. We agreed, amicably, that on that basis I would relinquish the editorship on October 1, 1983, but remain on the payroll as Director and with the risible new title of Editor Emeritus until my sixty-sixth birthday two years later. When shortly afterwards the news was announced, Murdoch issued a statement paying a personal tribute to 'an outstanding record in British journalism' and recalling that the handover of *The Sunday Times* to the new Editor would come at a time 'when the paper's authority stands high and its sales and advertising are buoyant.'

Whether Murdoch meant these words or not, he certainly recorded them and repeated something like them at the farewell party which he gave in my honour some time in the early autumn. He must have been pleased, I think, that I went without causing any uproar; very unlike the departure of Harold Evans, although the circumstances were so different that there could be no valid comparison between the two events. At the farewell party, attended by many members of the journalistic staff, I took great pleasure in saying that I believed that "the standards and quality of the paper have been upheld and that it has continued to be, what it has not always been in its long history, an independent-minded and fearless paper, unaffiliated to any political party or sectarian set of beliefs."

Of Rupert Murdoch himself, with whom I had had so alternating a relationship over the previous years, I took leave with mixed feelings. The beginning had been friendly, the middle rough, the end outwardly friendly again. He and I were different sorts of animals, as he would readily agree. In 1982, not long after the invasion of Lebanon by Israel, he paid a quick, non-publicised visit to Israel. Hearing of this by chance, I asked him, on his return, for his impressions. He said of Ariel Sharon, the then Israeli defence minister, a swashbuckling, contentious and charismatic personality, that he found him a fine character: "He's a man of action." But suppose (the obvious example was the foray into Lebanon) his action was wrong or misguided? "That's not the point – he gets things done." This just about sums up Rupert Murdoch. Not for him the finely balanced argument, the careful weighing of pros and cons, the cautious testing of the water. Supposing that he had heard of Hilaire Belloc's ironic couplet:

> Decisive action in the hour of need
> Denotes the hero but does not succeed

he would be likely to have cast it scornfully aside.

Not that he sees himself, I surmise, in the role of a hero. He is not even primarily a newspaper man, despite his predilection for slashing with a blue pencil at a page of newsprint, as though he were in charge of layout. A more likely and favoured stereotype would be that of a smart (in the American sense) operator, a man who by using his wits and staying close to the job gets the better of everybody, skirting or better still destroying by any means available the obstacles in his way. Such a person might not be likeable or agreeable to work with (although Murdoch, as Harold Evans rightly notes, is capable of turning on a good deal of charm when he wants to, and he has also performed unpublicised acts of kindness, especially towards his personal staff). But being liked is not a priority in the Murdoch philosophy. It probably comes low on the list of most would-be or real tycoons.*

Yet even that generalisation is not quite water-tight. Everybody is vulnerable to something or somebody and by chance I discovered one day Murdoch's capacity to let the mask slip. Among his real or assumed dislikes was the Monarchy; not the person of the Monarch or her family but the institution, which embodied for him all the stuffiness and elitism and immobility of the British Establishment. Soon after he had bought the papers, he held a small office lunch at which I was present, where both he and Gerald Long outbid one another in the strength of their Republican views. When I pointed out that if the leader columns of *The Times* and *Sunday Times* were to reflect such views, there would be a sharp drop in circulations, they both fell noticeably silent. Some considerable time after this, Murdoch appeared unexpectedly in my

---

* These judgements would seem to be upheld by Murdoch's tactics for getting the better of the print unions in early 1986. He deserves gratitude for trying to tame them, but his methods have been nothing if not ruthless.

office on a busy Saturday afternoon. He was not known to be in England and, anyway, this was much earlier than his usual visiting hour. It was immediately clear that he was in his most easy-going, unabrasive mood. In fact, he looked like the cat that has swallowed the cream. When I asked him what brought him to London, he replied that he and Anna, his wife, had flown from New York on the previous evening's Concorde for a luncheon engagement. Some sixth sense told me that he would like to be asked where or with whom they had lunched. The answer was Clarence House, with the Queen Mother. What had obviously happened was that that remarkable old lady, in whom shrewdness and perception underlay outward informality and high spirits, had charmed him as a bird is charmed off the tree. That Saturday afternoon's visit to my office was one of the most pleasant encounters I ever had with the new Proprietor of Times Newspapers.

So, amidst a flurry of valedictory dinners, drinks, presentations and some movingly generous tributes from my colleagues, my editorship of *The Sunday Times* and direct connections with it came to an end. The tributes included a splendid spoof front page of *The Sunday Times*, largely full of jokes for in-house consumption, but also carrying some exceptionally kindly observations from Brian MacArthur, my deputy, about myself and, especially appreciated, about Kitty, whom he described as being 'during some of the darkest moments of the last three years, a source of comfort, wit, happiness and superb hospitality to many members of the staff '. This was no more than the truth.

It had been an arduous, at times testing, experience, but one which I did not regret for a moment. Most reasonably ambitious people want to get to the top, however much they may profess otherwise. Often they get there – this was certainly true in my case – through luck. But there is nothing wrong with that. Schopenhauer listed three great powers – sagacity, strength and luck – and declared that it is the last which is the most efficacious. What the experience had taught was that to be a conscientious Editor, ever-watchful of his paper and those who work for it, calls for exceptional devotion to a cause. After being deputy-editor of the paper for so many years, often acting for the Editor over quite long periods of time, I was astonished how heavy the burden of full responsibility immediately showed itself to be. Father-Confessor to the staff (and journalists, like most artists, are often temperamental and difficult to handle), pundit and assessor (preferably omniscient) in all matters of public policy and interest, patient recipient of every complaint, from within and from without the office, above all, the guardian of the paper's standards and values: these are, or should be, among the attributes of an Editor who aspires to perform his task properly. Sometimes it seemed as though the only formula for the job was in the Collect for Whit Sunday, embodying the plea – surely the most extravagantly optimistic in the whole range of prayer – that we may be granted 'a right judgement in all things'.

★   ★   ★

Fate, in the shape of failure to pass the Foreign Office examination, decreed that my working life should be spent as a journalist instead of a diplomatist. Looking back with serenity, it is natural to try to draw up a balance sheet of profit and loss. Had I stayed at the Foreign Office, it is not too fanciful to suppose that I might have finished up as an Ambassador, perhaps, with luck, in a major post. It would have meant working my way up to that relative eminence by toiling conscientiously through the thickets of Whitehall, the forests of Africa, the deserts of Asia or the Middle East, the swamps of Latin America, with an occasional spell at one or more of the lusher watering holes in Western Europe or the New World. How would that have compared with nearly forty years in journalism?

In my experience, the members of the Diplomatic Service are for the most part clever, dutiful, hard-working, skilled professionals, as far removed as it is possible to be from the effete and dandified snobs of popular legend and the popular press, which blames them for every misfortune or untoward event in Britain's relations with the outer world. On the contrary, they often have to carry the can for the weakness or misjudgements of their political masters. A life in their midst would have been, like most lives, of varying interest, full of (mostly) pleasant colleagues, reasonably well-paid, providing the structure and security, and occasionally the constraints, of a large family. Always depending on circumstances, there could have been moments, especially near the top of the ladder, when real contributions might have been made towards the formulation of national policy. It would not have been a bad career at all, even though it would have come to an end, professionally, at sixty, the normal retiring age for civil servants. What it would have meant for Kitty and the children is less clear. Wives married into the Diplomatic Service are now permitted to take jobs of their own in capitals to which their husbands are posted. But before that concession, the burdens of constant moving of house, changing of schools, separations, bouts of loneliness, the tedium of diplomatic social occasions, could not for many women have been entirely or even partially offset by the attractions and intermittent glamour of existence in a privileged position in a foreign country.

Journalism, whether practised at home or abroad, imposes a minimum of such burdens. Nevertheless it has certain obvious affinities with diplomacy. Indeed, the two professions often overlap. In a large foreign capital, the British Ambassador and his staff will frequently meet the resident correspondents when the exchange of information and interpretation is something from which both sides, while carefully guarding their sources, can hope to benefit. This was certainly my experience in Rome and Paris. (Later, when travelling about the world, I would whenever possible call upon the Papal Nunciature in the capital of the country concerned. Though they will never say anything on the record, Papal diplomats are usually extremely well-informed and perceptive observers.) Occasionally, journalists may find themselves, however reluctantly, cast in a quasi-diplomatic role. In heated discussion (*their* heat) with Palestinian groups or Soviet editors or black African nationalists, I have been held answerable for the prevailing policies of the Government in London. Denials of playing any part whatever in the genesis of such policies cut no ice at all. In the eyes of his interlocutors, the travelling correspondent frequently becomes the representative of his race and nation.

Collection and analysis of information is something common to both journalism and diplomacy. The big difference, when it comes to getting all this material down on paper, is that the work of the journalist is read by hundreds, indeed many thousands, of people within a few hours or days of being written; that of the diplomat is read only by a few informed and interested professionals – until it is released for general consumption under the thirty-year rule. The comparison is with skilled private theatricals, put on for the chosen few, and a public performance open to instant criticism and judgement. On the other side of the coin, the diplomat's words, if they are about anything important, can have some sort of a life expectancy, while it is rare that a journalist's effusions will outlive the week, perhaps hardly the day.

It is this ephemeral nature of journalism, the fact that today's newspaper is used to wrap up tomorrow's fish, which inclines so many superior persons to look down upon it as a profession. One of my school reports from Wellington, referring to the first inklings of literary ability, carried a warning against 'slipping into journalistic ways'. The implication was clearly one of slapdashness, writing against the clock, playing to the gallery, disguising with external icing the lack of solid substance to the cake beneath. These are indeed ills to which Grub Street is often prone. (It was a real street in Cripplegate, described by Dr Johnson as 'much inhabited by writers of small histories, dictionaries and temporary poems, whence any mean production is called grubstreet.') But then much official writing, which must include Foreign Office telegrams and despatches, is guilty from time to time of pomposity and excessive use of what Ernie Bevin called the clitch. It is not, I think, because of literary infelicities or failings that in this country, compared with the United States, journalism is widely held in low esteem, whereas the Diplomatic Service is (or anyway used to be) the cherished goal of many middle-class parents for their supposedly gifted son. Certainly my own mother, the officer's widow, had her eye on the Foreign Office. Though she concealed her disappointment loyally, it must have been a considerable let-down when I finished up in Fleet Street, even if it was with *The Times*.

Among the real reasons for such attitudes is the fact that much of British journalism is of a low order, its constant purpose being to trivialise, sensationalise and thus (or so it is hoped) to sell more papers. Not that such sensationalism and so on always evokes the same, single reaction. There is a large element of hypocrisy here, bordering on schizophrenia, which has been well described by Bernard Levin* as 'simultaneous fascination and revulsion at the antics of the mass-circulation papers, with their gossip columns, their trivialities and their very remarkable ability to give the most detailed and colourful accounts of things that never happened'. He also refers to the 'popular hatred of journalists and the avidity with which the worst of them are read'. The reference to inventive journalism is apt. 'Journalists,' wrote Arnold Bennett, 'say a thing that they know isn't true, in the hope that if they keep on saying it long enough, it *will* be true.' This is not fair. Many journalists do indeed do this, but they do it generally at the urging and behest, spoken or tacit, of their Editor and beyond him of their proprietor. There is of course nothing wrong with the desire of these tycoons to make their papers pay (an aim made more difficult by the print unions). But living or dead, they must bear the major responsibility for the low standing of much of the British press, as well as for persistently and insultingly misleading the general public. If there is

* *The Times*, October 29, 1985

such a thing as the Day of Judgement, they will in the end be called to awful account.

Such comments are open to the charge of elitism. "It is fine for you," I can hear someone saying, "who have spent your life writing for an educated and informed readership. You have had virtually no limits placed on the length at which you write or the vocabulary you can use. The journalist on a popular paper has the far more challenging task of having to explain and simplify, within a short space, difficult matters to a less recipient public who simply wouldn't get through your sort of stuff at all. And as for misleading people, quality papers get things wrong, too, with far more potentially serious consequences."

These are valid points. Worthy, honest, professionally skilled men and women can and do work for popular papers. At the best, they do a laudable and demanding job of what in French is called *vulgarisation* – bringing the message to the masses. But at the worst – and it all too often is the worst – their efforts are offset and overtaken by their newspaper's relentless emphasis on triviality, its unfaltering adoption of the lowest and meanest common denominator. If these values earn journalism a bad name, it is not surprising.

But there is another reason for the bad name. This time we are dealing with a universal, rather than a specifically British phenomenon, affecting the world of the media in a way unknown to diplomacy and diplomats. This is the deep-rooted tendency to regard the bringer of bad news as the person responsible for it. In classical times, the messenger, the unfortunate herald of misfortune, was often put to death. Modern journalists are not called upon to pay this sacrifice, but they frequently find themselves the target of criticism and animosity for having dared to investigate and report in such a way that the final picture is unflattering or even repulsive. In the early seventies, *Sunday Times* reporters produced some disturbingly well substantiated accounts of impermissible excesses on the part of the army and the police in the struggle against terrorism in Northern Ireland. Some of this reporting showed signs of an in-built anti-military bias, better avoided. But for the most part, it was well-founded, as official inquiries subsequently showed. It brought down showers of reproof upon our heads – discreetly from the Ministry of Defence, less discreetly from Colonels of regiments, not discreetly at all from outraged members of the public. Yet I have no doubts that it was right and proper, a function, indeed an obligation, of a free press to have done it. Harold Evans, then Editor, was at his best on such occasions, withstanding the sticks and stones with courage and dignity. Popular papers, despite my earlier strictures, also enjoy a usually merited reputation (when they manage to forsake treatments which are meretricious or contrived) for similar revelations of injustice or impropriety. And of course the non-written media – radio and television – play a prominent part in the business of uncovering incompetence or wrong-doing in public and private places.

This indispensable watchdog function, provided it is carefully and honestly performed and avoids obsessional tendencies, provides a sizeable counterweight to the shortcomings and excesses, real or imputed, of British newspapers. I cannot in truth say that I was ever deeply involved in this function. Knowledge, analysis and understanding of a situation or a personality, in order to help other people to understand it or him, was always what drew me on. But the investigative process, when properly conducted, is deserving of respect and approval, even if it often evokes precisely the opposite reactions. This aspect of journalism is obviously something alien to the normal exercise of a diplomat's duties. Even if he does, exceptionally, stumble on some scandal or irregularity, the general public will be unaware of his discovery. It is one more instance of the difference between private and public performance. A journalist is in the business of spilling, or at least trying to spill, the beans. A diplomat is normally more concerned with preventing them being spilt.

There remains the question of job-satisfaction. Would I have had more as Ambassador than as Editor of *The Sunday Times*? The answer must necessarily be subjective. It is possible, indeed quite common, for Editors to suffer the delusions of power, to suppose that their words and their influence can play a dominant role in the ordering of human affairs. Sometimes they can; but not often. Generally the Editor's ideas and the contents of the paper for which he is responsible will do little more than add another grain to the mountain of sand called British public opinion. But the delusions are harmless and can give rise to deliberations as serious as any which take place around a Cabinet table or an Ambassador's desk (the seriousness is usually and fortunately punctured by moments of farce and mirth, difficult to imagine as a regular feature of Cabinet meetings). Presiding over a leader conference on a quality paper, knowing that the power of final decision is yours, is surely just as great and possibly greater a satisfaction than that of an Ambassador at his daily meetings with his staff ('prayers').

If the scales are fairly equally balanced as between the satisfactions of an Editor and those of an Ambassador, at an earlier stage they come down heavily in favour of the journalist. What young Embassy Second Secretary could have talked man to man, as I did at the age of thirty-one, to the Prime Minister of Italy or to the future Pope? Even in later years, few senior diplomats would have thought it fitting to ask the Shah the sort of questions I put to him, or had the chance to listen to Lyndon Johnson's verbal extravagance. There is no doubt about it; journalism is a wonderfully rewarding profession for the younger man or woman who makes good fairly early. Later on, things can become more uncertain. There is not much career structure in the profession. By definition, a newspaper can only have one Editor, one foreign editor, one literary editor, one chief Paris correspondent. Given a certain degree of talent, promotion to these posts is often a question of luck, of being in the right place at the right time. By contrast, ambassadorships, though they may not fall off trees, are numerous and, contrary to what the Book of Ecclesiastes tells us, the race is usually to the swift. Perhaps the last word on the two professions – the one I meant to follow but did not and the one I never contemplated but in which I spent a working lifetime – is that neither is likely to fall within the scope of Thoreau's gloomy observation that 'the mass of men lead lives of quiet desperation'. Both diplomatist and journalist may, like almost everyone, experience moments of disillusion or depression. But they are unlikely to last for long. The fascination and variety of the scene and scenes they are paid to become familiar with sees to that.

Index